T0290755

美国博物馆国家标准及最佳做法
National Standards & Best Practices
for U.S. Museums

美国博物馆国家标准及最佳做法
National Standards & Best Practices
for U.S. Museums

美国博物馆协会
The American Association of Museums

伊丽莎白·E·梅里特　评述
Commentary by Elizabeth E. Merritt

外文出版社
FOREIGN LANGUAGES PRESS

First Translated Edition 2010

Originally published by The American Association of Museums,
Washington, DC, USA.
ISBN 978-1-933253-11-4
© American Association of Museums

ISBN 978-7-119-06416-1
© Foreign Languages Press, Beijing, China, 2010
Published by Foreign Languages Press
24 Baiwanzhuang Road, Beijing 100037, China
http://www.flp.com.cn

Printed in the People's Republic of China

序

亲爱的中国博物馆同仁：

    作为美国博物馆协会的主席，我非常高兴能让您和您的博物馆同仁们得到本书。我们这些在美国博物馆协会工作的同行希望本书以及该套丛书的其他书籍能够帮助您以及贵馆更好地为公众服务。

    虽然我们是"美国"博物馆协会，但我们的 — 以及你们的 — 工作并不会只停留在任何国境线内。博物馆拥有并保存属于全人类的艺术品和文物，我们的观众来自世界各个国家。我们的职责是欢迎他们，教育并激励他们，或许还能让他们对我们所共同生活的这个世界有更多的了解。我知道您作为博物馆的专业人员有着相同的职责。

    我希望本书能够成为美国博物馆专业人士与你们—我们在中国的朋友兼同仁—之间长期而丰富合作的第一步。我相信我们可以从你们那里学到许多东西，我们也非常愿意与你们分享我们的知识。

    我欢迎您和您的同仁加入我们的行列，成为美国博物馆协会的国际会员。请访问我们的网站 www.aam-us.org 了解更多的信息，或者翻到本书最后一页，以便对我们有更多的了解。

福特·W·贝尔
美国博物馆协会主席

新中国建立以来，特别是改革开放以来，中国博物馆事业进入了一个新的蓬勃发展的阶段。随着中国社会经济的快速发展，博物馆的数量和质量也在发生巨大的变化。根据国家文物局最新公布的统计数据，2008 年全国通过省级文物行政部门年检备案的博物馆已达到创纪录的 2970 座。

面对当前中国博物馆事业迅速发展的大好形势，特别是博物馆免费开放政策实施所带来的前所未有的机遇，博物馆如何提升其管理水平，更好地实现其"为社会和社会发展服务"的目标，已成为中国博物馆界所共同面临的、亟待解决的课题。

作为世界上博物馆事业高度发达的国家之一，美国在博物馆管理方面曾经进行了许多有益的探索和实践，积累了许多宝贵的经验和做法。此次我们与美国博物馆协会合作，引进、翻译并出版"美国博物馆协会博物馆管理丛书"的目的，就是希望把美国博物馆的这些经验和方法介绍给中国博物馆界。该系列丛书内容广泛，涉及博物馆的标准和认证、机构规划、职业道德准则、藏品规划与保护和教育与观众服务等诸多领域。

"他山之石，可以攻玉"，希望该套丛书的翻译、出版能推动中国博物馆界的思考和深入探讨，并在学习和借鉴美国同行经验的基础上，最终形成具有中国特色的博物馆管理体制和机制。

张柏

中国博物馆学会理事长

博物馆作为近代外来的文化形态之一，在中国已经走过了一百多年的历程。一百多年来，中国博物馆事业由小变大，由弱变强，发生了翻天覆地的变化，现已初步形成了一个具有中国特色的博物馆体系。但从总体上来说，博物馆行业仍然还有许多全局性、深层次的问题未得到很好地解决，其服务公众与社会的功能还未得到充分发挥。特别是在当前全国博物馆实施免费开放的新形势下，面对公众日益增长的精神文化需求，中国博物馆正面临着诸如体制机制如何创新，服务水平如何进一步提升，教育工作如何更好地开展，认证评估如何科学地进行等一系列亟待解决的新问题。

而作为近代博物馆发源地的西方发达国家，其博物馆在二十世纪后半叶以来正经历着巨大的变革，博物馆与社会之间的联系更加紧密，之间的互动也更为密切，其在博物馆管理方面也处于领先的地位。因此，当美国博协主席福特·贝尔先生提出用中文翻译出版一套"美国博物馆协会博物馆管理丛书"的想法时，我们感到非常高兴。

湖南省博物馆与美国博协经过长达半年多的反复沟通与协调，最后从美国博协完全拥有版权的图书中总共挑选出十本我们认为对当前中国博物馆具有重要参考、借鉴价值的书籍。考虑到通过中国博物馆学会这个平台向全国同行推介将使该套丛书更有价值，在征得学会同意并在张柏理事长的大力支持下，我们最终决定以中国博物馆学会的名义组织丛书编委会，并由湖南省博物馆博物馆学研究所具体负责该套丛书的翻译出版工作。

愿该套丛书能给我们带来有益的启示。

陈建明

湖南省博物馆馆长

中国博物馆学会副理事长

前　言

　　什么样的博物馆能算得上是伟大的博物馆？我们见到它的时候肯定都能知道。可如果你去某个博物馆，向一位董事、助理研究员、馆长、营销部的某个人以及随意挑选的几位观众提出几个基本问题——该博物馆的目标是什么，该博物馆如何实现这些目标，该博物馆的目标应该是什么——你可能会发现对于这些大家都知道的问题，每个人的回答不尽相同。

　　因此，我们需要本书。美国博物馆协会的一个核心作用便是给博物馆界提供讨论、教育和交流的平台，这既可以是年度大会和职业教育研讨会，也可以是这样的出版物。《美国博物馆国家标准及最佳做法》将一流专业人员的经验和最佳思路综合在一起，不仅探讨博物馆如何经营，而且探讨博物馆在大千世界里应该发挥的作用。我们的目标是：提供具体的方法，让大家更加深入地思考如何将自己的机构办得最好，也提供各种工具，让大家将自己的想法变为现实。

福特·W·贝尔，兽医学博士
美国博物馆协会主席

致 谢

　　本人深感荣幸，能够为《美国博物馆国家标准及最佳做法》一书撰写评述。我在美国博物馆协会（AAM）的一部分工作便是帮助董事会搜集数十年来所积累的分散在各处的各种标准和最佳做法文件，并且将它们汇集成一个整体。多年来，美国博物馆协会的《博物馆职业道德准则》、认证项目标准以及美国博物馆协会的其他文件一直在指导着美国博物馆的行为。然而，美国博物馆协会董事会直到2006年（恰好是美国博物馆协会创建一百周年之际）才正式将这些文件指定为该领域的国家标准。这一过程还在不断完善中，因为美国博物馆协会正努力将协会下属十三个常设专业委员会制定出的标准和最佳做法汇集到一起。新的标准将在未来几年中问世，以满足人们对博物馆新的要求以及应对新出现的各种挑战。

　　本书的第二部分主要介绍这些标准和最佳做法。在相应的章节中，本人依据自己在博物馆领域的工作经验，介绍各种标准所适用的具体情况。本人已经在博物馆领域工作了二十三年，最后这八年一直在美国博物馆协会工作，主要负责认证与博物馆评估项目，以及美国博物馆协会董事会的职业道德特别工作组。我在这个位置上曾花大量的时间与人们探讨博物馆应该以及实际如何表现。如果有博物馆馆长对认证结果感到不快，他们会给我打电话。如果有媒体联系美国博物馆协会，询问某博物馆是否违反了博物馆标准，公关部的人员也向我汇报。每当认证委员会为哪些标准合适以及这些标准应该如何应用感到难以抉择时，我会倾听并鼓励他们更加深入地探讨这些难题。

　　对于这些标准应该在哪些真实环境中得到检验，博物馆如何将这些标准运用于实践以及最大的问题有可能出现在什么地方，我已经对自己的观察结果进行了总结，其中的许多结果都来自于我与全国各地博物馆专业人士的真实交谈内容。换言之，这一切都已经过同行们的实际检验。我希望大家也能觉得这对自己有用。

　　本书的评述部分反映了博物馆界无数人的集体智慧，任何完全属于我本人的评述也是依据于我从他们那里学到的东西。这些人当中最主要的是认证委员会的成员，他们每年要花数百个小时阅读并讨论他们所评估的博物馆材料。我尤其要感谢该委员会所有前任以及现任负责人，感谢圣玛丽城历史遗址博物馆馆长马蒂·沙利文和沃切斯特艺术博物馆馆长吉姆·维鲁。在我们做出这些艰难的决定时，他们的耐心指导对我而言不啻为难得的教育过程。

　　我要感谢我的同事伊琳·戈尔德斯皮尔、朱丽·哈特、金·伊戈、埃里克·雷德贝特和海伦·威赫斯勒，他们对认证标准、国家以及国际博物馆职业道德、政府规定和新闻学等领域有着深刻的理解，因而对本书的细节以及保证本书的准确性做出了巨大的贡献。任何错误或疏漏 — 万一有什么逃过了他们敏锐的眼睛 — 均为本书作者之过。我还要特别感谢维多利亚·加文，正是她在将近十年前出任美国博物馆协会的第一位标准研究者／起草者时首次提出了这个问题："这些标准究竟在哪里？"（美国博物馆协会当时还没有正式批准任何行业标准！）虽然她早已另谋高就，我在撰写本书时脑海里仍然能时常听到维多利亚评价行文时的声音，激励我在做解释时尽量表达清晰、精确。

　　我已经明白了一个道理，好的写作能力来自好的编辑，因此我要感谢约翰·斯特兰德和丽莎·梅耶洛维兹的精心努力，将原先松散的书稿变成了流畅的行文。在他们的指导下，我的写作和思维能力都有了提高。我还要感谢科斯腾·安克斯和苏姗·V·列文，他们在设计方面的专业知识给本书增添了美感。

　　我要感谢我的丈夫克里夫·杜克，感谢他在多个早晨当我感到需要详细评论《纽约时报》上刊登的关于博物馆以及博物馆行为（或错误行为）的报道时耐心地聆听。最后，感谢我的花剑教练维塔里·波卡伦科，感谢他不断地提醒我不要过于严肃。我希望我在本书中接受了他的建议。

伊丽莎白·E·梅里特
"博物馆未来"中心的创建主任

目　录

第一部分　简介

本书的适用对象及使用方法

本书为国家博物馆标准（所有优秀博物馆都应该做的事）和最佳做法（博物馆会为此得到额外加分的行为）的一个概述，介绍了这些标准的制定过程、适用对象和目的，以及博物馆如何运用这些标准来指导经营。本书将各种标准和最佳做法集中在一起，再从常人的角度去探讨它们在实际应用中的具体情况，为认真探讨博物馆能够以及应该从事的活动定下基调，因此请尽可能多地将本书与那些和你们探讨这些问题的人分享。你们可能想把本书分送给：

- 治理机构[1]成员：帮助他们了解各种标准，让他们更好地指导员工制定决策，可以据此更好地让外界对他们作为董事会成员的业绩进行评价；
- 博物馆的员工：创建一个共有的文化，并且为制定博物馆政策和各种规定创造一个良好的基础；
- 参与制定博物馆规划的人：将达到博物馆标准定为各项长期目标的指导原则；
- 上级单位的主管（如果有上级单位的话），如大学、市政府、营利性公司或基金会：营造出一个能让博物馆发展、主管能够帮助博物馆实现目标的环境；
- 新闻记者：让他们知道如何报道博物馆，让他们掌握更多知识来向公众介绍博物馆；
- 出资人和资助机构：让出资人和机构知道博物馆了解这些标准，帮助他们制定恰当的评判标准来确定博物馆是否值得他们资助。

第二部分将详细介绍这些标准，首先介绍至关重要的"优秀标准"的特征，然后介绍这些"特征"所针对的七个业绩评估领域。此后的七个小节将分别介绍这七个领域的"特征"，介绍各个领域所涉及的更为详细的标准，对经常造成问题或者引起疑问的一些事情进行评述，并大致介绍一些相关的最佳做法。

---

[1] 参见术语表中"Governing authority 治理机构"条。——译注

何为博物馆？

> 博物馆是一个以特殊方式邀请人们对人类为追求真、善、美而做的努力进行反省和思索的场所。这种反省与思索一方面能够让我们明白自己多么无足轻重和昙花一现，另一方面能够加深我们与永存之物之间那种神秘联系和关系的体验。
>
> ——F.J.C.J.努言，荷兰社会学家，1981

多年来，人们曾无数次试图为"博物馆"的种类确立一个固定的界限，明确界定哪些机构属于博物馆，哪些机构不属于博物馆。人们曾经考虑过的一些方面包括：

- 该机构（私人所有或政府所有）属于非营利性，而不是以营利为目的。依据这个评判标准而被排斥在外的机构有国际间谍博物馆、巴尔的摩庄园、超级歌星猫王的故居、美国国际响尾蛇博物馆和性博物馆，更不用提数不清的还没能正式成为非营利机构的小型博物馆（如位于亚利桑那州苏必利尔市的"世界最小博物馆"，其室内总面积只有 134 平方英尺）。博物馆界的行家们可能会坚定地认为非营利性质是一个重要的方面，能够确定绝大多数博物馆的主要目的是为公众服务，从街头走进来的普通人可能会认为上述机构完全符合他心目中的博物馆这一概念。

- 该机构是否将教育视为自己的核心功能。几乎每个人都赞同将这定为一个合适的评判标准，可当你一旦意识到教育可以包括各种获得知识的形式，那么这个评判标准就会因包罗万象而变得毫无意义。对于广告偶像博物馆、乐倍饮料博物馆及自由企业制研究院[2]、侏罗纪技术博物馆这种机构而言，你能否认他们的教育本质或内容吗？它们可能没有展出传统艺术、历史或科学，但它们在各自选定的领域均提供了令人惊叹的知识。还有华盛顿州拜恩布里奇岛的布鲁德尔保护区呢？它宣传自己的目的是"让人们有机会通过在花园和林地静静地散步来欣赏大自然"。这显然是一座公共花园，因而也是一座博物馆，但它的教育作用极为有限。因此，这种评判标准又如何有助于人们将博物馆与图书馆、学校、舞蹈工作室或其他明显具有教育作用的机构区分开来呢？

- 保管、保护和展出各种物件。这条评判标准在过去显然没有错，但二十世纪

---

[2] 位于美国得克萨斯州韦科市的乐倍饮料博物馆成立于 1988 年，旨在全面介绍软饮料的历史以及相应知识；自由企业制研究院为该博物馆为感谢乐倍公司首席执行官 W·W·克莱门茨而于 1997 年创建的研究院，旨在"向得克萨斯州的学生及成年人介绍美国所采用的自由企业经济体系"。——译注

末出现了大量被视为博物馆却并不保管、拥有或使用藏品的机构——例如，许多儿童博物馆和科学中心虽然将物件用作道具，却并不将这些视为受公众之托而拥有的藏品[3]。目前有百分之十的博物馆声称自己不拥有也不使用藏品。

- 该机构是否有具体场所（其本身可能就是历史遗址），是否在该场所让人们通过体验来了解其诠释的内容。然而，越来越多的博物馆都是虚拟的，只存在于互联网上。它们可能有具体的场所，拥有不对外展出的藏品，但有些人可能觉得它们并不"存在"。这些完全是传播知识和图像的虚拟机构，没有真实场所（除了容纳网站的服务器）。（如国际宇宙飞行博物馆，它就"位于"互联网上的"第二人生"这个虚拟世界中。）就连一些有馆舍的传统博物馆也正通过自己的网站为越来越多的人提供服务——这些网站的浏览量远远超过去馆舍实际参观的人数。如果真实世界中的博物馆关闭或者转移，但其网站仍然存在，难道该博物馆就会因此不再被视为博物馆吗？

我们可能不得不接受这样一个事实："博物馆"这个概念是许多复杂类别的相交点，结果是人们可以凭直觉判定一个机构为"博物馆"，但却无法给它下一个清晰明了的定义。

那么对于这些难以下定义的机构，我们该如何制定标准呢？美国博物馆协会采取了迎合多种不同观点的"大帐篷"政策。如果一个机构认为自己是博物馆，那它就算这大帐篷里的一份子。这就意味着从我们的角度来看，美国博物馆界既包括少数营利性博物馆也包括绝大多数非营利性博物馆，既包括传统意义上的收藏性博物馆也包括非收藏性博物馆，既包括保管活体藏品的机构（动物园、植物园、水族馆）也包括艺术、历史和科学博物馆。我们将这些看似千奇百怪的机构归入到同一类别中，这种直观判断依据于这样一个事实：它们的确能够就适用于所有机构的标准达成一致意见。

为什么需要制定标准？

标准：能够充当进行比较、规范或模型之物；所需或所认同的质量水准或成就。
——《简明牛津英语辞典》

与他人进行比较是人的天性——我们想知道自己没有做错事，想知道自己达到了什

---

[3] 伊丽莎白·E·梅里特主编，2006，《博物馆财务信息》（美国首都华盛顿：美国博物馆协会，2006）

么样的标准。就个人行为而言，我们比较的对象是文化规范 — 习惯的行为、道德规定；以及社会基准 — 如智商测验、教育学位、业绩评估、薪水。从大众杂志的内容来看，美国人无法抗拒"我表现如何"等各种自我评价的测试的诱惑，自我评价的内容五花八门，既有约会、外表和性行为的表现，也有人生目标的实现程度。

我们自然也将这一套引入到了我们的工作中。每一个专业领域从创始之初就开始制定自己的专业评估准则。对于个人而言，怎样才能算一个优秀的机械师、医生或精神病专家？对于机构而言，怎样才能算一个优秀的大学、兽医院或有机农场？有些机构相对比较容易判定。如果它们要求根据结果进行评定，那么它们所达到的效果比较容易描述：学生通过考试并找到工作；宠物被治愈并在生命的最后阶段得到关怀；产品不含化学物质。博物馆作为一个领域却比较难确定我们力图达到的效果，至少无法以任何清晰、可以量化的方法进行评定。作为非正式学习途径的提供者，我们不一定能搜寻到并测量我们对人们的认知所产生的影响。我们所提供的知识也不总是一个具体的事实或者一种思维方式，它常常是一种体验 — 视觉、听觉、嗅觉、触觉和情感的总和 — 能够丰富我们的生活经历。

目前，美国绝大多数博物馆都是非营利机构，需要得到某种形式的公众支持，作为对公众提供服务的回报。因此我们的行为是否能够在很大程度上接受公众的问责就显得非常重要，公众不仅指我们的服务对象，而且是指整个社会。尽管有些博物馆单独评估并报告它们对观众和服务对象所产生的影响，但这类博物馆的数量少之又少，而对整个博物馆领域进行的研究依然十分缺乏。因此，制定出公认的标准，能够说明什么样的博物馆算是"优秀"博物馆，值得公众支持和信任 — 这就越发显得重要。

而且，由于我们负责管理45亿至60亿美元的政府和私人资助资金，博物馆理所当然地成了执法人员关注的对象[4]。恪守相互认同的标准可以让博物馆在很大程度上进行自我约束，以灵活且适当的方式满足我们领域多样性的特点。一旦博物馆某个重要经营领域的标准阐明得不够明确，或者某座博物馆的行为违反了普遍接受的（即便是不成文的）公共标准，政府便会出面干预，我们就得面对联邦政府、州政府或者地方政府的法规，而这些法规不一定合理并适用于各种类型和规模的博物馆。

最后但也是最重要的一点，美国媒体的6.7万名从业者正密切监视着博物馆，他们便是自封的公众利益和政府疏漏的监督员。新闻记者是社会的监督员，虽然我们作为被监督的对象可能不喜欢他们，但他们对博物馆行为（博物馆的错误行为的确会成

---

[4] 根据《2005年博物馆财务信息调查》收集到的数据以及美国人口统计署关于雇主机构数据的估计。

为重大新闻）的狂热关注能让我们时刻保持警觉。他们不断地测试我们，看我们是否能令人信服地解释我们的行为，是否能够向公众说明为什么这些行为按照我们自己制定的标准是合理合法的。

标准的特点

标准能够反映一些普遍公认的领域。如果人们没有达成一致意见或者比较接近的意见，任何标准都不会问世，因为大家没有就任何问题达成共识。当博物馆尝试不同类型的经营行为，观察他们的同仁、公众、执法人员和媒体对这些尝试有何反应并随之调整。它们可能会发现一些非常重要的经营领域根本没有标准。这种对标准的探讨有时会持续几十年而仍然无法达成一致意见。

标准能够反映一些确实会出错的领域。人们不会为不可能发生的行为制定标准。最近出现的一件事便是，洛杉矶现代艺术博物馆在日本艺术家村上隆作品展览的中央搭建了一个路易威登的时装店。村上隆以探索艺术与商业之间模糊不清的界限而著称，尤其是与路易威登进行过多次合作。该专卖店的利润属于路易威登公司，而不是博物馆。有些人开始质疑这样做是否符合道德规范。这种行为违反博物馆标准吗？答案是否定的。目前的博物馆标准并没有涉及营利性公司在展览中央开设商店的内容。就我所知，以前从来没有博物馆这样尝试过，因此这个问题从来没有出现过，自然也就没有人探讨过它所涉及的更广泛的道德问题。

标准会与时俱进。博物馆标准来自人们对技术的了解（如何将事情做好，如保护或教育）以及人们对正确和合适行为的态度（职业道德）。对技术的了解以及人们的态度又随着时间的变化而不断发展。当我们逐渐了解相对湿度以及温度对物件和建筑物产生的影响有多么复杂时，我们制定的控制博物馆环境的技术标准也越来越精细。我记得当初最高层直接下达了规定，将湿度控制在"55％±3％"。没有任何商量余地。但我们现在知道，对于加利福尼亚州毕晓普市（平均相对湿度为20％）某座砖结构里的博物馆而言，你根本无法要求它保持55％的室内相对湿度，否则砖头就会碎裂。社会也在发生着变化，因此博物馆标准随着更大的文化环境发展。五十年前，人们普遍认为博物馆可以拥有来自其他文化的人类骸骨和圣物，而现在人们正进行着激烈的辩论，这样做是否符合道德标准以及什么时候符合道德标准。由于博物馆在这方面落后于社会期待，没有能够制定出并应用令人信服的标准，美国国会通过了《美国原住民坟墓保护与归还法》（NAGPRA），以法律的形式规定博物馆必须如何与联邦政府认可的原住民部落和夏威夷原住民组织打交道。该法律成效显著，但如果博物馆在这之前就已经主动与部落代表协商，寻找到双方可以接受的解决方法，这种方法从效率和效果的角度来说可能会更好（效率和效果正是政府规定通常所缺乏的两个特点）。如果从相互信任和美好意愿的前提出发，双方在具体实施解决方法时也会容易一些。

因此，本书可谓是对千变万化的景色拍摄的一张快照。大家在使用本书时还要阅读专业期刊，参加地方、州和地区的博物馆会议，登陆美国博物馆协会和其他博物馆行业协会的网站，与同行进行交流，以此来关注下一周、下一月、下一年可能会出现的变化。

标准源自广泛的对话。博物馆标准若想做到适用而可信，就需要通过一定的程序来制定，该程序必须综合将来会遵守这些标准的人员以及那些对标准有所期待的人的意见。正是由于这一点，大家应该积极参与目前的讨论，并最终以书面形式制定出标准 — 这些标准若想适用于所有博物馆，就需要各个类型和各种规模的博物馆里的专业人员集思广益。由于我们面临着来自公众的越来越大的问责压力，因此我们也需要听取公众、政策制定人和媒体代表的意见，他们将运用这些标准来评估博物馆是否达到了他们的期望。大家还可以向你们博物馆的出资人、地方政策制定人、媒体以及国会议员宣传博物馆标准，将他们也吸引到标准的讨论中来。

何为"标准与最佳做法"？

如果说人们很难确定哪一点可以算博物馆的特点，那么我们很容易说出博物馆从业人员的特点：我们都特别喜欢就词语的意思进行辩论。如果我们就"标准"一词的定义展开辩论，那么本书的篇幅可以比现在大上十倍却刚刚开始言归正传。为了预先阻止这场辩论（然后迅速转入到确定这些标准这一重要任务上），美国博物馆协会董事会批准了下列定义。当然，我们无法让博物馆领域的其他部门统一采用这一定义，但它至少为理解本书的内容确定了一个定义。

*标准*是为人们普遍接受、所有博物馆都应该达到的业绩水平。*最佳做法*为值得称赞的行动与理念，能够表明人们了解这些标准，能够成功地解决难题，可以被复制，可以被适用的博物馆仿效。

翻译成通俗语言：标准是所有优秀博物馆都应该达到的水平，如果博物馆没有达到这一水平就会受到同行、出资人或媒体的批评。标准不是只有少数几座博物馆能够达到的高不可攀的目标，而是博物馆成为一流机构、成为一个负责任的经营良好的非营利机构所必须具备的条件。最佳做法为"奖励分"。博物馆如果将这些付诸行动就会得到称赞，但如果没有也不会受到批评。有些最佳做法可能并不符合某座博物馆的特殊情况，某些博物馆则可能缺乏所需的资源来实施最佳的做法。

标准来自何处？

美国共有 17,000 多座博物馆，20 多万从业人员[5]。这些博物馆的大小不等，有些博物馆只有志愿者，有些博物馆的正式员工就超过三百人。它们每年的经营成本也从几百美元到上千万美元不等。这些机构包括历史遗址和故居、动物园、艺术博物馆、历史博物馆、科学中心、儿童博物馆、自然中心和植物园（略微列举了一些）。创建一个体系，制定出适用于所有这些机构的标准，这真是难以想象的重任。

幸运的是，博物馆界不必立刻创建这样的体系——它已经通过近四十年的探索自行发展了起来。这个方法的概念非常简单：召集能够代表这些不同博物馆的人相互交流，让他们有机会去近距离观察大量不同的博物馆和这些博物馆的经营方式，让他们交流哪些做法行得通、哪些做法行不通，讨论哪些适用、哪些不适用，将这些记录下来，报告给整个博物馆界，看看哪些为人们所接受或者遭到人们的拒绝因而需要修改。这一过程通过代表博物馆界不同部门利益的几十个专业协会的活动来进行，美国博物馆协会则代表其整个博物馆界。

在美国博物馆协会内部，负责探讨行业标准的主要是博物馆认证项目、由美国博物馆协会董事会任命的职业道德特别工作组和常设专业委员会（代表着博物馆行业的各个不同人群：研究人员，登录人员，教育人员，安全人员等等）。

其中博物馆认证项目对于制定博物馆书面标准产生的影响最大。我们将在第 11 页进一步介绍认证项目在认定成绩和执行标准中所起的作用，此处只集中介绍它在制定博物馆标准方面所起的作用。认证项目总共包括约 800 座博物馆（已经通过认证的有 770 多座，另外有十多座博物馆提出了申请）。要想通过认证，这些博物馆必须首先对自己经营的各个方面进行详细的自我评估。两位业内评估专家（来自相似机构的高级馆员）阅读它们递交的自我评估报告，去这些博物馆实地考察，然后撰写报告总结他们的观察结果。最后，博物馆递交的自我评估报告和评估人员所写的报告由志愿参加认证委员会的九位博物馆专业人士进行评审。该委员会根据这些信息决定让该博

---

[5] 博物馆与图书馆服务协会估计美国有 17,000 座博物馆，见 www.IMLS.gov；从业人员估计值来自美国博物馆协会对 2000 年人口调查结果的分析，见密苏里人口普查数据中心 http://mcdc2.missouri.edu/。

物馆通过认证，或者搁置决定但同时要求该博物馆在它没有达到标准的方面进行整改，或者否决通过认证。大家可以想象得到，委员会、博物馆和业内评估专家之间还会就这些决定进行大量后续讨论。

该项目在二十世纪七十年代初开始时还很不正式。博物馆方面为业内评估专家提供很少的文字材料，而且主要集中在博物馆经营的某些方面，不过当时也没有任何成文的标准。当业内评估专家、委员会和等待着自己命运的博物馆，努力解决如何做出公正合理的决定时，人们逐渐意识到必须创建一套能够对博物馆进行评估的客观标准——一些大家事先都能知道的规定，以便让委员会在做出决定时有一个共同参照点。这些规定逐渐发展和增加，变成了后来的《美国博物馆国家标准和最佳做法》的核心。

对于博物馆国家标准至关重要的另一个文件是《博物馆职业道德准则》。这份文件于1978年起草，最近一次修订是2000年。它指导不同博物馆创建了自己的内部道德准则。这份文件以及美国博物馆协会董事会批准的其他职业道德文件在正式通过之前被分发给了整个博物馆界，供大家讨论（甚至热烈辩论）。这个过程可以采取多种形式，包括就某一议题召开全国学术报告会（如2002年和2005年召开的学术报告会便分别探讨了藏品规划和藏品诠释规划的制定过程）；专业大会的特别会议；正式讨论期；参考其他机构特别行动组或委员会的做法。

各种按专业划分的博物馆协会也采用了相同步骤，它们为自己所代表的博物馆制定了适用的标准——美国州和地方历史协会、儿童博物馆协会、科技中心协会等等。这些已经成文的标准合在一起后构成了一个相互重叠、适用于所有博物馆的指导原则，然后再细分为适用于某些特殊、具体领域的做法和道德规范。

总而言之，博物馆标准是经过漫长而又艰难的对话之后得到的结果，将各种意见综合在了一起，并且得到了整个博物馆界的一致认同，因为出席这场对话的代表都是积极参与各自专业协会的员工。只有这样才能确保这些标准适用于各种类型的博物馆，确保这些标准在这些博物馆中得到落实。

博物馆如何运用这些标准？

治理和经营博物馆的董事、员工与志愿者来自不同背景和文化，接受过不同的培训。员工可能接受过博物馆学的培训，懂得非营利性机构的一般经营模式；他们也可能有着各自专业（艺术、科学、历史）的大学教育背景，但是缺乏或者根本没有非营利机构经营的法律和道德基础知识。有些人主要在工作过程中学习，但各个博物馆的做法又不尽相同，尤其是在一些小型或偏远的机构中，标准和规范可能与整个博物馆界的标准和规范相去甚远。有些员工、许多董事和志愿者 — 更可能是馆长本人 — 都来自营利性机构，因而对自己的机构或雇员的行为是否正确与合适有着完全不同的看法。一些隶属于非博物馆实体（如大学、市政府或州政府）的博物馆可能需要向一些人报告，而这些人的本能是将该实体的习惯做法应用在博物馆身上，根本不考虑这些做法是否会与博物馆的习惯做法相冲突。

博物馆的经营过程之所以会出现许多冲突，部分原因是人们想当然地认为大家都使用相同的语言，而实际上非营利性机构（尤其是博物馆）有着非常详细、非常晦涩的语言来指导这些机构的思维。为了确保领导和经营博物馆的各方都能理解博物馆的各种标准，我们首先就需要确定通用词汇。正如1981年出版的介绍艰难谈判技巧的经典著作《谈判力》指出的那样，为做决定而制定出客观标准能够帮助有着不同需求的各方达成明智而有效的解决方案。人们通常都会同意：一致认可的国家标准是指导他们做出各种决定的最佳办法。

下面这些机会能够让人们了解这些标准，帮助他们建立起一个共享的文化：

- 雇佣员工、选举董事或者招募志愿者时：在人事政策、董事会简介、志愿者手册或类似文件中加入一本《美国博物馆"优秀标准"的特征》。在新员工、新董事和新志愿者初次见面会上介绍这些标准。

- 博物馆制定规划时：博物馆标准要求博物馆在制定规划的过程中阐明自己的目标。有些博物馆会制定出自己应该达到的标准，或者借助达标认证让人们知道自己已经达到标准，而通过认证本身就是一个目标。当规划人员开始工作时，将博物馆标准以及他们可能会研究的其他重要文件一起交给他们（如上一个规划，博物馆最新的财务报告，可行性研究报告等）。

- 在员工和董事会制定政策时：博物馆管理方式中首先需要进行评估的是该博物馆是否遵守自己的各项政策，而这些政策应该与所有适用的国家以及行业标准相一致。虽然博物馆的行动可能会让一些个人感到不快，但只要这些行动没有违背预先制定并通过的政策，这些个人就很难将这些行动认定为"错误的"。当然，最重要的是这些政策必须在采取行动之前就已经制定了出来。（没有什么比事后补救更糟糕，因为这会让本来很正常的行动变了味。）还有一点同样重要：这些政策必须公之于众，让人们看到该博物馆相信自己的政策能经得起公众的审查。

- 在博物馆申请资助时：如果能让出资的个人和基金会、上级拨款机构和决策者明白什么样的博物馆算"优秀"博物馆，值得他们资助，这对于博物馆本身和整个博物馆界都大有益处。大家在与出资人联系、起草拨款申请和与地方、州或国家政府官员合作时，可以将关于这些标准的信息以及如何达到这些标准的做法纳入到文件中。

- 在做出重要决定以及在制定相应的沟通计划时：你是否能解释博物馆的行为如何与国家标准保持一致？正如第三部分所探讨的那样，每当有博物馆出现在新闻中，而且涉及的是媒体或公众认为有问题的事，他们就会给美国博物馆协会打电话，我们就会请他们参阅国家标准，以此来引导他们对博物馆的行为做出评判。因此，在既成事实之前一定要用这些标准来衡量一下你的决定。

- 在对博物馆的业绩进行评估并报告时：人们越来越频繁地要求博物馆公开解释它们究竟做了什么，为什么值得公众为它们出资。尽管最有意义的办法是以文件的形式解释博物馆如何实现其使命（即它给服务对象和观众带来的益处），但是向人们展示你们遵守了国家博物馆标准也是一种有效的方法，能够让公众、媒体、决策者和出资方了解你们非常负责地使用了他们所提供的支持。博物馆可以就这一点自行评估并提交报告，也可以请其他机构的咨询师，参加诸如博物馆评估和藏品保护评估等以同行评估为主的项目，或者以通过认证的方式接受其他机构颁发的符合标准的证书。

该标准的其他适用对象以及运用方法

出资方越来越多地运用国家标准来评估一些博物馆是否值得他们资助。有些出资方会考虑该博物馆是否通过认证，并且会将这种来自第三方的证书视为该博物馆达到国家标准的证明。例如，佛罗里达州要求博物馆必须通过认证才能获得某些种类的州政府拨款。克雷斯哥基金会和其他一些主要资助机构在研究资助申请时会考虑博物馆是否通过认证。美国博物馆与图书馆服务协会在给予拨款时会考虑该博物馆是否参与博物馆评估项目，并会优先考虑那些由行业专家依照标准进行过评估的博物馆。我们没有统计地方以及地区性出资方运用这些标准的频率，但我们知道这是一种趋势，而且这种做法将来会变得更加常见。

决策者在决定是否以及如何制定法规来规范博物馆的行为时也会参照这些博物馆标准。博物馆界之所以要主动制定标准，常常是因为要赶在政府法规出台之前。例如，《美国博物馆协会个人捐赠指导原则》便是在 1999 年布鲁克林艺术博物馆《轰动》展览举办前夕起草的，因为该展览带来了一个问题：展出作品的出借方查尔斯·萨奇是否对展览的内容以及展出形式施加过不当影响，博物馆方面在萨奇的资助和他参与的程度这个问题上缺乏透明度。纽约州政府在考虑是否将一些博物馆定为州立非营利性机构时会考虑这些博物馆是否通过认证。美国各州的总检察长在仔细考虑自己辖区内非营利性博物馆的行为时也会参照国家标准。一旦这些总检察长代表公众出面干预——可能是由于博物馆方面主动要求他们干预，或者是由于博物馆方面可能违背了公众的信任（如纽约市立博物馆建议大规模地出售其藏品时），他们在作出判决以及给博物馆方面提供指导意见时不仅要考虑国家法律，还要考虑道德和博物馆标准。

媒体从业者也会运用博物馆标准来进行新闻报道，尤其是涉及有些人觉得不道德或者纯粹是不喜欢的具有争议的行为时。经常有媒体从业者就这座或者那座博物馆的事联系美国博物馆协会，询问该博物馆的行为是否符合国家标准。我们不会对某博物馆的行为进行评述，但我们非常乐意利用这种机会向新闻记者介绍博物馆标准，帮助他们懂得如何将这些标准运用在他们的报道中。最容易引起媒体关注的话题为：出售藏品、藏品保护、高管的薪水、财务困境（尤其是由于财务管理不当造成的财务困境）、与捐赠个人或法人之间的关系以及利益冲突。

越来越多的公众也会参照博物馆标准，尤其是当他们对博物馆的某些做法感到不满并且想引起媒体的关注时。以前的情况是公众比较难接触到专业标准，除非有人非常投入地进入图书馆进行研究或者致信专业协会。现在有了互联网，任何人只要有浏览器，只要掌握了如何在互联网上搜寻到信息，就能轻而易举地得到这些资料。博物馆方面应该知道自己的服务对象和观众能够接触到这些信息，因此它们在做出任何决定并且向公众进行解释时应该牢记这一点。

博物馆认证

在美国，博物馆是否按照标准行事完全是自愿的。虽然博物馆方面可能面临来自出资方、政府部门、媒体和公众的压力，但最终决定是否选择遵守这些标准的还是博物馆本身。

不过，还是有相当多的博物馆正式取得了美国博物馆协会认证项目颁发的证书，以此来保证自己将遵守这些标准。在过去十年中，通过认证的博物馆数量一直比较稳定，介于750至770之间，约占美国博物馆总数的百分之五。我们应该赞扬这些博物馆勇于承担接受公众问责的重任。这些机构向同行开放自己的经营体系并接受他们的严密审查，从而提高了所有博物馆的声誉。它们也对完善这些标准起到了重要作用——认证本身就是一个考验过程，人们可以对一些重要问题进行认真研究，可以分析一些行为模式是否一直很成功，可以检验一些新制定的标准是否与已有标准保持连贯性、是否适用和恰当。

认证项目本身也在随着时代的变化而不断地改进，即使在本书写作过程中，该项目也在经历重大改革。不过，自二十世纪七十年代启动以来，该项目的整体框架一直保持不变，而且很可能会继续保持这样。在该认证项目中，博物馆：

- 首先开始全方位自我评估，详细记录经营的各方面情况。这种自我评估包括将所有重要文件汇总在一起，如各种规划和经过政府部门批准的政策；
- 接受由博物馆专家组成的委员会的评估。这些人将审阅博物馆的自我评估报告以及所附文件，去该博物馆实地考察，并且与董事会成员、员工和志愿者面谈；
- 接受认证委员会的最终评审。该委员会由博物馆专业人士自愿组成，他们将审阅博物馆递交的自我评估报告、所附文件以及专家的评估报告，然后决定该博物馆是否达到美国博物馆协会的标准。

美国博物馆协会的网站（**www.aam-us.org**）提供了很多信息，包括这些标准在认证过程中如何运用，以及接受认证的博物馆应该提供哪些文件来证明它们确实达到了标准。

多年来我一直与不同博物馆的员工交换意见，我估计只要有一座博物馆通过认证，就会另有十座博物馆自觉地运用博物馆标准来指导自己的规划和经营。有些博物馆希望最终能通过认证，其他博物馆则认为这些标准虽然实用，也值得它们关注，但它们并不需要或者不想要这种认证证书。还有几座博物馆则主动决定不参加，因为它们觉得自己的企业文化与其中一些标准不相符。

不过，所有非营利机构 — 包括博物馆 — 都面临着来自政府决策者和出资方越来越大的压力，要求它们遵守公认的正式标准并且向公众证明自己确实做到了这一点。考虑到这种趋势很可能会继续，博物馆认证 — 或者某种形式的证书 — 将来很可能会起到更大的作用。在这种情况下，本书提出的这些标准以及博物馆用来证明自己遵守这些标准的方法就越发显得重要。正是考虑到所有博物馆的最大利益，博物馆界才制定出这些标准以及评判这些标准的程序，免得博物馆被迫去遵守一些根本不符合这一行业特点的标准或者要求。

第二部分 标准与最佳做法

核心问题

参照博物馆标准对博物馆进行评估，必然会涉及两个核心问题：该博物馆在多大程度上实现了其阐明的使命和目标？该博物馆的业绩在多大程度上达到了博物馆界普遍公认并且适用的标准和最佳做法？

评述

这些问题对于在各种规模和类型的博物馆中灵活而恰当地运用国家标准至关重要。

使命与目标

非营利性博物馆为公众提供服务，这类博物馆会在其目标宣言中阐明自己的服务对象和服务方式。（详情请见第33页介绍目标宣言的内容。）因此，在对一个博物馆进行评估时，不管评估方是公众、媒体、出资方、认证专家还是其他机构，最主要的问题是看该博物馆是否成功地完成了自己的使命。博物馆在选择自己使命的同时也为自己选择了被评估的主要基准。

如果两座博物馆经营活动完全相同但有着不同的使命，那它们在评估方面可能会有完全不同的结果。一座小型历史博物馆如果为自己确定的使命是通过诠释所在地区的历史来服务当地社区，那它在完成这一使命方面可能会做得很好。另一座城市中与它一模一样的博物馆，虽然展览和项目也完全相同，但为自己确定了雄心勃勃的使命，要成为促进历史界学术发展的世界级博物馆，那它很可能无法实现这一目标。

目标宣言涉及的内容非常广泛，大多数博物馆都可以用不同方式实现自己的使命。每座博物馆通过自己的规划进行更加具体的选择，主要是机构规划（见第36页）。这些规划会确立具体的目标，如"三年内创建一个最先进的新展厅"、"通过博物馆认证"或者"通过各种项目服务将小学生的数量增加一倍"。博物馆在其规划中制定的目标成了该博物馆自我确定是否实现其使命的重要标志。

"符合自身条件"

一个主要由志愿者管理、每年经费只有五万美元的乡间艺术中心显然怎么也无法在规模或形式上与纽约的大都会艺术博物馆相提并论，然而这两个机构都可以达到国家级博物馆标准。这怎么可能呢？这是因为它们都能明智地利用已有资源做好自己的工作，从而让专家们认定其工作符合各自的条件。这个小型艺术中心可能只有一间400平方英尺的库房，陈列架为镀锌管所制，冬天配有一个手动加水的增湿器，夏天配有一个除湿器（同样需要人工倒水）。门上配有坚实的锁，钥匙掌握在兼职的馆长和志愿者研究员的手中。展品的文字说明牌由激光打印机清晰地打印出来，贴到泡沫塑料上后再用双面胶粘贴到墙壁上。照明主要采用白炽灯，几盏荧光灯均装有滤光器，以免有害的紫外线伤及艺术品。博物馆的教育项目非常出色，授课的是一群兢兢业业的志愿者，个个都完成了艺术史的自学课程。他们每年为社区举办一次开放日，以在停车场举办烧烤活动为特色，并且聘请当地的消防队员和警察。博物馆的董事包括该地区迅速增长的移民代表。还有什么不让人喜欢呢？

"符合自身条件"也要考虑到博物馆的地理位置、观众和社区的价值观。大多数博物馆不太可能将不要的藏品退还给最初的捐赠人。从法律的角度来说，捐赠人与任何人一样对这些藏品不再享有任何所有权。博物馆的主要责任——利用其资源来服务公众——通常仍然可以得到体现，最佳的办法就是将藏品捐赠给另一个非营利性机构，让藏品继续为公众服务，或者通过公开出售这些藏品来得到最佳价格，使博物馆有更多的资源来开发和保护其藏品。不过，一些主要服务于社区的小博物馆却发现，在有些情况中，将藏品退还给捐赠人非常合适。否则他们该如何告知一位捐赠人，说他祖母的婚纱卖给了千里之外的某位收藏家？或者他家祖传的《圣经》现在到了400英里外的州档案馆中？

美国博物馆"优秀标准"的特征

以下三十八点分为七大类，最初由博物馆认证委员会起草，能够让大家对国家博物馆标准有一个全面的了解。大家可以从这些特征着手，认真地研究国家标准与最佳做法。其他更加详细的说明都源自于此，本章节将详细地介绍每一大类。

I. 公众所托与可问责性

- 博物馆受公众之托保管好它所拥有的资源。
- 博物馆确定其服务的对象，并且就如何为他们服务做出正确的决定。
- 尽管博物馆有明确的服务对象，它仍然要努力为其所在社区做好服务。
- 博物馆应具有包容性，为不同人群的参与提供机会。
- 博物馆注重其为公众提供服务的作用，并且将教育列为该作用的核心。
- 博物馆致力于为公众提供条件，让他们在身心和智力上都能够接触并了解博物馆及其资源。
- 博物馆致力于接受公众的问责，并保持其使命和经营的透明性。
- 博物馆遵守地方、州和联邦政府对其设施、经营和管理的各项法律、准则和规定。

II. 使命与规划

- 博物馆对自己的使命有清晰的认识，能够阐明自己存在的理由以及从中获益的对象。
- 博物馆经营中的各项工作都围绕实现其使命开展。
- 博物馆的治理机构和员工获得、开发和分配资源要从战略的角度思考和行动，以便促进博物馆使命的发展。
- 博物馆为自己制定能够体现其机构特点、可持续的规划，这些规划包括观众和社区的参与。
- 博物馆建立衡量其成功与否的标准，并且用这些标准来评估和调整它的各项活动。

III. 领导与组织结构

- 治理机构、员工和志愿者的结构以及处理事务的程序能够有效地推动博物馆的使命。
- 治理机构、员工和志愿者对自己的作用和责任有着清晰而一致的认识。
- 治理机构、员工和志愿者合法、合理、有效地尽到自己的责任。
- 博物馆的领导层、员工和志愿者的组成和资格的多样性能够确保博物馆完成其使命，实现其目标。

- 治理机构与给博物馆提供支持的任何组织之间有着明确而正式的责任分工，不管这些组织隶属于博物馆、在博物馆内经营还是博物馆的上级机构。

IV. 藏品保管

- 博物馆拥有、展示并使用与其使命相符的藏品。
- 博物馆合法、合理、有效地管理、记录、保护和使用藏品。
- 博物馆在开展与藏品相关的研究时必须遵守相应的学术标准。
- 博物馆为其藏品的使用和开发制定战略规划。
- 博物馆遵守其使命，在确保藏品得到保护的前提下让公众接触藏品。

V. 教育与藏品诠释

- 博物馆清晰地阐明其总体的教育目标、理念与思想，并且证明它的一切活动均符合这些目标与理念。
- 博物馆了解现有和潜在观众的特点和需求，并且将这种了解应用在其藏品诠释中。
- 博物馆的藏品诠释内容所依据的是相应的研究。
- 博物馆在开展研究时要遵守学术标准。
- 博物馆可以使用与其教育目的、内容、观众和资源相符的各种技术和方法。
- 博物馆应向不同观众提供精确、恰当的藏品诠释内容。
- 博物馆在其藏品诠释活动中要始终保持高质量。
- 博物馆对自己的藏品诠释活动进行有效性评估，将评估结果用来规划和改进其活动。

VI. 财务稳定

- 博物馆合法、合理、负责任地获得、管理和分配其财务资源，促进博物馆使命的发展。
- 博物馆的经营必须对其财务状况负责，必须确保博物馆长期可持续发展。

VII. 设施与风险管理

- 博物馆通过分配空间和使用各种设施来满足藏品、观众和员工的需要。
- 博物馆有相应的措施来确保人员、藏品／物件和设施的安全。
- 博物馆采取有效措施来保护和长期维护各种设施。
- 博物馆要保持整洁、维护设施，并根据观众的需要提供其他条件。
- 博物馆采取相应措施来预防潜在的风险和损失。

上述三十八点中的每一点都体现了参与制定这些标准的所有人的大量思考。每一个用词都经过仔细斟酌，每一个意思和含意都经过详细讨论。然而这些标准给人的整体印象仍然让人不寒而栗。人们有时候正是由于其中的措辞才迟迟不愿意做出尝试——他们能感觉到制定这些标准时人们耗费了大量精力，因而他们竭力分析其中的每一个"the"、"and"和"so"。

为了越过这个障碍，帮助大家将注意力集中在这些严谨措辞背后的意图上，美国博物馆协会的工作人员大胆地将这些《特点》从官方语言翻译成了大白话。这个版本虽然有些不敬，却是一个非常有用的办法，能够让大家明白这些《特点》完全是一些常识，不仅能够实现而且必须能做到。大家在向新的观众人群介绍博物馆标准时可能想向他们散发这个版本。

翻译成"大白话"的《美国博物馆"优秀标准"的特征》

I. 公众所托与可问责性

可问责性

- 一定要好。
- 还不够——不仅要合法，而且要合乎道德准则。
- 要主动让大家看到你确实很好，确实很合乎道德准则（不要等到他们开口提出要求）。

社区活动

- 为社区服务。
- 了解服务对象……
- 各种措施要尽量稳妥：
  — 友好对待其他所有人……
  — 尤其是近在咫尺的人。

多样性与包容性

- 避免所有员工或董事都为同一类人。
- 尽量让他们很像你的服务对象……

- 或者像你的邻居。
- 让别人决定玩什么游戏⋯⋯
- 以及游戏的玩法。
- 和大家分享你的玩具。

II. 使命与规划

使命

- 知道自己想做什么⋯⋯
- 知道这会给他人带来什么样的不同。
- 然后将它写出来。
- 坚决照办。

规划

- 决定你下一步想做什么。
- 在决定自己的行动时，多听听他人的意见。
- 然后将它写出来⋯⋯
- 照办。
- 如果行不通，千万不要再尝试。
- 如果行得通，将它付诸行动。

III. 领导与组织结构

一定要确保每个人都知道自己该做什么。

- 董事会知道自己负责治理。
- 馆长知道自己负责经营（董事会也知道这一点）。
- 员工知道其他该做的事都属于他们。
- 将这些写下来。

IV. 藏品保管

- 知道自己拥有什么。
- 知道自己需要什么。
- 知道这些东西在哪里。

- 将它们保管好。
- 确保有人从中受益……
- 尤其你所关心的人。
- 以及你的邻居。

V. 教育与藏品诠释

- 知道自己的说话对象。
- 问他们想知道什么。
- 知道自己想说什么（以及自己在说什么）。
- 使用恰当的语言（或者图像，或者音乐）。
- 确保大家听懂了你的话。
- 问他们是否喜欢。
- 如果他们不喜欢，换个方式。

VI. 财务稳定

- 将钱用在博物馆的使命上。
- 钱够用吗？
- 明年还会有吗？
- 知道自己什么时候需要更多的钱吗？
- 知道自己可以从哪里得到钱吗？
- 不要做假账。

VII. 设施和风险管理

- 不要人满为患……
- 也不要到处堆满东西。
- 确保观众的安全……
- 以及员工的安全。
- 保持清洁。
- 给卫生间装满卫生纸。
- 万一其他一切都已失败，知道出口在哪里（并且确保出口有明显标志）。

I. 公众所托与可问责性

公众所托与可问责性的标准
公共所托与可问责性"优秀标准"的特征

- 博物馆受公众之托保管好它所拥有的资源。
- 博物馆确定其服务的对象,并且就如何为他们服务做出正确的决定。
- 尽管博物馆有明确的服务对象,它仍然要努力为其所在社区做好服务。
- 博物馆应具有包容性,为不同人群的参与提供机会。
- 博物馆注重其为公众提供服务的作用,并且将教育列为该作用的核心。
- 博物馆致力于为公众提供条件,让他们在身心和智力上都能够接触并了解博物馆及其资源。
- 博物馆致力于接受公众的问责,并保持其使命和经营的透明性。
- 博物馆遵守地方、州和联邦政府对其设施、经营和管理的各项法律、准则和规定。

评述

公众所托与可问责性是《特征》于 2004 年新增的一个部分,它反映了公众越来越期望他们能参与自己所资助的博物馆的决策过程,也反映了公众和决策者越来越期望博物馆能够向人们阐明自己的行为以及这些行为背后的原因。由于这些特点是新增的,我们很难准确说明博物馆应该采取哪些措施来达到这些标准。下面的评述反映了这些标准背后的依据与价值观。在缺乏"判例法"的情况下,这或许有助于大家决定如何才能最好地将这些应用到博物馆的经营中。

从大局来说,《"优秀标准"的特征》新增加的这一部分包含了一个博物馆领域第一批需要处理的标准:道德准则。以合乎道德的方式经营对于获得公众信任和资助至关重要。本书将从第 25 页开始介绍整个博物馆领域的道德准则以及涉及每座博物馆各自道德准则的标准。

资源托管

"博物馆是公众托管资源的好管家。"大家可以将犹太学者希雷尔的这句话理解为"好管家就是所有优秀博物馆的标准……其他都是评述。"管家替别人照管东西。对于非营利性的博物馆而言，这个"别人"便是公众，而博物馆必须能够就如何管理公众的财产接受公众的问责。（这有些比喻性的解释，依据的是法律——若想详细了解托管过程中的法律义务，请参阅玛莉·马拉罗的《博物馆藏品管理的法律读本》。）

上述说法是一个言简意赅的好标准，可以用它来做任何可能的决定。一个理智的人会考虑博物馆的行动是否与管好藏品、资金、建筑或任何应该管理的事相一致。例如，馆长的报酬是否与该博物馆的总预算比例相符？博物馆保护委托藏品的工作是否令人放心？即便理智的人可能会不认可某个具体问题的答案，但用这种方法来阐明这一点有助于消除人们潜在的疑虑。

服务对象与邻居

博物馆的非营利身份是因为博物馆提供公益服务——作为对公众支持的回报，我们将"利润"用来创造更加美好的社会。不过，在过去五十年中，人们对谁应该从公众资助中获益有了截然不同的看法。仅仅吸引一小群特定的观众（如上了年纪、爱好铁路的男性白人），然后说"这便是从我们的工作中获益的人群"，现在已经远远不够。人们现在期待任何博物馆都能服务更加广泛的人群。

尤其是在过去二十年中，人们越来越认同一点：博物馆需要关注邻居们的需要——即在博物馆附近生活和工作的人。他们不一定是博物馆确定的服务对象。例如，一座位于某历史古迹中的小型植物博物馆，四周恰好是经济不景气、种族结构复杂的社区。该博物馆保存并诠释其档案、珍稀典籍和植物标本。它在使命中将自己的服务对象定为研究这些藏品的科学家、历史学家和艺术家。不过，即使居住在这座博物馆周围的人从来没有迈进过它的大门，博物馆仍然影响着他们的生活。博物馆的外观，来到这里参观博物馆的观众，由此产生的停车、交通状况、垃圾和噪音污染——所有这一切都影响着博物馆邻居们的生活质量。博物馆标准规定所有博物馆必须考虑这些影响。这座博物馆或许在与其使命相关的方面是个好邻居，如培训社区的花匠和帮助社区保护好一块公共绿地：它也可以开放自己配备有上网电脑的图书馆，将它变成周围孩子们傍晚时可以在里面做作业的一个安静、安全的场所。

令人高兴的是，当博物馆开始实施这条标准时，它们发现从业务的角度来说，这样做也能给它们带来最大的利益。与你所在的社区打成一片或许能让你的邻居们成为博物馆的观众，还可能让你与当地的一些企业建立起互惠的合作关系。这样做可以让你与那些支持你们博物馆的人和基金会建立起联系，这既是因为你对社区产生了影响，也是因为他们相信你的使命（尽管他们会逐步开始关心你的使命）。这样做甚至有可能激发周围的某个孩子长大后成为植物学家，为解决我们面临的下一个挑战尽力，这个挑战便是……

公众服务作用与教育

坦率地说，博物馆标准之所以要强调教育作为确定某机构是否属于博物馆的关键，其历史原因与金钱密不可分。政府对文化事业的资助在二十世纪六十年代急剧增加，伴随而来的还有税务改革，迫使一些基金会将自己的收益用在慈善事业上，但主要分配给了文化机构。在当时，博物馆仍然被美国国内收入署定性为"娱乐性"机构。获得税收资助和其他拨款的机会越来越多，面对这样的局面，要想有资格获得这些款项，博物馆就需要将自己牢固地定位在教育领域中。美国博物馆的历史记录了它们给社会各个阶级提供教育的雄心，直到今天仍然如此。同样，政府、所有出资的基金会和个人仍然期待着博物馆能够致力于承担这一重任。

多元性

越来越多的人开始认识到，博物馆应该在其治理机构、员工配置和观众开发等方面更好地体现美国社会的多元性。这种对话很快就会变成一场辩论，究竟哪些要素应该算多元性的一部分（民族、人种、性别、文化、残疾与否、年龄等等）。这些问题无法在国家层面上得到解决—"正确的"答案完全要根据每座博物馆及其环境的具体情况而定。很明显，位于南达科他州某个乡间小镇上的博物馆在招聘人员时肯定无法像位于芝加哥市中心的某座博物馆那样充分体现民族和文化的多元性。不管怎么说，对于南达科他州的这座博物馆而言，要想让董事会也体现多元性，那它面临的最大挑战将是找到六十岁以下的人来掌舵。

同前面提到的融入社区问题一样，这既是一个意识形态问题也是一个实际问题。根据美国人口普查局的预测，美国的人口到2050年将会是"多数人成为少数人"—白人或欧洲人的后裔在总人口中所占的比例将不足50%。如果你所在的博物馆目前的观众主要由创建美国的欧洲人的后裔构成，那么如果只有这一小部分人关心该博物馆，你所在的博物馆将会出现什么样的情况呢？支持你的基础会逐渐缩小，最后可能会缩小到博物馆难以维持的地步。反过来，如果博物馆的内容非常重要，能够吸引所有美国公民，你就能让更加多元化的观众关注你所做的一切。或许博物馆可以逐渐改变它的使命，开始介绍一些背景更广泛的移民问题，歌颂不同移民对象的"建国之父母"。无论是何种情况，由清一色人群组成的董事会和员工队伍即便有着再美好的愿望也很难与博物馆试图提供服务的对象建立起"街头信誉"[6]。人们希望看到有和他们一样的人在博物馆里工作，希望这些人能够就博物馆的经营方式发表他们的看法。如果没有这些人群帮助博物馆做决定，该博物馆很可能无法以最佳的方式来服务这些新观众群。

开放

由于所有美国公民都向博物馆提供了支持（即便他们没有提供任何捐款，博物馆也通过联邦或州政府的免税政策得到了补贴，更不用说地方政府的征税等等），因此每个人都应该在可能的范围内从博物馆获益。

除了法律规定外——尤其是美国的《残疾人权利保护法》——博物馆还有着道德上的义务，尽可能让公众接触到它们的资源。这包括建筑和场所等有形资产，也包括知识资产——藏品信息、博物馆的研究成果、展览、项目和网站。

博物馆的开放可能会有一些局限，常常源自于开放与保护之间的矛盾，但博物馆必须竭尽全力在这两者之间找到一个平衡点。无限制的开放会破坏博物馆为子孙后代保护其藏品、土地或历史建筑的能力（就展示活体动物藏品而言，无限制的开放对保护观众也不利）。无限制的知识开放也可能会以有害的方式披露信息。例如，博物馆如果披露捐赠人的信息，捐赠人就有可能遭遇风险，罪犯可能会盯上他们的个人藏品。如果博物馆透露其标本的来源地，一些濒临灭绝的物种就有可能在商业投机者或业余爱好者的捕捉下彻底灭绝。

但是限制开放现在只是个例外规定而不是普遍规定。博物馆应该意识到公众有参观的权利，如果这种权利受到了限制，那么博物馆就必须准备回答这些问题：博物馆有什么理由设定这种限制？博物馆还有什么更高的目标？任何人都不应该被迫向公众解释为什么某个对象应该得到特殊待遇才能进入博物馆，或者得到的尊重少于其他观众。例如，行动不便的观众不应该遭到冷遇，被迫使用货物装卸口或者货运电梯。

---

[6] 街头信誉：美国口语说法，指为人们尤其是年轻人所接受的新式或时髦做法。 ——译注

问责与透明

博物馆以前常说"别管幕后的人",但这样的日子已经一去不复返了。指导博物馆经营的政策和规定,博物馆为未来制定的规划,博物馆的业绩是好还是坏——任何人只要对这些信息感兴趣都应该能得到。收到书面请求后邮寄这些资料的传统做法已经越来越无法满足人们的要求。这意味着博物馆必须将这些信息变成供公众查阅的文件,必须以业务通讯的形式将它们公之于众或者将它们公布在博物馆的网站上。

坦率地说,这些信息大多都会以不同形式公之于众。Guidestar 网站(www.guidestar.org)公布了所有非营利性机构的 IRS990 报告[7]的电子版,而随着国内收入署开始要求所有机构提供电子文件,人们会更加容易、更加及时地看到这些报告。国内收入署知道许多人现在都使用这些报告来评估非营利性机构的业绩,因此它正在重新设计 990 表,以帮助人们进行分析。在互联网世界里,再机密的政策或规划都会泄露出去,张贴在网上,让整个世界去了解。这对于博物馆而言是件好事,它可以更好地控制媒体和所传达的信息,可以利用这种机会来提供信息,免得信息被人误读或误解。

守法

大家可能会感到有些意外,博物馆标准中居然会添加了守法的要求。许多用心良苦的人常常认为自己的所作所为是出于好意,因此可以不必遵守某些法律规定:儿童博物馆的某位志愿者可能不会意识到,他们上午接待儿童时的工作就像一个日托中心,因而必须遵守相应的准则和规定;员工们可能会认为,放在博物馆柜子里的东西最危险的也就是固体胶棒、丙烯颜料、丙酮、来苏儿、地板蜡和去污剂,因此他们不必给员工提供物资的安全数据以及如何训练他们来解读这些数据,就连一些大型博物馆的员工也会有这种想法;一些在国外进行实地考察后回国的博物馆研究员也会认为不必向海关、美国渔业和野生动物署或者美国农业部申报自己所携带的动植物标本,因为他们是科学家——他们这样做的目的不是谋利,而是为了促进人类的发展。一定要确保你的所有员工、董事会和志愿者熟悉与博物馆行为相关的法律和规定,并且知道"这些法规你要遵守"。

---

[7]IRS990 报告:即美国国内收入署规定的财务报告。——译注

职业道德标准
职业道德"优秀标准"的特征

- 博物馆受公众之托保管好它所拥有的资源。
- 博物馆致力于接受公众的问责，并保持其使命和经营的透明性。
- 博物馆遵守地方、州和联邦政府对其设施、经营和管理的各项法律、准则和规定。

评述

下面这部分将探讨职业道德方面两个普遍为人们所接受的标准：一个标准详细说明每座博物馆如何制定出指导其行动的并符合其特点的内部道德标准，另一个标准概述美国所有博物馆都必须遵守的普世道德准则。本书还介绍了其他几条标准，也可以被视为道德准则。有些人可能会有不同看法，认为所有全局性的标准都应该是关于职业道德的，而不是诸如应该使用何种档案墨水这样的技术标准。不管怎么说，这些反对意见都被归纳进了探讨实际经营问题的部分。第四部分藏品保管将探讨向非博物馆机构出租藏品和如何处理纳粹统治时期被非法侵占的物品等问题。第六部分财务稳定性将探讨如何管理企业与个人捐赠、缩减规模和裁员等问题。

美国博物馆协会的《博物馆职业道德准则》

博物馆收藏、保护并诠释我们这个世界的各种物品，以此对公众做出独特的贡献。博物馆在历史上曾经拥有并使用过有生命和无生命的自然物品以及各种形式的人工制品来增加人们的知识并陶冶人的情操。今天，博物馆所涉及的内容五花八门，而这正好体现了人类视野的范围之广。博物馆的使命包括收藏、保护、展示自己拥有或者租借和制造的物件，以此向公众传播知识。博物馆包括政府和私人所有的人类学、艺术史和自然历史博物馆、水族馆、树木园、艺术中心、植物园、儿童博物馆、历史遗址、自然中心、天文馆、科技中心和动物园。美国的博物馆界包括收藏型和非收藏型机构。尽管它们的使命各不相同，但它们均为非营利性组织，而且全都致力于为公众提供服务。它们的藏品以及它们借用或自己制造的物件是研究、展示和吸引公众参与的各种活动项目的根本。

总的来说，博物馆的藏品和展出物件代表着整个世界共有的自然和文化财富。博物馆作为这些财富的托管人，必须提高人们对各种自然物品和人类经历的了解。博物馆必须成为全人类的资源，并且通过它们的各种活动培养人们在掌握知识的基础上去欣赏我们所继承的这个富饶而多彩多姿的世界。博物馆还必须为子孙后代保护好这笔遗产。

　　美国的博物馆建立在为公众服务的传统之上。它们的组织形式为公益信托，藏品和信息要造福于它们创建时所服务的对象。董事会成员、雇员和志愿者们致力于为这些受益人的利益服务。博物馆经营的基本准则是各种相关法律。博物馆作为非营利机构，必须遵守相应的地方、州政府和联邦政府的法律以及国际法和有关公众所托职责的具体法律标准。本《博物馆职业道德准则》依据上述原则制定，但是遵纪守法只是基本要求，博物馆以及博物馆的负责人除了应竭力避免承担法律责任外，还必须采取积极措施来保持他们的诚信，以此来博得公众的信任。他们不仅要遵纪守法，还应具有职业道德精神。因此，本《博物馆职业道德准则》列出了一些道德准则，而这些常常比遵纪守法更为重要。

　　忠诚于博物馆的使命以及忠诚于博物馆所服务的公众是博物馆工作的核心，不管这种工作是义务的还是有报酬的。在发生（实际、潜在或察觉到的）利益冲突的地方，绝对不能把忠诚作为牺牲对象。任何个人都不能利用自己在博物馆的职位谋取私利，或者以牺牲博物馆、博物馆的使命、声誉以及博物馆所服务的公众的利益为代价来使另一方获益。

　　对于博物馆而言，为公众服务是至高无上的。为了确认这一道德准则，也为了阐述它在博物馆治理、收藏和活动项目中的应用，美国博物馆协会颁布了该《博物馆职业道德准则》。博物馆在签署该准则后将为其治理机构、雇员和志愿者在行使博物馆相关职责时的行为负责。博物馆此后将确认自己确定的目标，确保谨慎地使用自己的资源，提高自己的效率，保持公众的信心。这种集体性的努力将提升博物馆的工作，增加博物馆目前以及未来对社会所作的贡献。

治理

　　博物馆的治理无论采取何种形式均为受公众之托确保博物馆为社会提供服务。治理机构保护并扩大博物馆的藏品和项目，以及博物馆的实物、人力和资金资源；确保这些资源支持博物馆的使命，应对社会的多元化，尊重自然和文化共同财富的多元性。

　　因此，治理机构要确保：所有为博物馆工作或者代表博物馆的人员都理解并支持博物馆的使命和公众托付的责任；治理机构的成员理解并完成自己的托管责任，采取集体而不是个人行动；以支持博物馆使命的方式来保护、维护和开发博物馆藏品和项目以及博物馆的实物、人力和资金资源；响应并代表社会的利益；与员工保持关系，相互明确分工并尊重对方的职责；董事、雇员和志愿者之间的工作关系建立在平等和相互尊重之上；用职业标准和习惯做法来告知和指导博物馆的经营；阐明各项政策并进行慎重监督；治理行为促进的是公共利益而不是个人的经济利益。

藏品

博物馆的职业道德具有与众不同的特点，这是因为博物馆拥有、保管和使用代表着全世界自然和文化共同财富的物件、标本和活体藏品。对藏品的这种保管关系代表着公众最高的信任，也意味着博物馆必须合法拥有、永久收藏、保护、记录、开放和负责地处理藏品。

因此，博物馆必须确保：它所保管的藏品支持博物馆的使命和公众托付的职责；它所保管的藏品为合法所有且不受任何附加条件的制约，藏品的保护、安全措施和保养符合法律规定；它所保管的藏品来源明确并有文件记录；允许并管理藏品及相关信息的对外开放；藏品的获得、出售和租借活动在实施时尊重对自然和文化资源的保护和保管原则，严禁对这些资料进行非法交易；藏品的获得、出售和租借活动与博物馆的使命和公众托付的职责相符；通过出售、交易或研究等活动出售馆藏完全是为了提高博物馆的使命。出售非活体藏品后的所得在使用时与博物馆行业的现有标准相一致，绝对不能用于与藏品获得或直接保管无关的活动；明确人类遗骸、丧葬物和圣物的独特性质，并据此做出涉及此类藏品的所有决定；与藏品相关的活动促进的是公共利益而不是个人的经济利益；公开、严肃、积极地处理针对博物馆某藏品的索要请求，并且尊重各方的尊严。

项目

博物馆通过各种展览、研究、学术成就、出版物和教育活动来提高公众对人类共同自然和文化财富的了解和欣赏力，以此来服务社会。这些活动项目进一步提高博物馆的使命，并对社会的关心、兴趣和需求做出反应。

因此，博物馆应该确保：所有项目支持博物馆的使命和公众托付的责任；所有项目都建立在学术成就之上，不弄虚作假；所有项目都对外开放并且根据博物馆的使命和资源鼓励尽可能多的观众来参与；所有项目尊重多元化的价值观、传统和关注；创收性质的活动以及涉及博物馆之外其他机构的活动必须符合博物馆的使命并支持公众托付的责任；所有项目促进的是公共利益而不是个人的经济利益。

博物馆制定内部职业道德准则的标准

所有博物馆都应该拥有正式批准的、有别于国家标准的职业道德准则，它应该能阐明该机构作为一座博物馆和非营利性教育机构所承担的道德职业方面的基本义务

（而不仅仅是利益冲突等个人行为）；应该符合博物馆的实际情况（不能简单地重复美国博物馆协会的《博物馆职业道德准则》（2000），或者宣布采用美国博物馆协会的准则，或者简单地重复上级机构的类似准则）；应该与美国博物馆协会的《博物馆职业道德准则》（2000）相一致；应该说明这些准则适用于治理机构、员工和志愿者；应该是一个独立的文件，而不是一本文件汇编或者一份介绍其他文件的清单；应该得到治理机构的批准。

此外，博物馆自身制定的道德准则还应该包括下列内容，或者将下列内容添加到其他独立文件中并且在道德准则中有所提及：

- 有关个人道德、行为、利益冲突等方面的内容，应该对员工、志愿者和董事会有详细的规定。这些部分的内容可以单独添加在如人事政策中。
- 与藏品相关的职业道德内容。这些部分的内容可以单独添加在博物馆的藏品管理政策中。
- 博物馆还可以遵守具体针对某个专业／藏品（见下文）或博物馆某些专业职能部门（如《美国博物馆协会研究员道德准则》）的道德准则，但采用这些准则并不意味着博物馆就能不制定自己独立的准则。不过，博物馆一旦决定遵守上述准则，其道德准则要么应该包括这些准则中相应的语言，要么应该列举这些准则并且说明博物馆将遵守它们。

对于那些由更大的机构或组织治理的博物馆而言，如果这些机构或组织没有将博物馆管理当成它的主要经营目的，博物馆就必须制定出符合本标准且针对博物馆具体问题的道德准则。

目的与重要性

博物馆自己制定的道德准则非常重要，可以确保它接受公众的问责。非营利性机构是否能给人留下深刻印象与公众对其诚信的感觉程度直接相关。博物馆只要能正式公开它的道德准则，就能证明它经历了一个重要的内部决策过程——任何一个机构如果想起草内部职业道德准则,都必须集体讨论它所面临的各种问题,然后确定它需要哪些道德准则来指导它的经营和保护它的诚信。

它还能确保决策过程的透明性：制定并实施博物馆的内部职业道德准则能够带来透明的监督，能够在几个方面让该机构获益。它能够让博物馆内部就哪些行为符合其使命达成一致意见。它能够在博物馆做出抉择时充当一个参照点。它还是风险管理的一个实用、有效的工具——能够保护博物馆的资产和声誉。

　　博物馆自己制定的道德准则表达了该机构的政策，与它在目标宣言中所声称的服务于公众的使命相一致。它将公众利益放在了机构或个人利益之上，鼓励博物馆采用那些能够赢得公众信任的经营方式。它认同适用于博物馆的法律规定（包括博物馆自己制定的内部章程或宪章），并且借用针对博物馆具体专业的行规，以此来帮助博物馆实现或者超越其使命。

实施

　　博物馆的职业道德准则 — 或者作为其内部制定的准则的一部分，或者作为其他通过的政策的一部分（如人事政策、藏品管理政策等）— 应该阐明：治理机构、员工和志愿者的道德责任；治理机构与馆长之间的关系所涉及的道德问题；利益冲突（如：信息披露、礼品与纪念品、借展品、机构外兼职、个人收藏、购买博物馆的财产、资产的使用、保密）；藏品所涉及的道德问题（如：藏品的获得、除藏、保管、保护、鉴定、交易、对外开放、如实介绍等）；博物馆的管理方式（如：守法、知识产权或学术研究的所有权、人事管理）；以及博物馆应该对公众承担的责任。此外，被视为最佳做法的还包括制定出政策，（在适用的情况下）能够处理企业或个人资助的管理、商业活动和政治活动。博物馆自身制定的道德准则还应该包含一个阐明如何执行该准则的章节。

人们对遵守专业道德宣言的期待

　　人们期待博物馆能够遵守"博物馆界公认的标准和最佳做法"。一些专业协会还出台了道德宣言或准则，适用于自己的专业或该专业的从业者。所有博物馆都应该遵守这些道德准则，前提是：适用于所有博物馆中的特定部门；是非指定性的（描述理想结果，而不是强行推荐一些能够让人取得这种结果的特殊方法）；在可能的情况下，以博物馆领域为人们广泛接受的现有准则为依据；它的出台经过了一个广泛参与的过程，收集了不同博物馆对相应专业、地理位置、规模、治理模式和其他变量的看法。

　　例如，历史博物馆应该遵守美国州和地方历史协会的《职业标准与道德宣言》，那些属于艺术博物馆馆长协会的博物馆应该遵守该协会的《艺术博物馆职业规范》。综合性博物馆（那些包含两个或两个以上专业领域的博物馆）在制定道德准则时必须确定如何将这些针对具体专业的准则运用在自己的整体经营中，并且让人们了解做出这些决定的原因。

评述

　　美国博物馆协会的《职业道德准则》和《机构内部道德准则的标准》为博物馆制定内部职业道德准则定下了标准。尽管美国博物馆协会的《博物馆职业道德准则》列出了博物馆界认同的、适用于所有博物馆的道德准则，但其本身并不是可以被任何博物馆所采用的——每座博物馆都必须为自己制定出内部职业道德准则，不仅符合国家执行的标准，而且专门依据其特殊情况制定。

　　每座博物馆在起草与美国博物馆协会的准则相一致的内部道德准则时，都应该在美国博物馆协会的准则的基础上增加新的内容，以针对该博物馆的具体情况，确保所制定的准则适用于该博物馆。让治理机构、员工和志愿者参与到博物馆规则的制定中就会激励这些机构的工作人员和负责人促进和维护合理的政策和规定。

如何制定适用于你们博物馆的道德准则？

　　博物馆制定道德准则时最常见的问题（除了没有准则或者干脆说"我们遵守美国博物馆协会的《博物馆职业道德准则》"）是许多准则只涉及美国博物馆协会准则中所涉及的问题，然而美国博物馆协会的准则只涉及那些可能会影响所有博物馆的问题，整个博物馆界早已就这些问题达成了广泛共识。美国博物馆协会的准则和其他道德规范在许多问题上只是简单地说，"这很重要，各个博物馆必须依据下列原则为自己找到最佳答案。"某座博物馆可能会选择接受或者不接受或者以某些方式接受一些（有着道德含意的）行为，这些行为必须在该博物馆自己制定的道德准则中加以说明，比如：博物馆收藏了一些艺术家或工艺师的杰作，而博物馆的商店在出售这些艺术家或工艺师的作品；博物馆的商店出售自然历史标本（贝壳、蝴蝶、化石）是否接受来自某些特殊渠道的企业或慈善资金（如烟草公司、武器制造商、石油公司）；披露／保护藏品来源信息，如不愿意透露姓名的捐赠者的身份，或者濒危物种标本的采集地；聘用／管理某位现任员工或董事的亲戚；展出某位员工、董事或志愿者拥有或者制作的藏品。

针对具体专业的标准

　　博物馆面临的一个挑战是确定自己是否应该遵守具体专业的道德准则，以及何时遵守这些准则。我们以一座集合了艺术、历史和自然史的综合性博物馆为例，该博物馆是否应该遵守美国州与地方历史协会的规定 — 出售馆藏品获得的资金只能用于购买或者保护藏品？（"保护"一词的定义虽然有些含糊，仍然比美国博物馆协会限定性条款中所用的词语更精确。）将这种规定应用在自然历史藏品上是否恰当？该博物馆是否对出售藏品和出售后得到的资金有不同的政策？

再比如，你们的机构是一座艺术博物馆，但馆长并没有被邀请加入成员有限的艺术博物馆馆长协会。那么你们会不会遵守一个以部分博物馆为对象所制定的标准（尽管它所代表的是那些规模最大、最负盛名的博物馆）？

如何使用出售藏品获得的资金？

这是博物馆界引起极度争议的问题，值得我们在此进行详细探讨。1991 年修改后的美国博物馆协会《博物馆职业道德准则》规定这类资金只能用于购买新的藏品。这是两个引起极度争议的问题之一，最终导致美国博物馆协会被迫重新修改这种表述。（另一个引起极度争议的限定性条款是美国博物馆协会可能会强迫其会员遵守《博物馆职业道德准则》，但该条款没有任何实际效果。）经过大量争论后于 1993 年通过的新文字表述补充了一点，除了购买新藏品外，该资金还可以用于"直接保管"藏品，至于"直接保管"的确切含意只能由大家自己去理解。

这不仅是博物馆领域一个讳莫如深的问题，也是公众极度关心的热点问题。如果大家统计一下新闻中出现的涉及博物馆的各种争议，其中很大一部分都牵涉到如何使用出售藏品后获得的资金这一敏感问题。就连那些不熟悉博物馆标准的人凭直觉也能知道博物馆收藏的是公众托管的藏品，这些藏品不是金融资产，不能被用来平衡博物馆的收益或者填补博物馆的财政缺口。

更加复杂的是美国联邦政府 — 具体而言是美国国内收入署（IRS）、美国财务会计准则委员会（FASB）和政府财务会计准则委员会（GASB） — 正越来越关注这一问题。FASB 和 GASB 制定标准，规定审计师们如何确定财务报告中的藏品，IRS 则制定博物馆如何在纳税表中申报金融和非金融资产的规定。在二十世纪九十年代，FASB 强烈要求博物馆在其损益表中将所有藏品资本化，以金融资产的形式申报。美国博物馆协会和其他机构参与到了这场较量中，成功地阻止了将藏品资本化的动议 — 至少这一次是成功了。

这是一场艰难的较量，因为从国内收入署的角度来看，博物馆想两者兼得。博物馆从道义这个高度出发，声称藏品不是金融资产，不应该在财务报告中被视为金融资产，然而又希望能够出售藏品，将现金用于各种不同目的。因此美国财务会计准则委员会和政府财务会计准则委员会在这一点上只做了一点让步，规定博物馆必须做出一个选择：要么将处理藏品后获得的资金用于购买新藏品（以同级别的艺术／科学／历史资产保持其价值），要么将该资金用于其他目的，但必须以金融资产的形式体现在财务报告中。如果这两个政府机构察觉到大多数博物馆没有遵守这些规定（比如，将出售藏品后获得的资金用于维护或者更换锅炉却没有将藏品资本化），它们可以重新提出这一要求，而博物馆方面届时不一定会再次获胜。

既然出售藏品后获得的资金引起了这么多的争议，博物馆为什么还要出售藏品呢？博物馆的圈内和圈外人士经过很长时间后才认定博物馆可以出售其收藏的一些物品。人们长久以来一直强烈地感觉到，收藏某物就意味着该物应该永远留在博物馆中，尤其是捐赠物。无论捐赠书中的文字如何表述，博物馆接受捐赠无疑就是在向捐赠者保证，他们的珍宝将永远得到博物馆的保护。然而，人们在过去几十年中越来越清楚地看到，这一原则常常与博物馆应该承担的义务发生冲突，因为博物馆的义务就是充分运用它的资源来造福公众并且保管好它的藏品。人们有时候会做出错误选择，结果一些物件变成了某博物馆的藏品，而这些物件无法让任何人受益，只会浪费时间和资源。博物馆的使命随着时间的变化而变化，一百年前的正确做法如今已不再为博物馆所接受。有时候，某博物馆的发展已经超出了它的能力范围，它所收藏的物件已经多得让它无法保管好 — 将一些藏品出售给公共机构或者私人或许是正确行为，免得这些藏品由于缺乏管理而每况愈下。

但是，由于藏品属于特殊种类的资产（文化、科学、艺术资产，而不是金融资产），许多人都强烈地感觉到出售藏品后获得的资金应该用于这类资产的更新或使用。如果博物馆获准用这些资金来支付其他费用（如维修门前步行道、资助博物馆的教育项目或者贴补博物馆的期刊），它就有可能抵挡不住诱惑，不断地出售藏品来贴补经营资金或捐款的不足。博物馆界一致认为这种做法严重违背了博物馆以其他方式筹集此类资金的信托责任。将博物馆的藏品用作金融资产，以此来维持博物馆的经营需要 — 这种做法绝对不行。出售藏品来取得最大利润并且将出售藏品后得到的收益用来处理博物馆日积月累的财务不稳定局面 — 这种做法是公然抛弃公众的信任。

然而，具体该如何运用这条原则却令人难以确定。如果大家认同博物馆完全有理由不购买新藏品（因为市场上没有合适的物件，购买这种藏品不道德，或者博物馆不准备再添加新的藏品），那么应该如何使用这笔资金呢？用它来保护现有藏品似乎是个不错的选择，可这笔资金应该仅仅用于主动保护（处理）还是应该包括预防性保护（这在很大程度上取决于库房的物质条件、恰当的环境控制和虫害的定期检测）？它是否还能包括参与保护活动的员工的薪水或其他劳务费（如修复员、研究员或藏品管理员所付出的时间），即便此类支出属于博物馆年度经营预算的正常部分？既然使用这笔资金来改善库房的条件是合适的，那么为什么就不能用这笔资金来改善展区的条件呢？既然博物馆的建筑是一个不可分割的整体，改善博物馆的屋顶或者电器/机械/报警/消防系统难道对藏品没有好处吗？

　　博物馆还会遇到许多特殊情况，使得人们非常想破坏这项原则。如果博物馆破产了该怎么办？如果整个机构都已经破产，它自然无法保管好藏品。鉴于这种情况（而且这种情况已经发生过），万一博物馆想处理掉它的藏品，成为一个不再拥有藏品的机构，这该怎么办？这些问题很难回答，没有现成答案，但我们不能依据一些例外情况来制定指导博物馆主流行为的道德准则。

隶属于非博物馆上级机构的博物馆

　　博物馆职业道德指导着博物馆的经营方式。那么博物馆的上级机构呢？难道一所大学在为它的一座博物馆制定政策时必须遵守博物馆职业道德吗？从职能的角度来说，机构的一个附属部门（即博物馆）根本无法命令它的上级机构允许自己采取何种行为。博物馆最多只能游说其上级机构，让上级机构相信博物馆遵守博物馆标准是合乎道德的。博物馆还可以向上级机构指出，强迫博物馆违反人们期待博物馆应该遵守的道德准则将会带来媒体的抨击，也会危及大学与校友的关系。上级机构可能很看重认证，博物馆便可以运用参加认证这种机会来遵守这些标准。不管怎么说，大家不妨在这种情况演变成问题之前主动与上级机构进行沟通。上级机构通常只会在面对重大（经济或政治）刺激因素时才会认真考虑博物馆认为不道德的行为，一旦这些刺激因素不复存在时，我们就很难让该机构就博物馆的行为标准进行公开、公正的探讨。

II. 使命与规划

博物馆目标宣言标准
博物馆目标宣言"优秀标准"的特征

- 博物馆注重其为公众提供服务的作用，并且将教育定为这种作用的核心。
- 博物馆致力于接受公众的问责，确保其使命和经营的透明性。
- 博物馆对自己的使命有清晰的认识，能够阐明自己存在的理由以及从中获益的对象。
- 博物馆经营中的各项工作都围绕实现该使命开展。
- 博物馆的治理机构和员工获得、开发和分配资源要从战略的角度思考和行动，以便促进博物馆使命的发展。

目的与重要性

所有博物馆都应该有正式阐述并获得通过的使命，说明该博物馆的工作性质、服务对象以及背后的原因。博物馆的目标宣言是对博物馆业绩进行评估的主要基准。在评估某博物馆是否遵守国家标准时，我们必须考虑两个核心问题，其中之一便是：该博物馆在实现其宣布的使命与目标过程中表现如何？强调这一点意味着认同有效、可效仿的做法：那些运用清晰表述的目标宣言来指导其活动与决定的博物馆更有可能高效地经营。

清晰表述的目标宣言可以向人们告知博物馆的目的 — 它存在的原因，因而能够指导博物馆的活动与决定。这种目标宣言能够确定博物馆的独特身份和目的，为博物馆提供一个明确的中心。目标宣言能够表明该博物馆很清楚自己对公众和藏品应该发挥的作用与应该承担的责任，还能够反映该博物馆生存的环境。博物馆的所有活动都应该直接或间接地支持该使命。

评述
长度

博物馆在理解这条标准的过程中有时会为所用语言犯难。今天的博物馆有时会创作出言简意赅的目标宣言，并且将它印制在名片上或者博物馆信笺的最下方。这些宣言在激励人的同时偶尔也会在具体内容上显得有些含糊：

为人类增加并传播知识。

— 史密森学会，1826 年

邀请所有年龄段的求知者通过科学来体验周围不断变化的世界。

— 明尼苏达科学博物馆

这样的目标宣言过于简洁，在描述博物馆的目的、表明它的独特身份和焦点等方面可能存在一些问题。这并不是说就没有地方可以印制这样的目标宣言（比如名片或信笺）。博物馆在书写如此简洁的目标宣言时可能还会有另一个文件（有时称为目的宣言），更加详细地介绍博物馆的工作、服务对象以及背后的原因。这种做法是可以接受的，条件是博物馆在其他地方能足够详细地表达它的使命。"足够"一词足以指导博物馆做出具体的选择，也足以指导公众对博物馆是否完成其使命进行评估。其他一些解决方法包括将简短的目标宣言用做更加详细的目标宣言的导言，在恰当的时候引用它；或者写一个较长的目标宣言，然后再写一句简洁明了、能够反映博物馆使命精神的非正式口号。

一致性

人们在起草目标宣言时最常遇到的问题之一是，如果目标宣言由于时代的变化而改变，不同的地方就会出现不同版本的目标宣言永久定格在某个通过的文件中。当前的目标宣言可能出现在该博物馆的规划中，但十年前最后一次修订的收藏政策中却可能写有老版本的目标宣言，而筹款计划中还可能出现另一个版本的目标宣言（制定计划的员工可能自作主张地想让文字表达更灵活一些）。如果不同版本之间的差异很小，博物馆只需稍做处理即可，但如果不同版本之间的差异较大，反映了博物馆在其工作、收藏或服务对象方面的政策改变，这就会变成一个非常严重的问题。这些相互矛盾的目标宣言或许能反映出更大层面上的问题，即该博物馆没有能全面地审核各种规划和政策，没有能确保所有这一切都服务于同一个目标。这还可能导致一部分员工在这些文件中寻找前进命令时被送往不同方向。

切合实际

目标宣言所涉及的另一个严重问题是博物馆为自己制定的目标超出了博物馆的资源范围。虽然力图成为全国最重要的自然历史博物馆之一是件好事，但你们是否有藏品能够保证自己做到这一点？如果没有，你们是否有庞大预算来创建这样的收藏并且支持所需的研究？按标准对博物馆进行的评估所依据的是它们为自己确定的使命和目标——如果博物馆没有能完成它们的使命，它们从一开始就搞砸了。

比较正确的做法是博物馆起草自己能够掌控的目标宣言，将其"不切实际的"想法纳入该博物馆的未来规划中。这样一来，该博物馆在接受评估时的参照标准就会是它目前的能力，同时它还能给人留下一个深刻的印象，即一旦有了足够支持它还能实现哪些目标。

与上级机构的一致性

隶属于某个较大机构 —— 如学院、大学、基金会、宗教机构或政府部门 —— 的博物馆面临着特殊挑战。由于这类博物馆可能没有单独的机构章程，它们不必为了获得非营利性地位而确定一个正式的使命。这就带来了一些问题：谁起草目标宣言，谁批准该目标宣言，该目标宣言具有何种权威性。一些不同性质的问题也会由此产生。

如果博物馆员工或者顾问委员会有一定的自由空间，他们或许会认同一个比较现实的目标宣言，并且会将它贯彻得很好。这种自由空间有时看似好事，可一旦资金、场地或员工配置吃紧，上级机构常常会对博物馆说，"哈！这就是你们所做的一切？这对我们并不是那么至关重要，所以先将你们裁掉。"在另一方面，上级机构也有可能严格管理博物馆，为博物馆起草目标宣言，然而这种目标宣言会常常忽视博物馆员工清楚地看到并且希望利用的一些大好机会。例如，某学院可能会要求其博物馆将注意力全部放在为学生提供服务上。这在表面上看似乎很合情合理，但博物馆有可能是该学院与周围社区潜在的最佳联系纽带，如果学院与社区的关系比较紧张，博物馆完全可以发挥重要作用。

要想解决这些问题，最佳的办法就是确保上级机构中某个拥有相当权力的人或对象（如大学的教务长、院长、副校长）与博物馆的员工和顾问委员会（如果有的话）密切合作，审定并通过博物馆的使命以及依据该使命而制定的规划。双方必须在制定规划和分配资源等决策出台之前对博物馆的使命都有明确的理解。

制定博物馆机构规划的标准
制定规划的"优秀标准"的特征
- 博物馆经营中的各项工作都围绕实现其使命开展。
- 博物馆的治理机构和员工获得、开发和分配资源要从战略的角度思考和行动，以便促进博物馆使命的发展。
- 博物馆为自己制定能够体现其机构特点、可持续的规划，这些规划包括观众和社区的参与。
- 博物馆建立衡量其成功与否的标准，并且用这些标准来评估和调整它的各项活动。

目的与重要性
制定战略规划能够带来大家一致认同的远景，让大家知道博物馆的发展方向和希望实现的目标。它能确保该使命满足观众和服务对象的需求，确保博物馆阐明为了实现这一远景将如何获得各种资源。制定规划还将使博物馆根据经营环境的变化做出正确的决定。

　　博物馆通过制定规划来确定自己的目标，并且制定实现这些目标的战略；确保博物馆以促进其使命和保持其经济实力的方式来获得、开发并分配其（人力、财力和馆舍）资源；收集相应的信息来指导它的行动，包括来自股东的意见和来自基准评估机构的数据；确定博物馆评估自己业绩的标准。

实施

　　博物馆应该为自己的未来发展制定现时的、全面的、及时和正式的规划。只要制定的规划是最新的而且能够反映机构目前的情况，它就是现时的；只要制定的规划涵盖了博物馆经营的所有相关方面（不只是某个设施的总体规划），它就是全面的；只要制定的规划符合博物馆盛衰周期中的一些重要事件（如规模、范围、目的和治理等方面的变化），它就是及时的；只要制定的规划正式成文并且由博物馆的治理机构投票通过，它就是正式的。制定规划的过程应该包括所有股东：员工、治理机构、观众和服务对象；应该是不间断的、经过认真考虑的、成文的。

文件记录

　　作为机构制定规划的证据，博物馆应该以文件的形式记录其制定规划的过程（如委员会成员名单、会议纪要、制定规划的日期），以及一个包含了博物馆战略和经营要素的现时的、全面的、及时和正式的规划。每座博物馆的书面规划都应该包括一个多年规划和一个经营规划，或者一个兼容二者的规划，或者功能相仿的文件。

　　记录每个博物馆规划的文件应该各不相同，但这些规划应该：成文并且得到治理机构的通过；以博物馆的使命为依据；与其他规划文件相关（如财务规划、发展规划、藏品诠释规划、藏品规划）；确定重点项目，帮助博物馆做出选择和分配现有资源；阐明博物馆如何将资源和目标结合在一起，以此来确保实施规划时所需的人力和财力；是现行文件，由员工和治理机构使用并不断得到更新；确定可量化的目标以及博物馆评估自己是否成功的方法；涵盖具体行动步骤，确定具体实施时间表，分配应该承担的职责。

隶属于非博物馆上级机构的博物馆制定规划的过程

　　对于那些由上级机构经营的博物馆而言，如果上级机构（如大学或者政府机构）并不重视博物馆的管理工作，博物馆应该有具体针对博物馆制定规划的程序和方案，这两者都应该与上级机构制定规划的过程一致。上级机构制定规划的过程和文件也应该体现对博物馆使命的支持，应该确保博物馆的具体目标能够得以实现。

评述

为何需要规划？

经常有人问我，"我的博物馆为什么需要规划？我们没有规划也干得非常出色呀。"这个问题的答案太多，我都不知道该从何说起。如果你们作为一个对象（董事会、员工、股东）都没有决定自己该干什么工作，那你们又如何知道自己干得不错呢？如果这个决定没有写下来并获得通过，你们又如何知道大家全都明白自己的目标以及如何实现目标呢？如果馆长（通常是博物馆的动力所在）离职，博物馆会出现什么情况？接任的馆长如何知道博物馆的规划是什么，如何平稳地朝着正确方向发展？如果没有书面规划，你们又如何让公众、地方政府、慈善家、慈善基金会或拨款机构相信你们打算做的事值得他们支持呢？这还只是几个问题，其他的原因更是不胜枚举。事实上，制定规划是博物馆继续生存所必需的，不仅能增加你们走上正确方向的机会，而且能给你们带来更多支持。除非你们有一个符合本标准所列特点的规划，否则如今很少会有基金会、公司或者拨款机构给你们提供资金。

进程

规划的价值有一半（或许不止一半）来自制定规划的过程。虽然一个人可以将自己锁在房间里，构想出类似博物馆规划的东西，但这很可能是一个空洞无物的文件。如果制定规划的过程包括不同股东对象，其中有董事会成员、员工、主要出资人、博物馆自己确定的服务对象以及博物馆的邻居，规划就更有可能比较现实、成功而且得到很好的实施。为什么？博物馆的服务对象是评价博物馆服务是否到位的专家，也是就如何提高服务质量问题不断提醒博物馆面对现实的最佳人选。而且，一群有着不同背景、经历和专业的人士会从更加广泛的角度来考虑各种可能性，并且会更好地分析各种可能性的优缺点。员工、董事、志愿者和服务对象成员如果参与了规划的制定过程，就会更加支持规划，更好地实施这些规划。

内容

制定规划的标准是美国博物馆协会出台的最具体的标准之一。为什么要如此详细？这是因为这部分的标准主要是认证委员会起草的，而认证委员会每年都要评估大约一百座博物馆，每十年去这些博物馆看一次，其中一些博物馆他们已经跟踪了三十多年。因此，他们有着广泛的经验，能够观察到是什么原因让博物馆成功（或者失败），这些原因与博物馆规划中的一些要素之间有什么联系。本标准之所以要具体列出每一个要素（重点、时间表、资源、责任分配），是因为人们发现缺少规划正是限制许多博物馆发展的拦路石。大家可以将认证视为一个长期的科学大试验，通过认证的博物馆便是代表所有博物馆的试验品，需要在这些专家们看来都是全国业绩最好的博物馆身上测试哪些标准行得通，哪些标准行不通。既然制定规划对这些博物馆的成功至关重要，那么制定规划为何就会对其余95%的博物馆不那么重要呢？

如果你刚刚开始制定规划，那么我建议你运用这些标准为规划的内容确定一个大纲。如果你已经有了一个规划，那么我建议你按照这些标准重新研究一下你的规划，看看有些地方是否需要再详细一点。

III. 领导与组织结构

博物馆治理的标准
博物馆治理"优秀标准"的特征
- 治理机构、员工和志愿者的结构以及处理事务的程序能够有效地推动博物馆的使命。
- 治理机构、员工和志愿者对自己的作用和责任有着清晰而一致的认识。
- 治理机构、员工和志愿者合法、合理、有效地尽到自己的责任。
- 博物馆的领导层、员工和志愿者的组成和资格的多样性能够确保博物馆完成其使命，实现其目标。
- 治理机构与给博物馆提供支持的任何组织之间有着明确而正式的责任分工，不管这些组织隶属于博物馆、在博物馆内经营还是博物馆的上级机构。

目的与重要性
好的治理是确保博物馆成功的基础。博物馆的有效经营建立在一个功能齐全的治理机构之上，而且该治理机构与博物馆馆长保持着密切的工作关系。治理机构与馆长一起确定博物馆的发展方向，获得并管理博物馆完成其使命所需的资源，确保博物馆能够接受公众的问责。无论博物馆的管理模式、结构或名称如何，所有博物馆都应具备这些特点。

实施

治理机构尽到自己作为一个非营利性机构的基本管理责任，通过：制定该机构的使命与目的；选定该机构的首席执行官并支持和评估他的业绩；确保该机构制定有效的规划并确保它拥有充足的资源；有效地管理资源（包括对藏品和历史建筑进行良好的保管）；确保该机构的各种项目和服务能够促进其使命的发展；提高该机构在公众心目中的地位；确保该机构在法律和道德上保持廉正，并能接受公众的问责；招聘治理机构的新成员并帮助他们熟悉自己应承担的义务；评估治理机构的业绩。对于那些接受非直接治理的博物馆而言，上述责任可以通过具体的行政管理系统来实现。在这种情况下，各种职责必须明确地被分配给不同部门。对于那些接受联合治理的博物馆而言，可以将上述职责明确地划分给不同的上级单位。请参阅下文介绍的这些情况中的国家标准。

接受联合治理的博物馆的标准

对于那些接受联合管理的博物馆而言，即由两个或者两个以上的对象分担博物馆的基本治理责任（如某个市政府和某个非营利性私人机构，或者某所大学和某个顾问委员会），或者某个独立实体提供了对博物馆经营至关重要的资源时（如土地、藏品、建筑物、员工），国家标准要求该博物馆必须明确说明参与治理或者提供这些重要资源的所有对象，并且说明每个对象必须承担的责任。上述关系应该以正式书面文件的形式详细说明（如协议备忘录、谅解备忘录、经营协议）。

文件记录

为了证明博物馆有着良好的管理方法，也为了证明该博物馆满足了"优秀标准"的特征，博物馆应该拥有下列文件：目标宣言；机构规划；机构章程、宪章、授权法或其他创始文件；管理博物馆所依据的内部规定、章程、遗嘱或其他文件。如果该博物馆有上级机构，它应该拥有阐述该博物馆对上级机构重要性的文件，能够证明上级机构会全力支持博物馆（如上级机构通过的永久性决议，上级机构的内部章程或部门设置文件，谅解备忘录或上级机构与博物馆达成的管理协定）。博物馆应该拥有相关文件，说明博物馆和其他与之管理或经营密不可分的机构之间的经营关系（如谅解备忘录或其他正式文件），拥有能够证明授予博物馆馆长或类似人员博物馆经营权的文件。

治理机构人员结构方面的标准

　　治理机构应该：不断吸纳新的成员和新的想法；反映博物馆所服务的社区的多元性；提供机会来听取外界的意见，使治理机构能够更好地接受服务对象的问责；确保治理机构成员接受业绩评估，确保没有业绩的成员被淘汰。虽然博物馆不必规定治理机构成员的任期，但许多博物馆一直运用这一方法来实现上述目标。

　　在治理机构本身无法实现博物馆目标的情况下（如博物馆隶属于上级机构，博物馆接受非直接治理，或者博物馆接受政府部门的治理），博物馆需要寻找到其他方法来实现上述目标，包括建立一些所需的支持团体来协助治理（如顾问委员会、辅助工作组、服务对象理事会）。

评 述

无报酬治理机构的职责

　　制定该标准的目的是让治理机构的成员将精力集中在他们应该做的事情上。第 40 页"实施"部分列出的非营利性治理机构的基本职责引自理查德 • 英格拉姆的经典著作《非营利性治理的十个基本职责》，目前已经为所有非营利性机构普遍接受，包括博物馆。不过，尽管政府和公众对于博物馆接受监督的程度有着更高的要求，真正对博物馆进行监督的却主要是未受过专业训练的志愿者（他们可能在各自专业领域接受过高水平的培训，但很少接受过非营利机构治理方面的培训）。非营利性机构（尤其是博物馆）在过去十年不断陷入到丑闻之中，其中许多丑闻的原因都是治理机构没有能有效地行使自己的监督权，普遍情况包括：首席执行官的报酬过高，特权太多，在报销费用等方面公然造假和滥用职权；治理机构没有能发现博物馆的财务困难并采取措施，或者没有能发现员工的财务造假和财务报告；允许博物馆参与或亲自参与一些会引起员工、董事会成员、个人或企业捐赠者、借展方或营利性机构利益冲突的行为。由于治理机构中很少有人接受过非营利性机构治理或博物馆标准方面的培训，博物馆员工通常有义务将这些职责告知他们，或者至少帮助治理机构创建新董事接受培训的程序。

反映服务对象的多元性

　　国家标准可以在许多方面给博物馆提供指导，多元化便是其中之一，但每座博物馆必须自行决定应用这些标准的正确方法。只有博物馆和它所在的社区能够确定哪些多元要素与他们的环境相关，哪些要素可以构成博物馆管理中的多元性。我们可以简单地介绍一下多元性的对立面 — 单一性 — 的常见模式，它的起源和发展，以及它对博物馆出色表现所造成的障碍。

博物馆的创办者常常在他们去世多年后仍然对博物馆产生着影响，大家只要观察一下董事会的成员就能看出这一点。由于大多数 501（C）3[8] 博物馆的董事会大多自行延续（虽然有些博物馆的董事会由董事选举而成），董事们通常挑选与他们相似的新成员。这很自然 —— 人们通常更愿意和那些背景和经历与自己相同的人一起工作，而且他们通常从他们现有的熟人圈子中吸纳董事会的新成员。但这也是一个问题 —— 请参阅第 22 页和第 58 页对多元性的阐述。这种董事会能够自行延续，是因为当博物馆终于向从来没有被邀请担任过董事的对象敞开大门时，它会发现这些对象根本没有担任董事的兴趣。我们经常在博物馆中看到一些这种单一性的模式：富裕、上了年纪的白人社会名流，偶尔有来自负有盛名、拥有相当资金资源的机构的女性；热衷者 / 知识渊博的业余爱好者 —— 如铁路爱好者或者老爷车收藏家；学者 / 研究人员 —— 如历史学家或科学家；人种单一的对象 —— 尤其是如果该博物馆诠释的是某个特别的文化或民族；相互有联系的世家成员 —— 尤其是那些由某特定对象经营的博物馆，如"美国革命之女"、"殖民时期的夫人"、"南部联邦之子"等等。虽然这些对象都能给博物馆的治理带来力量，但如果董事会是清一色的这种人，他们在宏观规划、开发新的不同资源、接受新的服务对象、培养下一代博物馆观众和董事会成员方面的能力会受到严重制约。更为糟糕的是，上述变数（种族、民族、职业、兴趣）还可能会带来其他意想不到的单一性。例如，由研究者和学者组成的一个董事会可能会提高博物馆主题的专业水平，但他们可能资金资源有限，或者很少有机会接触拥有资金的人。

联合治理

美国至少有 4% 的博物馆存在某种形式的联合治理。这种形式可能是某学院或某市立博物馆与一个独立的非营利性民间资助社团联合治理，该社团为博物馆筹集主要资金，甚至雇佣一部分员工并实际拥有藏品。也有可能是某城市与某个非营利性民间资助社团联合治理，该城市拥有博物馆的馆舍和藏品，而社团则按合同负责招聘员工并经营该博物馆。有时候合作双方关系非常密切，人们无法指着其中一方，说"你就是博物馆的主人"。此类博物馆其实是大家齐心协力合作的结果。

随着博物馆开始寻找成功的资金来源模式，上述治理形式也变得越来越常见，而且经常很成功，然而联合治理双方的结合点很脆弱。万一联合治理博物馆的双方（三

---

[8] 501（C）3：为美国税法中的一项条款，规定博物馆等非营利性机构享有免交联邦政府税的地位。
　　—— 译注

方或四方）就这种安排发生矛盾该怎么办？万一市政府说它想收回藏品，在别处另建一座博物馆该怎么办？万一提供资助的社团决定不再每年向博物馆提供经营经费，除非博物馆展出该社团负责人的藏品——万一出现这种情况该怎么办？

这种联合治理的形式常常在一开始非常顺利，因为合作双方许多关键职位上的负责人之间有着相当程度的信任。当这些人最终离开后，一切都会发生变化。人际关系常常转瞬即逝——但法律协议却能延续（至少可以延续到双方同意废除这些协议或者由法院判定协议无效为止）。有些机构迟迟不愿意提议与联合治理博物馆的机构签订一份正式协议，是因为"现在一切经营良好，如果我们提出这种要求，结果可能会适得其反"。这种想法其实很难让人对联合治理形式的稳定性充满信心。博物馆若想确保这种关系平稳发展，最佳的做法就是以法律文件的形式将它书写下来，让双方在出现矛盾之前就明确说明各自的要求。

授权的标准

所有博物馆都应该有一个兼职或全职、有报酬或完全义务的馆长或类似人员，治理机构可以以将博物馆日常经营工作相托的一个对象。不仅如此，治理机构、员工和志愿者都应该明白自己的地位和应承担的职责。

目的与重要性

治理机构能够明确授权就意味着它对自己应该承担责任的领域非常清楚。这些领域包括：集体确定博物馆的使命，制定博物馆的经营政策，确保博物馆宪章和内部章程得到执行，为机构制定规划，批准博物馆的预算，建立财务管理体系，确保有足够的资源来促进博物馆的使命。

授权的结果是明确治理机构和管理层各自的职责，带来有效的领导和组织结构；这种明确职责的做法能使每个人将注意力集中在各自要做的工作上。大家相互之间有交流和协作，但不会有重复劳动。由于董事会已经任命了馆长（或相应官员），而且馆长有能力经营博物馆，因此就应该让馆长在不受干扰的情况下行使自己的职责。

这种不受干扰的行使权力的方式能够让博物馆取得更大的成就。它能够使人们更好地运用各种资源，包括时间。馆长有权独立行使自己的职责，管理日常经营工作，而治理机构则花时间来制定指导博物馆经营的各种决定。各级员工应该很清楚行政管理系统。

文件记录

我们可以在博物馆的下列文件中看到授权规定：博物馆的内部章程，正式批准的馆长（或相应官员）工作内容介绍，以及 — 为了告知所有员工 — 常常阐述各自职责的博物馆员工手册。

评述

授权

向馆长授权有一整套标准，这一点是导致博物馆紧张局面的主要原因。治理机构成员之所以要这样做，是因为他们非常热衷博物馆的工作。但是治理机构的职责 — 批准各项政策和预算，制定规划，寻找资金 — 看似非常枯燥。如果治理机构成员运气不错的话，他们就会成为藏品委员会的成员，有机会用别人的钱去购物。不过真正有意思的工作 — 设计各种展览和项目，为新展厅挑选地毯 — 都属于员工。因此，治理机构成员常常插手员工们负责的这些工作就不足为怪了，只是这样做会严重损害馆长的权力以及员工的职业精神。

对于那些主要或完全由志愿者经营的小型博物馆而言，授权尤其困难，特别是在董事会的一些成员本身就是志愿者的情况下（如担任博物馆的研究员、布展师、开发部或营销部官员，等等）。这种双重职责使他们同时既凌驾于馆长之上（作为馆长的老板和上级）又充当馆长的下属（作为博物馆的员工）。许多小型博物馆都采用这种经营模式；只要这些带着两种截然不同帽子的个人能够记住适时更换帽子，这种经营模式就会非常成功。

对于那些隶属于某个更大的上级机构（如某个大学、某个市政府或州政府机构）的博物馆而言，授权也会带来一些问题。有时候，管理者可能会抵挡不住诱惑，会笨手笨脚地插手博物馆更有意思的工作（展览总是那么有吸引力，藏品和收集藏品也一样）。这项标准能够帮助博物馆馆长向大学教务长、市政府官员、市长或州长解释直接干预博物馆经营是多么不合适。

IV. 藏品保管

藏品保管标准

藏品保管"优秀标准"的特征

- 博物馆拥有、展示并使用与其使命相符的藏品。

- 博物馆合法、合理、有效地管理、记录、保护和使用藏品。
- 博物馆在开展与藏品相关的研究时必须遵守相应的学术标准。
- 博物馆为其藏品的使用和开发制定战略规划。
- 博物馆遵守其使命，在确保藏品得到保护的前提下让公众接触藏品。
- 博物馆通过分配空间和使用各种设施来满足藏品、观众和员工的需要。
- 博物馆有相应的措施来确保人员、藏品／物件和设施的安全。
- 博物馆采取相应措施来预防潜在的风险和损失。

目的与重要性

保管指小心、完好、负责地管理托付给博物馆保存的物件。拥有藏品就意味着要承担法律、社会和道德义务，要为藏品提供恰当的存放、管理和保管的场所以及相应的文件记录，以及对藏品知识的恰当管理。拥有藏品意味着接受公众的信任，因此博物馆必须让藏品服务于公众。有效的藏品保管能够确保博物馆拥有、租借、临时托管或使用的物件能够让我们和子孙后代接触到。藏品是博物馆实现其使命、服务公众的重要手段。

实施

博物馆应该：就藏品保管问题制定战略规划并且采取合乎道德标准的行动；合法、合理、负责地征集、管理和处理藏品，并且知道自己拥有／托管哪些藏品，藏品的来源，博物馆获得这些藏品的原因，藏品目前的状况和地点；让人们经常合理地接触和使用它所拥有的藏品／物件。

要想达到这一标准，就必须彻底了解藏品保管所涉及的所有问题，这样才能确保制定出深思熟虑、负责的规划并做出决策。考虑到这一点，国家标准要求博物馆系统地制定并定期评估它为自己的目标、活动以及藏品需要所制定的各种政策、规定、习惯做法和规划。

博物馆如何评估自己的藏品／物件是否符合自己的使命？

要想确定这一点，就必须将博物馆的使命 —— 博物馆如何正式确定自己的独特身份和目的，如何理解自己的角色和对公众的责任 —— 与下列两点进行比较：（1）博物馆使用的藏品；（2）博物馆为开发和使用藏品而制定的各种政策、规定和习惯做法（请参阅博物馆目标宣言的国家标准）。

对博物馆藏品保管进行评估时需要检查：博物馆的目标宣言或涉及藏品的文件（如藏品管理政策、藏品规划等）是否明确，是否能指导博物馆做出藏品保管方面的决定；博物馆拥有的藏品和借展的物件是否符合博物馆的使命和与藏品有关的文件；博物馆的使命和其他涉及藏品保管的文件是否与博物馆的习惯做法相一致，是否能指导博物馆的习惯做法。

对藏品保管工作进行评估

由于博物馆所采用的媒介和使用藏品的方式以及博物馆自身的规章制度、规模、设施、地理位置、资金和人力资源各不相同，因此管理、存放、保管、记录和保护藏品的方法也不尽相同。人们必须考虑博物馆经营的多个方面，因为只有对这些方面进行全盘考虑才能反映该博物馆的藏品保管政策、规定和习惯做法是否有效，才能在各种变化因素的基础上对其进行评估。例如，许多博物馆可能有不同种类的藏品，分别根据不同目的和用途进行归类 — 永久性藏品、教育性藏品、档案性藏品、研究性藏品等等 — 可能有着不同的管理和保管要求。这些特点应该在涉及藏品保管的政策和规定中明确阐明。而且，不同博物馆的规章制度可能会带来不同的藏品保管方法、问题和与该专业相关的需要。博物馆应该遵守与自己的规章制度相符并且适用于自己的国家标准和最佳做法。

国家标准要求：

- 博物馆具有现行的、得到批准的、全面的藏品管理政策，并且积极地用它来指导博物馆的藏品保管工作。
- 博物馆有充足的人力资源，员工接受过相应的教育和培训，有足够的经验，能够完成博物馆藏品保管工作的各项责任和藏品本身的要求。
- 员工被赋予一定职责，能够执行藏品管理政策。
- 博物馆具有一套文件记录、档案管理和库存详单体系，能够描述每个物件和它的入藏情况（永久性还是临时性）、目前的状况、存放的地点以及流通情况。
- 博物馆定期检测其环境状况，采取积极措施来减少紫外线、温度和湿度的变化、空气污染、人为破坏、虫害和自然灾害对藏品的影响。
- 博物馆应该有相应的方法来识别各种要求，并且确保藏品保护/保管的首要任务得到完成。
- 博物馆预防紧急情况/灾难的规划中应该包含记录、实施并处理涉及博物馆托管藏品安全的规定和方案的内容。
- 博物馆应该定期评估、规划藏品的各种需求（开发、保护、风险管理等），并且给藏品保管分配充足的财力和人力资源。

- 博物馆应该有合适、详细和成文的藏品保管政策和规定，涉及藏品的展示、存放、外借和运输。
- 博物馆藏品保管的工作范围包括对其财产实物和知识的管理。
- 博物馆的相关政策和规定应该包括对藏品保管的道德考虑。
- 博物馆的规划和其他相关政策文件还应该包含对未来收藏活动的考虑。

评述

藏品保管：整体印象和细节

这是制定博物馆标准时技术文献最多的一个领域，将各个细节探讨到了极致。反过来说，也正是因为这个原因，人们才更难将这些标准应用到"两个核心问题"所具体规定的博物馆的使命、目标和条件中去。关于温度和湿度对不同物质的影响，人们已经发表了大量研究论文。就消防系统应该采用湿的水管还是干燥的水管（更不用提预防措施了）进行的辩论可谓无休无止。但这一切根本无法帮助一个小型地方历史协会来回答这个问题："我们这个只有一间屋子的具有历史意义的校舍应该采用何种环境控制或消防系统？"由于这一切很容易陷入到过于关注细节的泥沼中，我们在此不妨先从整体上分析这些标准，采用我们前面对标准特点进行通俗说明时所使用的文字：

知道自己拥有什么。

知道自己需要什么。

知道这些东西在哪里。

将它们保管好。

确保有人从中受益……

尤其你所关心的人。

以及你的邻居。

这种全局观念能够让大家将注意力集中在结果上，而不是集中在方法上。博物馆员工可以认真思考选择什么样的基准来衡量所期待的结果，然后从基准的角度出发，倒过来构想正确的详细执行方案，充分利用博物馆的人力和财力资源。

例如，"知道自己拥有什么"当然指藏品登记和库存。博物馆需要（纸质和电子）的藏品登记册，记录自己有什么藏品以及这些藏品的来源、重要性、使用历史、存放地点和条件。大家在登陆 Museum-L 网站、就藏品编目软件的相对优点与同事们进行在线辩论之前，先停下来思考一下自己的收藏规模以及采取的措施。你们的博物馆是不是一座全部由志愿者经营的小型历史建筑，只有二百件藏品，既不外借自己藏品也不向其他机构借用藏品？你们或许只需复制一份自己的目录卡（当然是使用档案登记卡）备用就足够了。相反，如果你们拥有的是古生物藏品，有几十万个标本，而且使用者主要是来自各国的研究人员，你们可能需要制作一流的相关数据库，能够以供人查询的格式在网站上公布目录数据，而且符合相应数据标准。如果你们所在的是艺术博物馆，你们可能需要以数字图像的形式来记录每一件艺术品，其质量应该达到学术研究和保险公司的要求。如同藏品保护的所有领域一样，博物馆在编目领域采取的方法只能从藏品、藏品要求、藏品使用者以及博物馆的使命和资源的角度来进行评估。

环境控制

环境控制是引起极大争议的方面，一方面是因为相关的机械系统在设计、制造、调试和维护过程中会耗费大量资金，另一方面是因为目前还没有为"正确的"环境控制制定出绝对标准。这是因为博物馆通常收藏并陈列不止一种材质的藏品，而不同材质（陶器、纺织品、板面油画、家具、剥皮动物标本、矿物、液体标本）对于温度和相对湿度有着不同的最佳环境要求。要求博物馆具备一个能够为各种材质单独调节环境的库房是不现实的。即便大家能够装备一个环境控制系统，能够精确地保持所选定的温度和相对湿度，这种环境也是不同藏品要求之间的一个妥协。

从另一个角度来说，环境控制是"完美是良好的敌人"这句格言的一个经典例子。环境控制系统非常昂贵，非常复杂，很难伺候，也很难维护。许多博物馆其实只需安装一个经久耐用的系统，只要这个系统能够保持某个温度和相对湿度，上下波动处于可接受的范围内，然后将没有花在"最先进"系统上的资金用在材料和劳务上，创造出多个小气候环境（箱子、塑料袋、干燥剂）或者提供高质量的虫害控制或者保安系统上。"保管良好"是用权衡的方法处理所有这些问题后所积累起来的效果。

对于那些主要设在历史建筑或遗址上的博物馆而言，环境控制系统甚至会带来破坏作用，不仅会破坏这些地方的历史意义，而且会对建筑物本身造成实际破坏。虽然历史古迹领域的专家们仍在努力为这个问题制定标准，人们已经一致认定，对于某些历史建筑而言，尽可能少地控制环境常常是最恰当的做法。在每年恰当的时候打开和关闭窗户，运用建筑物设计时所依赖的"被动控制"系统，这从历史的角度来说可能是保护某些建筑物的最有效的方法。那么这样一个建筑物里陈列的家具、服装、档案和其他材料呢？如果这个机构能够做出战略决策，陈列复制品或者在另一个装有环境控制设施的现代建筑里陈列一些藏品，这倒是更加负责任的做法。

即便在那些与其说具有历史价值不如说具有历史象征意义的建筑中，理论上的"最佳温度和湿度"既不切合实际也不需要。在湿度很低的自然环境中，竭力在博物馆里保持55%的相对湿度不仅会给博物馆带来巨额电费账单，还会给博物馆的建筑带来灾难。当室内的潮湿空气透过墙壁进入到外面更加干燥的环境中时，砖瓦结构的建筑真的会因此变成碎片。

制定收藏规划

对于藏品保管而言，好消息是博物馆遇到的大多数问题（库房里的藏品过多，需要进行环境控制，需要员工对藏品进行编目，藏品的保护、清洁和虫害控制等等）都可以简单地用金钱来解决。这并不是说博物馆就很容易得到资金，但至少正确的解决方案就这么直截了当，大家只需查阅一下参考文献，听取同事们的意见，然后进行合理的选择。这不大像博物馆工作的其他一些领域，如治理——该领域涉及的主要是人际关系和政治方面的问题，因而难解决得多。（例如，创建博物馆的董事会可能不太愿意让位给年轻人，或者不太愿意去适应博物馆不断变化的需求——这些都不是可以简单地用金钱解决的难题）。

不过，藏品保管工作也有一个无法用金钱解决的棘手的大难题："知道自己需要什么。"许多博物馆（或许是绝大多数博物馆）都要花费一部分宝贵的资源来保管一些既不会促进其使命或服务于观众、也无法为展览、教育或研究项目提供支持的藏品。这其中的原因是可以理解的，许多博物馆都有继承下来的藏品，其历史可以追溯到博物馆的创办人身上，而这些人当初对博物馆的看法可能与该博物馆目前所起的作用大相径庭。许多博物馆的藏品都是几十年慢慢积累起来的，它们接受人们捐赠的一切物品，其指导思想常常为："这东西与我们的使命相符，而且东西不错。"如果博物馆拥有无限的资源，这些物品当然不会构成问题，甚至可能（我们在此不妨引用最常见的说法）"将来某一天会有用的"。然而任何博物馆（即便是史密森学会或盖蒂博物馆）都不可能拥有无限的资源——博物馆用来保管和开放藏品的时间、空间和金钱都是有限的，而博物馆保管的所有藏品都在争抢这些资源。

制定藏品规划是一个主动做出理智选择的过程，它需要从博物馆的使命、目的和观众的角度来选择哪些物品应该入藏，能够确定哪些藏品可以帮助博物馆讲述它力图告诉公众的故事或者回答观众提出的问题。虽然国家标准还没有要求所有博物馆制定藏品规划，越来越多的人都认同一点：藏品规划是一个核心文件，能够帮助博物馆做出明智的选择并且让关键资助人相信博物馆在使用他们提供的资金时都经过深思熟虑。在今后十年内，藏品规划可能会像藏品管理政策一样成为必不可少的文件。

向非博物馆机构出借藏品时的最佳做法

博物馆拥有公众托付的藏品。作为保管人，博物馆通过保护、保管和让公众接触到藏品并从中获益来完成自己受托和道德上的义务。美国博物馆协会注意到一些博物馆将自己的藏品出借给了非博物馆机构，因而敦促这些博物馆一定要考虑藏品保管和对外开放以及公众问责等方面的最佳做法。

在有些情况中，将藏品出借给非博物馆机构可能会损害这些藏品的保管级别。这可能有悖于博物馆在接受公众信任时所承担的责任，并且被视为不当或不道德地使用本该用来让公众受益的藏品。将藏品出借给非博物馆机构还有可能造成藏品文件记录中出现不当或不充分记录的结果，并且影响公众与这些藏品的接触机会。

如果某博物馆习惯将藏品出借给非博物馆机构，那么该博物馆应该考虑这种做法是否与它的使命相一致；应该极其小心，依照藏品保管最谨慎的做法来管理藏品，以确保外借的藏品至少能够得到它们在博物馆时所享有的同等保护、文件记录和环境控制；应该有明确阐述并获得通过的内部政策和规定对外借藏品进行管理，包括藏品管理政策和道德准则。

评述

博物馆常常面临来自主要资助人的压力，要求它们将藏品出借给非博物馆机构，如另一个非营利性机构（学校、大学、医院、基金会）、一个营利性企业或者一个政府机构。例如，当地一家给博物馆提供了大量赞助的银行可能会要求博物馆出借一件艺术品，悬挂在该银行的总部。市立博物馆可能会被要求出借其收藏的画作或装饰艺术品给市长的办公室或官邸。虽然有些人希望博物馆方面能够认定这样做是错误的，会让员工在拒绝这些请求时列举国家标准，实际情况远非如此简单。在有些情况下，外借藏品有助于博物馆使命的发展，可以让博物馆接触到一些关键观众，从而增加博物馆展示藏品的机会；在有些情况下，外借藏品是不得不面对的政治现实。比较负责的做法是博物馆应该区分服务于公众的、可接受的外借要求（例如，在学校、公司或政府建筑等有环境控制、安全的公共场所）与牺牲公众利益、仅仅对某些个人或私人公司有益的外借行为之间的区别。

关于纳粹统治期间非法侵占物件的标准和最佳做法

藏品管理工作的这一领域非常敏感，也非常重要，因此需要博物馆制定单独的标准并提出最佳做法。博物馆界之所以要制定这些标准就是要为博物馆尽到公众托付的职责提供指导。

关于纳粹统治期间非法侵占物件的标准

读者最好登陆美国博物馆协会的官方网站（www.aam-us.org），上面有这些标准的详细内容，包括这些标准制定的过程以及美国博物馆协会坚决执行该标准的决心。

总则

美国博物馆协会（AAM），国际博物馆协会美国国家委员会（ICOM-US）以及美国博物馆界都致力于不断确定并执行藏品保管方法中合乎法律和道德规范的最高标准。美国博物馆协会的《博物馆职业道德准则》规定"藏品保管肩负着公众最高的信任，因而必须合法拥有、永久保管、保护、记录、开放和负责地处理藏品"。

一旦面临这样一个局面，即博物馆收藏的某个物件有可能是纳粹集团令人深恶痛绝的做法造成的非法侵占物件，博物馆就必须承担合乎道德规范的藏品保管责任。博物馆应该制定并执行合乎上述指导原则的政策和规定来处理这个问题。

这些指导原则的目的是协助博物馆处理有可能属于非法侵占物件所涉及的问题。这些物件有可能是纳粹统治时期（1933 — 1945）对犹太人实施大屠杀行动进一步升级后非法侵占的，或者被纳粹分子和他们的合作者抢占的。为了便于大家理解这些指导原则，我们可以根据具体情况将通过盗窃、充公、强制交易或其他非法侵占手段获得的物件视为非法侵占物。

为了帮助大家鉴别和发现博物馆藏品中可能含有的非法侵占物件，美国纳粹大屠杀资产总统顾问委员会(PCHA)，艺术博物馆馆长协会（AAMD）和美国博物馆协会（AAM）一致同意博物馆应该努力：（1）鉴别所有产生于1946年前，并于1932年后由博物馆获得的藏品、1932年至1946年间易手的物件以及在此期间有可能属于欧洲大陆的物件（下文简称为"所涉及的物件"）；（2）公开目前所藏物件和这些物件的来源（原拥有人）信息；（3）在资源允许的情况下优先进行藏品来源研究。AAM，AAMD和PCHA还一致认定首要的研究重点应该是欧洲画作和犹太文物。

由于世界各地都能接触到互联网，我们鼓励博物馆在互联网上更多地开放藏品信息，这或许能帮助人们发现纳粹统治期间非法侵占后没有归还的物件。

　　AAM 和 ICOM-US 承认在第二次世界大战期间以及战后数年中，创建物件来源和证明物件所有权的许多信息都已散落在各地或者遗失。在确定某件物件是否属于尚未归还的非法侵占物时，我们必须考虑由于时间流逝和大屠杀期间特殊环境所造成的物件来源的空白和模糊信息。AAM 和 ICOM-US 支持博物馆更多地开放其档案和其他资源，也支持博物馆创建有助于跟踪和组织信息的数据库。

　　美国博物馆协会敦促博物馆认真考虑这个问题的复杂性，逐个解决每件藏品的来源问题。博物馆应该努力提供有用信息，确定一些无法确定身份的物件是否出自纳粹统治时期。出现利益冲突时，博物馆应该努力营造合作、妥协和达成一致目标的气氛。

　　美国博物馆协会要求博物馆在获得、展示和研究物件时考虑公众利益。这些指导原则旨在促进博物馆合法、合理地保管物件的意愿和能力，不应该被理解为给博物馆实现其目标增加的不必要的负担。

标准

1. 获得藏品

　　美国博物馆协会的立场是在获得藏品之前 —— 无论是通过购买、捐赠、遗赠还是交换，博物馆应该采取一切合理措施来确定这些物件在纳粹统治时期的来源问题。

　　1)　对博物馆欲收藏的物件所进行的规范研究应该包括要求卖家、捐赠人或遗嘱执行人尽可能多地出具物件来源的信息，尤其是物件在纳粹统治时期的情况。

　　2)　如果博物馆欲收藏的物件在纳粹统治时期的来源问题不完整或者无法确定，博物馆应该考虑在获得该物件之前还需要进行哪些研究来进一步解决物件在纳粹统治时期的来源问题。这种研究可以包括查询相关信息渠道，如现有记录和跟踪非法侵占物件信息的其他数据库。

　　3)　如果没有证据能证明该物件为非法侵占后没有归还的物件，博物馆可以着手收藏该物件。博物馆在获得物件后应该尽快公布该物件以及物件来源的信息。

　　4)　如果有确凿证据证明该物件为非法侵占后没有归还的物件，博物馆应该将证据的性质告知捐赠者、卖家或遗嘱执行人，并且中止交易，直到采取进一步的措施来解决这些问题。由于具体案例的具体情况各不相同，慎重而且必要的行动可以包括向有资质的法律机构咨询以及将博物馆了解到的情况告知其他相关各方。

5) 美国博物馆协会认为：在某些情况下，获得来源无法确定的物件可能会进一步揭示该物件的信息，有助于解决其身份问题。在这种情况下，博物馆可以选择继续收藏该物件，只要其收藏过程合法、合适、慎重，只要博物馆在获得该物件后尽快公布该物件及该物件来源的信息。

6) 博物馆应该以文件的形式记录自己对所获物件进行的纳粹统治时期来源的研究。

7) 博物馆应该遵守博物馆界目前的习惯做法，公布、展示或让公众接触到最近接受的捐赠和遗赠物以及购买的物件，以此让人们对所有新获藏品进行进一步的研究、查验、评估和问责。

2. 借展品

美国博物馆协会认为，博物馆作为借展品的临时托管人应该知道自己有道德上的义务来考虑借展品的身份，知道自己临时保管的某件借展品有可能会遭遇索要请求。

1) 对借展品进行的规范研究应该包括请求出借方尽可能详细地提供借展品来源信息，尤其是纳粹统治时期的情况。

2) 如果借展品在纳粹统治时期的来源信息不完整或者无法确定，博物馆在借用该借展品前应该考虑还需要进行哪些研究来进一步解决借展品在纳粹统治时期的来源问题。

3) 如果没有证据能证明该借展品为非法侵占后没有归还的物件，博物馆可以着手借用该借展品。

4) 如果有确凿证据证明该借展品为非法侵占后没有归还的物件，博物馆应该将证据的性质告知出借方，并且中止借用行为，直到采取进一步的措施来解决这些问题。由于具体案例的具体情况各不相同，慎重而且必要的行动可以包括向有资质的法律机构咨询以及将博物馆了解到的情况告知其他相关各方。

5) 美国博物馆协会认为：在某些情况下，公开展示无法确定来源的物件可能会进一步揭示该物件的信息，有助于解决其身份问题。在这种情况下，博物馆可以选择继续借用该借展品，只要博物馆能够确定借用程序合法、合适、慎重，并且能够公布该物件及该物件来源的信息。

6) 博物馆应该以文件的形式记录自己对借展品进行的纳粹统治时期来源的研究。

3. 现有藏品

美国博物馆协会认为，博物馆应该认真地分配时间和资金，对来源信息不完整或不确定的藏品中所涉及的物件进行研究。考虑到物件来源研究费时费力，用于这种研究的资源非常有限，博物馆应该在考虑有限资源和藏品性质的前提下制定优先研究的对象。

研究

1) 博物馆应该鉴别藏品中所涉及的物件并且公开目前已经掌握的物件和物件来源的信息。

2) 博物馆应该仔细研究藏品中所涉及的物件，鉴别出那些特点或来源有问题的物件，以便确定这些物件是否是纳粹统治期间非法侵占后没有归还的物件。

3) 在进行物件来源研究时，博物馆应该彻底查找自己的记录，并且在必要时联系有可能提供纳粹统治期间物件来源信息的现有档案机构、数据库、艺术品经销商、拍卖行、捐赠人、学者和研究人员。

4) 博物馆应该将对纳粹统治时期物件来源的研究纳入到对藏品的规范研究中。

5) 在寻求资金举办展览或进行公共项目研究时，博物馆应该将对纳粹统治时期物件来源的研究纳入到申请书中。由于各自的情况不尽相同，博物馆还应该寻求特别经费来开展纳粹统治时期物件来源的研究。

6) 博物馆应该以文件的形式记录自己对此项研究所开展的工作。

发现非法侵占的物件的证据

7) 如果在研究过程中发现确凿证据，能够证明某物件属于被非法侵占后没有归还的物件，博物馆应该在征求合格律师的意见之后采取慎重而必要的措施来解决物件的身份问题。这些措施应该包括公布信息，如果可能的话通知潜在的所有人。

8) 万一有确凿证据能够证明某物件确系非法侵占后没有归还的物件，但没有合法主人出面索要，博物馆应该在征求合格律师的意见后采取慎重而必要的措施来解决该问题。这些措施应该包括继续保留该物件，或者将其处理掉。

9) 美国博物馆协会认为：博物馆收藏可能属于非法侵占后没有归还但又无人索要的物件后可以继续保管、研究和展示该物件，以此让更多的观众获益并且提供机会让公众了解该物件的历史。如果博物馆保留了这类物件，它应该在展品说明和出版物中注明物件的历史。

4. 所有人的索要请求

美国博物馆协会认为：博物馆在处理与其保管的物件有关的索要请求时应该做到公开、认真、积极，并且尊重各方的尊严。每一个索要请求都应该根据具体情况单独处理。

1) 如果有人声称博物馆的某件收藏品系纳粹统治时期非法侵占后没有归还的物件，博物馆应该立刻全面分析这种说法。

2) 博物馆除了自己进行研究外，还应该请求索要人出具拥有该物件的证据，以便协助确定该物件的来源。

3) 如果博物馆确定某藏品确系纳粹统治时期非法侵占后没有归还的物件，博物馆应该尽量以公平合理、双方可接受的方式与索要人一起解决问题。

4) 如果博物馆收到索要请求，认为其临时保管的某件借展品系非法侵占后没有归还的物件，博物馆应该立刻通知出借方，在征求合格律师的意见后尽到其作为该物件临时保管人所应负的法律义务。

5) 只要有可能而且能够做到，在接到认定博物馆某藏品为纳粹统治期间非法侵占后没有归还的物件的索要请求后，博物馆应该努力寻求法律诉讼之外的办法（如调解）来解决问题。

6) 美国博物馆协会认为，为了合情合理地解决索要问题，博物馆可以选择放弃某些辩护权。

5. 信托义务

许多博物馆声称自己在采取上述行动时是受公众之托来保管藏品。它们的保管职责和它们对自己服务的公众所承担的责任都要求它们就获得、借用或处理物件做出决定之前必须首先采取正确措施并经过仔细考虑。

1) 为了实现这一目标，博物馆应该制定政策和处理方法来解决上述指导原则中所涉及的问题。

2) 博物馆应该对公众和媒体的垂询快速做出正确的回答。

纳粹统治期间非法侵占物件的最佳处理方法

公众越来越了解纳粹统治期间被非法侵占的文化财产问题。虽然许多文化财产被重新发现并归还，或者所有人得到赔偿，但仍然有大量财产下落不明。因此，博物馆界应该努力鉴别这一期间入藏的藏品，以便归还它们。

由于博物馆是受公众之托来保管藏品，博物馆必须鉴别这部分藏品。正如美国博物馆协会的《博物馆职业道德准则》中所述，藏品保管"意味着合法拥有、永久保管、保护、记录、开放和负责地处理藏品"。美国博物馆协会将纳粹统治期间非法侵占物件的问题视为对所有博物馆都意义重大的问题。

博物馆应该关注美国博物馆协会董事会和ICOM-US董事会任命的一个联合工作组于1999年制定的《处理纳粹统治期间非法侵占的物件之标准》。博物馆还应该关注美国博物馆协会的《公开纳粹统治期间欧洲物件转移信息的推荐做法》，其内容与美国博物馆协会、艺术博物馆馆长协会（AAMD）和美国纳粹大屠杀资产总统顾问委员会（PCHA）于2000年10月达成的协议完全一致。

博物馆应该注册并加入"纳粹统治期间物件来源互联网门户"（NEPIP），该网站（www.nepip.org）提供物件注册服务，可以搜索美国博物馆在1946年前收藏的以及在纳粹统治期间（1933－1945）欧洲大陆易手的物件。那些拥有此类藏品的博物馆在加入该门户网站之后依照本章节介绍的指导原则以及博物馆界普遍采纳的《推荐做法》尽到自己的义务，公开纳粹统治期间物件来源信息。

评述

努力解决纳粹统治期间非法侵占物件所涉及的道德问题为博物馆界解决更加普遍的文化财产索要问题打开了序幕。处理纳粹统治期间资产的标准为如何解决此类道德问题提供了一个典范。

至少每一座博物馆都应该知道自己可能获得的藏品的来源，研究这些问题，并且做出符合其使命、政策和价值观的决定，能够而且愿意接受公众的问责。请大家牢记翻译界的标准——出色不仅仅意味着遵守规则。博物馆有义务认真思考其行为的道德含意，权衡自己所追求的结果是否能经得起公共舆论以及法院的考验。

博物馆处理索要请求的方式为处理各种关系定下了基调——可能会决定该事件是通过调解还是通过法院解决。对索要请求迅速做出反映并且尊重对方，可以营造出比较友好的气氛，带来对双方有利的结果。博物馆可以采取的正确措施包括立刻分析索要请求，自己进行研究并请求索要方也进行研究。如果该物件确实是博物馆的藏品，而且有确凿证据证明为非法侵占后没有归还的物件，博物馆应该设法与索要方解决问题。

在许多情况中，博物馆可能会声称自己合法拥有该物件，并且在法庭上提供站不住脚的技术性辩护论点（如过了有效期）。除非博物馆在分析全部现有研究结果的基础上做出合乎道德标准的决定，否则博物馆不应该采用上述为自己辩护的方法。技术性法律辩护不会促使法庭做出违背道德标准的判决结果。

V. 教育与藏品诠释

教育与藏品诠释标准
教育与藏品诠释"优秀标准"的特征

- 博物馆清晰地阐明其总体的教育目标、理念与思想，并且证明它的一切活动均符合这些目标与理念。
- 博物馆了解现有和潜在观众的特点和需求，并且将这种了解应用在其藏品诠释中。
- 博物馆的藏品诠释内容所依据的是相应的研究。
- 博物馆在开展研究时要遵守学术标准。
- 博物馆可以使用与其教育目的、内容、观众和资源相符的各种技术和方法。
- 博物馆应向不同观众提供精确、恰当的藏品诠释内容。
- 博物馆在其藏品诠释活动中始终要保持高质量。
- 博物馆对自己的藏品诠释活动进行有效性评估，将评估结果用来规划和改进其活动。

评述

　　考虑到教育与藏品诠释是所有博物馆活动的核心，人们可能会为这部分标准的详细内容之少感到有些惊讶，因为除了上述介绍博物馆必须采取哪些措施来完成它在这一经营领域基本义务的《特征》外，本章节没有太多其他内容。（请参阅 59 页的《展示借展品的标准》部分，该章节的确对一个微妙但重要的问题提供了额外评述）。作者在此简单介绍一下对这一情况的思考。

　　首先，博物馆普遍在教育和藏品诠释领域表现出色。请记住我在本书开头部分的阐述：制定标准是为了解决确实已经成为难题的问题。博物馆界没有为这个领域制定详细标准或许是因为我们觉得这个领域没有什么需要解决的难题。其次，大家无法就评价"优秀教育"或"优秀藏品诠释"的客观标准达成一致意见。从狭隘的技术层面来看，目前已经有了撰写和设计展览说明牌或者布展的指导原则，可难道撰写展览说明牌真的只有一种好的方法吗？如果组织一个教育项目呢？通过网站宣传博物馆的内容呢？最后，这又是一个只能从博物馆的使命、观众和资源的角度来评估"好"的领域。我们无法用量化的标准来对其进行评估 —— 一座小型博物馆每年组织一个展览，准备四个公众参与项目，它可能会比另一座规模相同但将其财力和人力用到极限：每年组织三个展览、推出十二个项目的博物馆更好地发挥其作用，更好地运用其资源。

　　不过，我还是可以就教育和藏品诠释问题发表几点看法，因为这些方面常常给许多博物馆带来挑战。

观众的多元性

有些博物馆创建的目的是服务某个特定、有时非常局限的对象。将这些人聚集在一起的可能是文化（瑞典裔美国人）、兴趣（飞行爱好者）或家庭背景（美国革命之女）。从某个角度来说，这是博物馆的选择——每座博物馆确定自己的使命和服务对象。不过，许多人认为如果服务对象过于局限，博物馆其实是将那些有可能对其专题感兴趣的人排除在外，结果并没有在广泛意义上服务于公众利益。毕竟博物馆在获得免税地位时，公众是作为一个整体对博物馆提供了支持的。从实际的角度来说，很少有博物馆能够仅仅凭借服务有限的观众群而得以生存，尤其是任何社区的人口结构都会由于年龄老化、迁徙、兴趣的改变和时代的变迁而发生变化。博物馆服务的对象越小，它就越可能发现自己被边缘化，缺乏可以维持下去的支持。

因此《优秀标准的特征》具体规定博物馆"理解潜在观众……的特点和需求"，"博物馆应该努力具有包容性，为不同人群的参与提供机会"。这给我们描绘了这样一个机构：它应该竭尽全力让不同对象使用博物馆的资源，而这又会影响博物馆选择讲述的故事和传达的信息以及向观众传达这些信息的方式。比方说，如果一座历史建筑博物馆将自己的讲述内容完全针对富有的白人男性的商业和政治成就上，它就有可能缺乏吸引其他观众的宣传内容——管理家务的妇女的故事，或者让这种生活方式得以实现的仆人或奴隶的故事。对铁路情有独钟的人可能会只关心其技术成就，而实际上可以讲述的故事要广泛得多，如铁路对经济、迁徙、社会和地域流动性的影响等等。

评估

在缺乏明确的教育和藏品诠释标准的情况下，最有意义的评估方式是衡量博物馆的做法是否成功。美国博物馆认证委员会在努力为博物馆的藏品诠释工作制定标准时经常采用同一条思路，即一切都没有问题，只要博物馆（1）通过藏品诠释活动来明确自己想实现的目标（制定藏品诠释规划）；（2）评估博物馆是否实现了自己的目标；（3）必要时采取纠正行为。遗憾的是，评估对许多博物馆——甚至拥有大量资源的大型博物馆——都是一个挑战。不过，目前已经有大量文献、众多顾问和数不清的评估方案，能够在这领域给博物馆提供协助。对于那些希望展示自己在教育和藏品诠释工作方面有出色表现的博物馆而言，我给它们的最佳建议就是创建一个系统、正式、不断改进的评估项目，对博物馆的展览、活动和其他藏品诠释工作进行评估，并且用评估结果来指导这一领域的改进。

展示借展品的标准

读者最好登陆美国博物馆协会的官方网站（www.aam-us.org）来了解这方面的标准，其中包括导言和该标准制定的过程。

博物馆在考虑展示借展品之前应该有得到治理机构批准、公众提出要求时可以看到的正式书面文件，专门处理下列问题：

1. 藏品借用

博物馆的政策应该包含下列规定：

1) 确保博物馆认定借展品与博物馆的使命之间有明确联系。借用该物品与展览的学术品德相符。

2) 要求博物馆仔细审查出借方与博物馆的关系，以确定是否存在潜在的利益冲突或者的确有利益冲突，如出借方与博物馆的决策过程有正式或非正式的联系（比方说，出借方是博物馆的董事、员工或捐赠者）。

3) 包含指导原则和规定来处理此类冲突或存在冲突的迹象。这些指导原则和规定可以要求那些确实有或者感觉有利益冲突的人退出决策制定过程，对决策者进行特别监督，公开利益冲突或者拒绝借展品。

4) 禁止博物馆接受借展方出售借展品后提供的佣金或其他资金。这条禁令并不适用于为出售此类物品而专门组织的展览，如手工艺展。

2. 出借方的参与

博物馆制定的政策应该确保博物馆保持展览的学术品德和对展览的控制权。博物馆在遵守该政策时：

1) 应该保留对展览内容和展示方式的决策权；

2) 可以在保留全部决策权的前提下与出借方商谈从出借方的收藏中挑选哪些物件以及这些物件在展览中享受的地位；

3) 如果出借方也是展览的出资人之一，应该公开展览的资金来源。如果博物馆收到请求，要求博物馆不透露对方的身份，而如果这样做又会掩盖（实际或潜在的）利益冲突或者会带来其他道德方面的问题，博物馆就应该避免这种保密做法。

评述

我们为什么在涉及教育和藏品诠释工作的众多领域中单独为展品借用制定详细的标准？因为这常常让博物馆见诸报端，而且是负面报道。它常常涉及多个敏感问题，足以引起媒体、公众、执法人员和出资人的关注：利益冲突，利用公共资源谋取私利，影响展览内容的公正性与可信度。

这也反映了这样一个事实：我们制定标准来处理实际发生的情况。最著名的实例是起草该标准前布鲁克林博物馆举办的《感觉》展。查尔斯·沙弛这位专门收藏英国年轻前卫画家作品的著名收藏家将自己的藏品出借给博物馆，举办了一个大型展览。该展览在两个方面引起了极大的争议 — 公众抗议的其实是展览的内容。（天主教会尤其对克里斯·奥菲利的作品《圣母玛丽亚》提出了抗议，因为这幅作品中添加了大象粪便和从色情杂志上剪切下来的女性生殖器的图片。）不过，该展览还引起了人们对举办过程的争议。博物馆方面起初并没有透露沙弛除了出借这些作品外还对展览内容享有很大的自主权，并且为此提供了大笔资金。如果再考虑到沙弛对"糟糕"艺术品情有独钟（等到这些艺术品升值后再将它们出售）——（这在收藏家中很少见），媒体、公众以及纽约市长都觉得沙弛是利用接受了市政府人笔资助的博物馆来谋取自己的私利。

这个实例也是我们要求博物馆制定自己标准的原因之一。这种引起极大争议的事件会给博物馆界带来最大的风险，即（联邦、州或地方）政府会出面干预，强行对博物馆滥用公共信任的行为进行控制。尽管《感觉》展看似一个非常具体（而且极端）的例子，但这类问题仍然频繁出现。其他一些例子：某员工、志愿者或董事愿意为某展览出借一件藏品。人们是否会觉得这样做有可能提高该藏品的售价？出借方是否对博物馆施加了压力，让其展出该藏品？博物馆在讨好某大收藏家，希望该收藏家将来能把自己的藏品捐赠给博物馆。为了讨好这位收藏家，博物馆举办了一个展览，全部展品均来自该收藏家的藏品。收藏家希望自己能够在很大程度上对展出的作品、展览的形式以及展品的内容介绍有决定权。这种影响在什么程度上可以被视为对展览的学术内容施加了不恰当的影响呢（尤其是如果博物馆员工不同意对方的选择……）？

VI. 财务稳定性

财务稳定性标准
财务稳定性"优秀标准"的特征
- 博物馆合法、合理、负责任地获得、管理和分配其财务资源，促进博物馆使命的发展。
- 博物馆的经营必须对其财务状况负责，必须确保博物馆长期可持续发展。

评述

言简意赅。虽然博物馆界以外有许多标准也影响着博物馆经营的这个领域（如《美国财务会计准则委员会标准》，《专业筹款人员协会道德准则和职业行为标准》，《非营利行业出色治理与符合道德标准的习惯做法的指导意见》），博物馆最关心的是：（1）它们有足够的资金；（2）资金是通过正当渠道筹集的；（3）依照博物馆的使命运用资金。其他一些单独标准则涉及资金不足时如何经营以及如何确保资金来自正当渠道（即没有任何附加条件）。见下文对这些标准的详细介绍。

执行官的报酬

上文第三点"依照博物馆的使命运用资金"需要我们特别关注。在过去十年中，媒体、公众和执法者对非营利机构执行官的报酬问题越来越敏感。如果某博物馆长的报酬远远高于其他博物馆馆长，与博物馆的总支出不成比例，或者包含过于奢华或与其职责不相关的特殊待遇，媒体和公众尤其对特殊待遇感到愤怒。最近出现在新闻中的一些实例包括游泳池维修、为馆长家中配备高端纯手工制作家具、坐头等舱飞机旅行和入住高档宾馆。

不过，更加恶劣的是薪水过高问题。博物馆越来越多地进行大型扩建工程，请著名建筑师设计新建筑，开展新的业务以及涉及大笔资金的活动。这意味着馆长需要面对许多压力，需要筹集到大笔资金。有些董事会认为最佳的解决办法就是聘请来自私企的首席执行官，有着法律或财务管理背景的人。这些人对于薪水也有着与商界水平相同的期待。此外，有些来自非营利机构的馆长认为接近高端资助人的最佳办法就是采用他们的生活方式。尽管财务数据显示得非常清楚（"如果我们付给这个人 X 美元的报酬，他利用自己的各种关系可以带来 Y 美元的资助，我们仍然属于净盈利"），我们还是不能忽视公众的看法。公众将非营利性博物馆视为福利机构，期望博物馆馆长在保持博物馆非营利性地位的时候能够表现出一定的节俭，毕竟博物馆使用的资金大部分来自公众。博物馆应该认真研究，为首席执行官制定合理的报酬标准，包括以其他博物馆馆长和社区其他非营利机构负责人的报酬为基准。

寻求和管理企业及个人捐赠的标准

读者最好登陆美国博物馆协会的官方网站（www.aam-us.org）来查阅完整原文，其中包括记录捐资的推荐规定，以及应承担的法律和税务义务。

基本原则

- 忠诚于使命。为了确保能够接受公众的问责和做出明智的决定，博物馆应该制定经治理机构批准的文件政策，指导博物馆寻求和管理来自企业和个人的资助，做到既能保护自己的资产和声誉，又与自己的使命相符。
- 公众信任与问责。博物馆界认同并鼓励与各种利益共享者进行正当合作，包括博物馆的捐赠人。这类捐赠人常常希望能参与博物馆的经营活动。博物馆必须考虑自己对公众信托所承担的职责，必须时刻控制各种项目、展览和活动的内容与学术品德。
- 透明度。博物馆应该向捐资的企业和个人提供其使命、财务和项目的准确信息。
- 严格尊重捐赠方的意愿。博物馆应该将来自捐资企业和个人的资金应用在双方商定的目的上。
- 道德与利益冲突。在寻求和管理来自企业和个人的捐资时，博物馆应该遵守美国博物馆协会的《博物馆职业道德准则》和它的内部职业道德政策，尤其要留意潜在的利益冲突。
- 保密。博物馆应该保证按照捐资人的意愿来处理捐资金额信息，并且在法律允许的范围内为捐资人保密。

目的与重要性

非营利机构、慈善机构、教育和科学机构以及它们服务的对象一直从企业界和捐资个人的义举中获益，捐资企业和个人也从他们与博物馆服务对象的关系中获益。企业希望通过与博物馆的联系来提高自己的正面形象，让人们看到自己也致力于非营利事业，以此在它们经营的社区内制造好感，提高自己的知名度。捐资的个人则通过自己的义举再次向人们证明他们支持艺术、科学、历史和毕生求知的努力，支持通过让公众接触到藏品和信息来创造一个更加强大、更加文明的社会。此外，捐资的个人常常与他们所支持的博物馆保持着家族式的或者其他形式的个人密切关系。

考虑到博物馆与捐赠人之间的关系过于密切，美国博物馆协会与整个博物馆界联合制定了寻求和管理企业和个人捐资的标准。虽然这些标准提供了基本指导原则，每座博物馆还是应该各自制定与其使命和项目相符的政策。

管理捐赠资金

博物馆应该以独立文件或者以其他博物馆政策一部分的形式制定关于企业和个人捐资的政策。博物馆在执行该政策时应该保持一致性；任何改动都应该源自标准和最佳做法的改变，或者源自博物馆使命和战略方向的改变。博物馆不能完全由于某个具体情况而改变政策。

这些政策应该：为寻求和管理捐赠的资金而确定博物馆的目标；明确治理机构以及员工就企业和个人捐赠的资金进行决策的职责，包括但不局限于提出请求、接受捐赠、要求兑现承诺、对捐赠人表示感谢以及接受公众的问责；确保博物馆有必要的人力和财力资源来兑现自己在接受捐赠时所承担的义务；处理利益冲突，尤其是涉及企业或个人捐赠机会而又涉及博物馆治理机构某位成员或员工利益的情况。

利益冲突

该政策应该涉及员工或治理机构成员有义务披露上述关系中任何利益的问题。这些披露并不意味着道德不当。博物馆可以要求与捐资企业或个人有联系或者有利益关系的个人回避博物馆涉及捐赠资金的讨论或行动，并且以文件的形式记录该人在由该资金资助的项目或活动的任何其他方面所起的作用。

与捐赠方的沟通和关系

该政策应该明确哪些员工或治理机构成员有权与捐赠企业或个人签署或修改协议。此外，博物馆应该有明确政策，规定向捐赠方提供财务、税务和法律信息程度，包括建议捐赠方向博物馆法律和财务顾问咨询的条款。

博物馆可以接受的捐赠种类

博物馆应该制定接受捐赠的政策，规定其可以从捐赠企业或个人处接受的捐赠种类，并且规定其从博物馆使命、经营、企业和法律的角度决定是否接受所提供的捐赠。博物馆应该根据本社区和观众的特点、价值观和看法以及博物馆自己的原则和使命来决定是否由于某些企业或某类企业的产品和服务项目而将这些企业或这类企业排除在外。在决定是否将某些捐赠者排除在外的过程中，博物馆可以考虑：企业的产品和服务类型；潜在捐赠方的企业行为；是否仅仅在某些活动中将这些捐赠方排除在外（如儿童参与的项目）。

致谢

博物馆应该考虑各种对捐助企业或个人表示谢意的方式，并且考虑根据捐赠金额对捐赠方表示谢意的通用标准，如使用和安放捐赠者姓名牌和其他标志以及这些姓名牌和标志的大小。

保密

博物馆应该尽可能尊重捐赠方和捐赠金额等信息的隐私权，确保与捐赠方建立并保持信任关系。博物馆可以考虑建立一个系统来管理捐赠方信息的披露与处理问题；规定哪些种类的信息可以或者不可以透露，以此在博物馆接受公众问责的义务和保护捐赠方隐私的义务之间保持平衡；只收集捐赠方或潜在捐赠方与捐赠相关的信息。

匿名

博物馆必须确定是否以及在什么情况下可以接受匿名捐赠。博物馆应该避免同意那些掩盖利益冲突或者引起其他道德问题的匿名要求。

没有兑现的承诺

有时候会出现捐赠方无法或者没有兑现承诺的情况。博物馆在决定是否强制对方兑现承诺时应该考虑法律和财务因素；这笔捐赠资金对博物馆的整体影响；博物馆的历史以及与该捐赠方以前的关系；以及公众对这种情况的态度。

文件记录

博物馆应该按照相关法律和文件保管政策要求保留与捐赠活动相关的所有文件。

政策的应用

博物馆应该明确规定哪些机构必须遵守关于接受企业和个人捐赠的规定，如博物馆之友社团、志愿者组织、博物馆系统内的机构等等。

公众问责

博物馆在面对公众和媒体就其接受企业和个人捐赠情况提出的质疑（包括博物馆方

存在不道德行为的说法）时，应该迅速、全面、坦率地向他们介绍情况，介绍博物馆的行为以及这些行为背后的原因。

专门涉及企业捐赠的问题
博物馆名称和标识的使用
博物馆应该为赞助企业使用博物馆名称和标识问题制定明确规定。博物馆在制定该规定时可以考虑：允许企业使用博物馆名称和标识的特定情况；批准使用其名称和标识时所承担的责任；严禁使用的具体情况；是否符合博物馆制定的保护知识产权（如商标、版权等）的政策。

对博物馆与企业关系的宣传
企业可能希望在其营销、广告和公关活动中宣传它与博物馆的关系。博物馆可以在它的政策中规定：企业可以宣传其与博物馆关系的广度与深度，博物馆在批准这种宣传活动时应该承担的责任。

供应商的捐赠
博物馆与提供物资或服务的某位供应商之间的现有或未来关系不应该由于该供应商提供了捐助而发生变化。

唯一赞助商
博物馆应该认真考虑是否愿意与某企业建立唯一赞助商关系，这可能会限制博物馆接受来自该企业竞争对手的赞助或者使用竞争对手的产品和服务。

评述
在期望值之间寻找平衡点
由于大多数非营利性博物馆都为免税机构，绝大多数资金来自公共资源（政府资金），因此它们必须符合很高的行为标准。然而，美国博物馆与欧洲博物馆不同，它们很少能保证获得政府资助，因此它们只能主动寻找其他资金来源，包括个人赞助。这些赞助者 — 个人或企业 — 也给这种关系加入了自己的期望值。公司越来越将赞助视为一种业务，而不是慈善行为。提供赞助的个人非常关心博物馆和博物馆的使命，可能会对博物馆的某个项目非常感兴趣，希望能参与重要决策的制定过程。虽然这些标准具体针对的是个人赞助者，它们也适用于这些个人捐赠者创建的家庭基金会。

这些动机本身没有错，属于人的天性。但是博物馆有义务以合乎公众信托的方式承认并处理好这些期望值。一个需要认真思考的典型情况是博物馆为了讨好大收藏家而举办其藏品展览。公众或媒体有时候会质疑这种展览是否会因为提高了展出作品的价值而让收藏家获益。有些人更是质疑这些展览是否能代表博物馆布展的最高质量以及博物馆馆舍和时间利用的最高水平。另一种情况是公众可能会觉得某赞助公司能从展览传达的信息中获益。例如，一家石油公司赞助介绍美国阿拉斯加州环境保护的展览，或者一家制药公司赞助介绍对付病毒的传统药物的展览。公众（不管是对是错）可能会认为赞助商影响了展览内容。这种怀疑会逐渐削弱博物馆最宝贵的资产——即博物馆作为"精确"和"客观"代言者的名声。在上述例子中运用博物馆标准能够帮助博物馆在潜在冲突演变成公众争议之前就发现它们，做出与博物馆政策和博物馆界惯例相符的决策，以令人信服的方式向公众和媒体证明自己行为的正确性。

捐赠人的意图

如果博物馆在遵守捐赠物最初条款的同时努力对不断变化的环境做出合理的反应，捐赠人的意图便会引起人们的争议。极端的例子是引起公众高度关注的位于宾夕法尼亚州梅里昂市的巴恩斯基金会。虽然阿尔伯特·巴恩斯将该机构搬迁至费城市中心是确保它继续存在下去的唯一办法，有些人仍然认为巴恩斯的真实意图（以及他中止这个艺术机构的粗暴决定）是想彻底摧毁该机构。有些人就像对美国宪法进行死板解释的人一样，认为捐赠人的意图不可更改，哪怕人们提出的新用途完全符合捐赠物的精神。遗憾的是，捐赠人一旦过世，我们根本无法询问他的真实意图，尽管我们有时候可以联系捐赠者的家人，请他们代表捐赠者对捐赠物的使用目的进行合理更改。到了一定时候，这种事情就会闹上法庭，因为负责监督这些捐赠品管理工作的是博物馆所在州的检察总长。不过，正如本书所涉及的众多问题，博物馆应该在检察总长介入之前努力解决任何决策所涉及的道德问题。

缩减规模或裁员的标准

在这个经济面临挑战的时代，许多博物馆多个渠道的收入都在急剧减少，如政府拨款、上级机构的拨款、提供资金的机构的拨款、门票和博物馆商店的营业收入。为了应付这种局面，许多博物馆都对其治理模式、员工配备和经营进行了改革。博物馆必须采取这些恰当的步骤来确保它的未来。不过，裁员或缩减规模有时会被错误地视为管理失败的标志。本标准探讨裁员和缩减规模问题，以及这些做法如何影响博物馆。

裁员和缩减规模可以是收入减少后采取的负责的必要弥补措施。博物馆在准备缩减规模时应该：将重点放在保存完成其使命和为社区服务的能力上；采取与博物馆界最高道德、财务和管理标准相符的举措；认真考虑这些举措对员工、社区和为公众保管的藏品的影响。

博物馆在考虑裁员或缩减规模时常常会遇到一些问题，以下几点意见可以为运用博物馆标准来解决这些问题提供指导。

藏品

在博物馆缩减规模时，其藏品常常会特别引人关注，这是因为藏品保护涉及大量资金，也因为藏品是潜在的金融资产。考虑到藏品在博物馆缩减规模过程中所扮演的角色，我们为博物馆制定了下列指导原则。

博物馆受公众之托保管藏品，博物馆治理机构的主要职责就是要坚守这份信任。博物馆可以确定自己是否能够对其收藏的一些藏品进行长期有效的保管。如果博物馆无法做到这一点，最负责的行动就是出售馆藏，以保证藏品和相关文件通过安全的方式移交给另一家合适的保管机构。博物馆可以认真考虑究竟是让这些藏品继续保留在另一个非营利性公共机构中，还是可以本着对藏品负责的精神，通过公开出售来确保藏品的安全。不过，出售馆藏向来不是一个简单快捷的决定。博物馆常常需要花费大量时间和其他资源来研究这些藏品，确定它们的来源，明确所有权是否有任何限制，然后进行恰当而安全的移交。博物馆在短期内可能还要为进行必要的研究、准备各种文件、安排并实施移交增加额外费用。出售馆藏是经过漫长深思熟虑后做出的决定，博物馆必须决定采取何种最佳办法运用现有资源来完成它的使命。决策的过程必须符合博物馆标准和最佳做法，符合博物馆自身的道德准则，符合博物馆的藏品规划和藏品政策。

博物馆界的各种道德准则都对如何处理出售馆藏后获得的资金有专门规定。所有博物馆都必须遵守美国博物馆协会的《博物馆职业道德准则》以及博物馆各专业的道德准则。美国博物馆协会的《博物馆职业道德准则》明确规定，出售馆藏品后获得的资金只能用于购买和直接保管藏品。虽然不同博物馆和博物馆的不同专业对"直接保管"有不同理解，大多数人都同意这不包括用这笔资金来支付经营成本。艺术博物馆馆长协会（AAMD）的职业道德准则明确规定，艺术博物馆只能将出售馆藏后获得的资金用于购买新的藏品，而美国州和地方历史协会（AASLH）的职业道德准则规定历史博物馆只能将该资金用于购买或保护藏品。

博物馆正面临越来越大的压力，要求它们将藏品资本化，并且将藏品用作博物馆贷款的抵押品。美国博物馆协会的《博物馆职业道德准则》要求藏品"无抵押义务"，而这意味着藏品不能被用作抵押品。艺术博物馆馆长协会的职业道德准则同样禁止将藏品用作抵押品，并且禁止博物馆将藏品资本化。美国州和地方历史协会也发表过一个阐述其立场的声明，宣布将藏品资本化的做法违背道德准则。

博物馆藏品的价值在于它们向公众和学者开放，在于藏品本身所蕴含的信息通过文件记录和那些保管它们的人的知识得以保存。将藏品"束之高阁"，也就是说将它们放在库房内，对它们不进行或者尽可能少地进行研究和使用，看似减少成本的理想短期战略，其实这种做法具有一定的风险。许多种类的藏品在缺乏定期检查和照料的情况下会发生质变。藏品常常只有通过某位有经验、学识渊博的员工精心安排才能以有意义的方式对外开放，而博物馆的收藏一旦遭到破坏就很难重新建立起来。

人力资源

博物馆常常因为经费减少而裁员，结果不得不让一些岗位临时空缺，撤销一些岗位或者撤销某些部门和项目领域。博物馆在准备因缩减规模而裁员时应该考虑机构的短期和长期需要。某位员工离职后让他的岗位保持空缺虽然不像裁去现有员工那么痛苦，但也会造成关键时刻一些关键岗位无人的情况。博物馆在制定裁员决策时应该权衡员工的要求和博物馆的需要。

博物馆还应该考虑裁员对博物馆的经营和各个项目的影响。博物馆的使命主要通过它的员工来实现，但许多博物馆也依靠志愿者以及和其他机构的合作。制定裁员计划时应该考虑裁员对博物馆使命和活动的整体影响，而且应该成为恢复经营的整体战略的一部分，必须通过补充志愿者、增加合作或其他策略来达到博物馆的目标。

隶属于非博物馆上级机构的博物馆

隶属于某学院或大学或隶属于市政府、县政府或州政府的博物馆还会面临其他一些因素，影响它们应对经济危机的策略。当上级机构需要削减经费时，博物馆可能会承担与之比例不相符的损失。许多隶属于大型上级机构的博物馆都通过开发不同收入渠道来提高自己的财务稳定性。这一点对那些隶属于上级机构的博物馆尤其重要。那些能够从其他渠道获得大量经费的博物馆不像其他博物馆那样依赖上级机构的拨款，因而可以将上级机构减少经费后带来的影响降至最低，也可以减少上级机构将撤销博物馆视为诱人财务策略的可能性。

博物馆还可以单独与某个具有法人资格的友善机构建立关系。一个独立的501(c)3赞助团体可以提供大量资金，担任博物馆的宣传员，帮助博物馆缓解突如其来的机构变动。博物馆的上级机构与该友善团体之间签订的正式备忘录能够确保该团体在涉及博物馆未来的任何决策中具有发言权。

另一个策略是将博物馆纳入到上级机构的经营中。博物馆一旦成为上级机构不可分割的一部分，就不大可能立刻成为上级机构削减经费的目标。通过与上级机构服务的社区建立起密切关系，向更广泛的群体开放自己的资源，吸引新的资金来源，获得正面的公共形象，尤为重要的是为许多人所重视，博物馆就不会轻易受到削减经费的影响。一群积极、投入的支持者会敦促上级机构继续支持博物馆。

上级机构通常没有继续经营博物馆的法律义务。它们可能不会考虑博物馆会因为缩减规模而失去认证资格。美国博物馆协会代表着保管公共机构中藏品的公众利益，会敦促上级机构考虑下列道德、伦理和实际问题。首先，博物馆是上级机构与公众保持联系的长期战略的一部分。任何涉及博物馆未来的决定都应该考虑博物馆在造福广大公众方面所起到的长远作用。削减博物馆的经费虽然短期内可能会节省一些开支，但从长远的角度来看却可能会损害上级机构服务社区、接触广泛人群的能力。其次，博物馆的经营能够让公众获益，而它们收藏的藏品是一种公益信托。如果上级机构考虑裁员或者关闭博物馆，它必须承担确保公众利益不受损害的道德义务，必须认真考虑藏品的命运。一旦承担了保护藏品的义务，上级机构就必须规划如何以保证藏品和相关文件安全的方式将藏品保管权移交给另一个合适的机构。必须为藏品认真挑选新的保管机构，考虑该机构保管藏品和继续向公众以及学者开放藏品的能力。正如上文所提，这一过程可能短期内反而会增加开支，并不一定是立刻节省成本的好策略。

VII. 设施与风险管理

设施与风险管理标准
设施与风险管理"优秀标准"的特征
- 博物馆受公众之托保管好它所拥有的资源。
- 博物馆致力于为公众提供条件，让他们在身心和智力上都能够接触并了解博物馆及其资源。

- 博物馆遵守地方、州和联邦政府对其设施、经营和管理的各项法律、准则和规定。
- 博物馆通过分配空间和使用各种设施来满足藏品、观众和员工的需要。
- 博物馆有相应的措施来确保人员、藏品 / 物件和设施的安全。
- 博物馆采取有效措施来保护和长期维护各种设施。
- 博物馆要保持整洁、维护设施，并根据观众的需要提供其他条件。
- 博物馆采取相应措施来预防潜在的风险和损失。

目的与重要性

　　博物馆受公众之托保护它的各种资源，因而它有义务确保员工、观众和邻居的安全，维护好馆舍及场地，将它为子孙后代保管的藏品可能遇到的风险降至最低。博物馆应该积极主动地发现可能会对人员及藏品造成伤害的各种风险，而正确分配资源来减少这些风险对博物馆的管理更是至关重要。

实施

　　简而言之，博物馆应该管理好自己的设施（如建筑物和场地），确保这些设施清洁、得到精心维护、安全和对外开放。

　　风险管理涉及整个博物馆，包括建筑物和场地的治安、为观众提供的各项服务、虫害的综合管理、危险品的存放和使用以及保险。博物馆应该进行风险管理，以确保：精确发现和评估人员（观众、员工和邻居）和藏品可能遭遇的风险；采用适当的方法来避免、阻止、减轻、分担和承担风险，或者通过投保来预防风险；恰当地分配资源，将人员、设施和藏品风险降至最低。

　　博物馆还应该定期对员工进行彻底培训，让他们能够执行各种应急方案，包括练习和演习；应该对设施和各种风险（火灾、健康和安全，以及与博物馆情况相符的其他风险）进行检查；应该制定政策来处理检查过程中发现的不足之处；应该制定与博物馆情况相符的员工和志愿者的健康和安全培训项目。博物馆应该遵守相应的地方、州和联邦法律、准则和规定。

涉及承包商的设施和风险管理标准

　　当博物馆将一些设施的关键服务项目（如餐饮、博物馆商店、保洁、保安）承包出去时，它们应该要求承包商遵守设施和风险管理的国家标准。如果博物馆并不掌据管理这种关系的合同（如市政府聘用并监督在博物馆建筑内经营的承包商），博物馆应该向承包商介绍国家标准，并且鼓励他们遵守这些标准。

位于历史建筑内的博物馆标准

位于历史建筑内的博物馆应该在建筑的保护需要与为减轻人员和存放在建筑物里的藏品的风险而采取的必要行动之间保持平衡。国家标准并没有具体规定如何做到这一点，而是重点介绍采取必要风险管理后所带来的结果。例如，位于历史建筑内的博物馆需要考虑所有相关因素（使命、资源、对建筑物的影响、其他可采用的规避风险的技术），然后才能决定是否安装自动灭火系统。为了能接受公众的问责，博物馆应该能向公众解释自己的决定如何与具体情况相符。

文件记录

博物馆应该有最新、全面的应急/防灾规划，该规划应该符合博物馆的需要和博物馆的具体情况；应该考虑到所有可能出现的威胁；应该针对员工、观众、建筑物和藏品；应该包括人员疏散方案；应该具体说明遇到灾难时如何保护、疏散和抢救藏品；应该划分各自的责任。如果检查机构能够提供合格证书，博物馆应该拥有与其情况相符的、通过设施和风险检查的合格证书。

评述
应急方案

美国遗产保护委员会最近的研究表明，美国的防灾应急方案令人担忧。只有20%的博物馆具有涵盖藏品和员工培训内容的应急方案，然而这种方案对于博物馆完成其保管公众托付给它们的文化、艺术、历史和科学资源的重任至关重要。在博物馆努力达到国家标准的同时，美国博物馆协会强烈要求博物馆将重点放在制定应急方案和培训员工实施方案上。

保险

许多博物馆经常询问博物馆标准是否要求它们对藏品进行保险。答案是没有。国家标准只是要求博物馆制定一个全面、平衡的风险管理方法，为人员、设施和藏品提供全面的保护。对于大多数博物馆而言，安排一定程度的保险也是上述风险管理方法的一个部分。即便藏品的性质很独特，一旦损失后无法弥补，投保的博物馆在遭受损失时仍然可以获得新的藏品，继续让观众获益。不过，更好的做法是防止这种损失，博物馆在分配资源时应该认真权衡防灾和减灾（人工和自动报警系统、环境控制、灭火系统、藏品保护）与保险之间的关系。

第三部分　其他标准

博物馆标准和最佳做法汇总
其他标准什么时候适用于你们的博物馆？

属于和不属于博物馆界的大大小小的团体都制定出了各自的标准，而这些标准都有可能对博物馆产生影响，下文将介绍其中一些最重要的标准。不过，针对博物馆仍然会有来自不同渠道的标准。大家不妨仔细阅读下列参考意见，然后再决定这些标准是否能够正确地指导贵博物馆的政策和规定。

这些标准是否至少已经得到某个非营利性机构的采纳和批准，而该机构能够广泛代表该领域或者代表该标准所适用的领域的某个部门？这些标准是否能广泛应用于各个种类和规模的博物馆？如果只适用于某一类博物馆（如具体针对某一类博物馆的标准），那么这些标准是否广泛适用于所有此类博物馆？这些标准是否为非指定性的，即它们描述理想的结果，而不是大力推荐为取得这些结果所采用的特殊方法？它们是否（尽可能地）以博物馆界广泛接受的现有原则和习惯做法为依据？这些标准在制定时是否广泛采纳了不同专业、地理位置、规模、治理模式和其他相关变数的博物馆的意见？是否经过广泛评估，正式评审并吸收各种意见？这些标准是否仅限于一些习惯做法，而博物馆界对这些习惯做法已经达成了广泛共识？最后，这些标准是否与博物馆的整体健全管理相符？

认真考虑这些问题，看看制定这些标准的团体是否能够代表你们的博物馆，然后再决定你们是否自愿采用这些标准。例如，一座包含历史和自然历史藏品的综合博物馆应该考虑自己是否既遵守美国州和地方历史协会的标准又遵守美国保护自然历史藏品学会的标准。没有被邀请加入美国艺术博物馆馆长协会的艺术博物馆应该考虑自己是否愿意遵守该协会制定的标准，尽管这些标准在制定时只听取了该领域一部分博物馆的意见。

博物馆必须认真思考上述问题，因为一旦博物馆将来的任何决定都受到这些标准的影响，那么这些决定在现实世界里造成的后果便会对人们评判博物馆时的看法产生影响。此外，在某个引起争议的决定悬而未决时制定或修改政策，也会导致公众质疑这一过程的廉正性。

博物馆相关标准的其他主要来源

下面列出的是博物馆标准的其他主要来源，以及它们为博物馆界制定的最重要的政策文件。若想获得更详细的清单以及这些文件的链接，请登录美国博物馆协会网站。

与博物馆相关的（专业性或功能性、地区性）行业协会

美国州与地方历史协会（AASLH）

- 《职业标准和道德宣言》
- 《道德立场文件之一：藏品资本化》
- 《道德立场文件之二：某历史博物馆关闭时》

美国保护历史和艺术品学会

- 《道德准则与习惯做法的指导原则》

美国公园协会

- 《植物园和树木园自愿采用的行为准则》
- 《关于外来植物物种的规定》

艺术博物馆馆长协会（AAMD）

- 《艺术博物馆职业规范》
- 《关于圣物的报告》
- 《关于借用考古实物和古代艺术品的报告》
- 《关于艺术博物馆馆长协会成立收藏特别工作组的报告》
- 《关于艺术博物馆馆长协会成立阿登顿纳粹掠夺艺术品特别工作组的报告》

儿童博物馆协会

- 《儿童博物馆协会下属铁路博物馆协会标准》
- 《铁路博物馆推荐做法》

科技中心协会

- 《习惯做法》

动物园和水族馆协会

- 《职业道德准则》

国际博物馆协会

- 《国际博物馆协会：博物馆职业道德准则》

国际博物馆协会下属的藏品登记和注册委员会（CIDOC）

- 《博物馆藏品信息国际标准》

中西部露天博物馆协调委员会

- 《职业行为宣言》

博物馆商店协会

- 《职业道德准则》
- 《考古和人种学资源的道德政策》
- 《濒危自然遗产的道德政策》

全国网络化文化遗产和人文学科发起委员会

- 《文化遗产资料数字化展示和管理最佳做法指南》

国家公园管理局（东北地区）

- 《国家公园管理局：按照内政部长处理历史财产的标准而制定的处理历史古迹内部结构指导原则》

内政部长

- 《处理历史财产标准，包括保护、恢复、修复和重建标准》

保护自然历史藏品学会

- 《自然历史藏品保管指导原则》

东南地区学院艺术大会

- 《学院和大学博物馆及美术馆指导原则》

三州历史古迹联盟

- 《历史古迹管理标准与习惯做法》

代表更广泛非营利或学术机构的协会

美国历史协会

- 《博物馆展示历史藏品的标准》
- 《职业行为标准宣言》

职业筹款人协会

- 《职业行为道德准则和标准》
- 《可接受问责的非营利性机构》

美国优良企业局明智捐款联盟

- 《慈善捐款接受问责标准》

学院艺术协会

- 《兼职专业人员聘用指导原则》
- 《学院艺术协会采纳的博物馆聘用编外客座研究员、布展员 / 画家和图录撰文者的指导原则》
- 《艺术博物馆研究员专业习惯做法》
- 《关于收藏源自外国的文化财产的决议》
- 《关于博物馆出售和交换艺术品的决议》

独立机构

- 《良好治理与合乎道德习惯做法原则：慈善机构与基金会指导原则》

全国公共历史委员会

- 《全国公共历史委员会：道德准则》

美国博物馆协会各常设专业委员会及其制定的标准

　　美国博物馆协会目前有十三个常设专业委员会，代表博物馆界的不同专业领域（登录员、研究员、安全员、教育人员、管理人员、公共关系与市场营销人员、评估人员、媒体与技术人员、展览设计人员、负责发展会员的人员）以及小型博物馆、负责博物馆培训项目的专业人员和负责解决员工多元化问题的人员。其中许多委员会都为属于自己专业范围内的博物馆经营领域制定了标准和最佳做法。这些标准还没有经过美国博物馆协会董事会、认证委员会和常设专业委员会联合会的研究，没有被批准成为国家标准和最佳做法。正是由于这个原因，它们还没有被美国博物馆协会所承认。不过，它们代表着上述领域专业人员在努力解决工作中所面临的问题时所进行的思考。它们一旦经过美国博物馆协会治理机构的研究和修改并得到批准，就会被公布在美国博物馆协会的网站上，成为本书未来新版本的内容。

　　常设专业委员会制定的主要文件有：

　　登录员委员会（RCAAM）制定的《登录员职业道德准则》

　　发展与会员常设专业委员会（DAM）于1991年制定的《职业道德准则》

　　登录员委员会（RCAAM）制定的《博物馆藏品运输习惯做法准则》

　　研究员委员会（CurCom）于1996年制定的《研究员职业道德准则》

　　观众研究和评估委员会（CARE）制定的《博物馆进行观众研究和评估的专业标准》

教育委员会（**EdCom**）制定的《博物馆教育标准与最佳做法》

常设专业委员会联合会制定的《博物馆展览和优秀指标标准》

博物馆协会安全委员会与美国国际工业安全学会下属博物馆、图书馆和文化财产委员会联合制定的《博物馆安全建议准则》

趋势与未来可能出台的标准

我们无法预测未来，但我们可以通过跟踪博物馆领域的讨论、媒体的报道、政府官员的立法努力和出资人的期待对未来进行一些合理的推测。我们据此认为，下列趋势很可能会影响未来的标准。

透明度与问责

州政府和联邦政府的政策制定者将继续提高非营利机构接受问责的门槛。即便不会出现任何其他变故，只要来自艾奥瓦州的共和党参议员查尔斯•格拉斯里继续连任，所有非营利机构，尤其是一些博物馆，将继续受到密切监督。为了避免出现不当或过于强制性的法规指导我们行为的情况，博物馆需要制定出更加严格的标准来报告它们的财务和项目业绩以及给馆长和董事会成员的报酬。美国优良企业局明智捐赠联盟、慈善信息局和指南星网站（**Guide Star**）这样的团体正鼓励私人捐赠者在提供赞助前要求博物馆提供大量业绩信息。如果博物馆界不制定出关于向公众报告什么以及如何报告的自愿标准，类似标准很可能会强加在我们身上。

如何准备：认真思考公众、媒体、政策制定者和出资人想了解博物馆的哪些信息，以及你们希望他们了解哪些信息。着手设计一些方案来公开这些信息。互联网是一个很好的平台，能够以较低的成本分享信息。博物馆希望公开的文件可以包括目标宣言、机构规划、经过审计的财务报告、**IRS990** 纳税表以及一些重要的政策文件（职业道德、藏品管理等等）。考虑如何设计自己的业绩评估表 — 也就是说一张打分表 — 来引导服务对象对你们取得的进步进行评估。基本信息可以包括简单的"数据"：观众人数、新获藏品数、展览、项目和出版物数量。如果能根据评估数据来报告结果，效果会更好。你们的大型新展览如何改变了观众的知识、信念和态度？你们的高中实习项目如何影响了参与者对未来事业的选择？你们与当地商界达成的营销合作关系是否有助于增加观众对当地经济的贡献？做好收集和分享这些信息的工作既能够展示对公共资源的恰当保管，又能确保自己对博物馆的形象掌握主动权。

规划，规划，再规划

大家可能已经注意到了，翻译成大白话的标准中有一句话反复出现，重申博物馆应该"决定自己将做什么……并且将这些写下来"。提供资助的机构以及慈善基金会越来越关心自己赞助的对象是否能表明自己知道如何使用赞助的资金，关心它们的规划是不是博物馆可持续发展远景不可分割的一部分。博物馆与图书馆服务协会[9]以前经常提供综合经营经费，但那样的年代已经一去不复返了。美国《政府业绩与结果法》（GPRA）于1993年正式生效后，为联邦政府给该领域提供经费的时代划上了句号。联邦政府的拨款机构现在必须让人们知道属于公众的资金具体被用来达到什么目的。私人基金会正越来越多地采用相同方法。

如何准备：制定规划不像火箭技术那么复杂，也不需要聘请费用昂贵的顾问和占用员工大量的时间。小型博物馆可以将制定规划变成企业文化的一部分，在做出决定时将它们记录下来，并且确保这些成文的决定得到董事会的批准，为每个人所了解。这并不需要非常复杂的模板 — 只需从最简单的开始，然后一步步积累。规模较大的博物馆由于经营更加复杂，因此可以用更多的资源来制定正式规划，而且可能也必须这样做。博物馆的员工数量和预算越大，同时参与的项目越多（展览、活动、出版、研究、筹款），将这些活动综合在一起、按轻重缓急分类并且让所有参与人明白自己的职责就显得越发重要。在制定规划上投入的时间会带来回报，因为博物馆的各项活动会更加有效，博物馆筹集资金来实现这些规划的能力也将得到提高。

评估

在另一方面，提供资金的政府机构和私人越来越期待有正式评估数据来证明博物馆的规划很成功，并且达到了可以量化评估的地步（不管这种评估针对的是观众的知识和态度还是社区的经济状况）。坦率地说，博物馆界已经达成了强烈共识，认为必须对博物馆进行评估，而且评估是件好事。只有一个实际情况妨碍它成为国家标准的一部分：太多的博物馆（甚至那些通过认证的博物馆）无法立刻通过这些标准。通过认证显然是一件很难做好的事（就连那些有着许多资源的大型博物馆也不例外），但是在不远的将来所有博物馆都得想方设法来解决这一难题。

如何准备：评估也不像火箭技术那么复杂，倒是更像化学实验室 — 比制定规划

---

[9] 博物馆与图书馆服务协会（The Institute of Museum and Library Services）是美国联邦政府对全美博物馆、图书馆和档案馆等举行资助的专门机构。——译注

复杂一点，也更难以掌握。我们可以从整个博物馆界在采用评估方式方面的进展（或者说没有进展）这一点就能看出评估的复杂性。可以先采取一些小步骤，认真思考每一个项目或者每一项活动的理想结果，然后（至少在概念上）决定如何评估项目或活动是否成功。先确定最重要的项目和活动，然后对这些经营领域实施评估，至少要包括对这些项目和活动的预算进行一些科目的评估，明确哪些员工负责设计和进行评估，确保评估结果得到公布并且被应用于制定决策中。当地的大专院校通常可以提供帮助：了解一下相关研究领域的学生是否需要单独或者以班级的形式做项目，然后利用他们的资源。还可以使用网络上的免费项目评估资源，如博物馆和图书馆学会的评估表。

绿色设计

博物馆正面临着来自博物馆界内外的越来越大的压力，要求它们在其经营和设计中采用环境友好原则，为环境健康承担更大的责任。目前还没有任何涉及"绿色"设计的国家标准，但在未来十年中这将成为整个博物馆界讨论的话题。

如何准备：与董事会和员工探讨他们是否重视并且觉得博物馆应该采用一些环境友好型经营模式。这些模式是否与博物馆的使命相符？即便答案为"不"，人们是否觉得这些经营模式与博物馆作为一个企业所具有的价值观以及博物馆所在社区的期望值相符？如果是这样，那么博物馆应该开始将生态影响视为决策的一个方面，开始确定哪些小措施能够带来变化。最初的措施可以很简单，如在公共区域和员工区域提供可回收垃圾的收集桶，在办公和举办活动时使用再生材料，鼓励员工采用低环境影响交通方式（拼车、使用公共交通设施、骑自行车），使用低能耗的装置和办公设备。一旦出现能给环境带来更大影响的机会（房屋维修、新的建筑项目、对建筑系统进行升级），就可以将绿色设计理念加入到决策和预算中。有些博物馆不管是否会有正式证书，都在按照领先能源与环境设计(LEED)标准设计建筑。

制定藏品规划

目前还没有每座博物馆必须具有藏品规划的要求，但在不远的将来这很可能会成为国家标准所要求的文件之一 —— 而且会像博物馆规划或职业道德准则一样必不可少。（请参阅《藏品保管》章节对这一问题的探讨。）

如何准备：可以考虑在藏品规划成为国家标准之前开始制定藏品规划。藏品规划有助于博物馆更好地向人们宣传它的收藏计划，明确优先收藏的物品和保管工作的改进，说服收藏家们捐赠具体藏品或者说服赞助者提供藏品保管所需的资金。即便你觉得自己已经有了这样的规划，将它变成正式文件并得到治理机构的正式批准会有助于你以此获得资助。它可以在博物馆进行必要、恰当（但通常让人感到不快的）的出售馆藏活动时给博物馆带来所需的能量补充。当你请员工、董事会成员和外部人员参与规划讨论时，你很可能会发现他们的看法根本不像你想象的那么一致。

文化 / 生物 / 知识财产问题

大家如果看新闻就一定会注意到，国际社会越来越关注文化财产的所有权和归还问题。意大利、希腊和秘鲁最近都在强烈要求一些博物馆归还文物，它们认为这些文物是在违反来源国法律的情况下为博物馆获得、带出境或扣留的。这种情况所涉及的法律问题已经超出了我们的讨论范围。博物馆当然应该守法，而在文化财产问题上，在国家和国际法以及各种条约之间谨慎行事本身就是一个挑战。然而我们需要认真思考道德方面的问题，因为这些问题也将影响法律界的行动，可能会导致新条约或规定的出台，也可能会导致外国政府（或美国政府）选择依法行事。博物馆界目前正努力解决一些藏品所涉及的道德问题以及对古物和考古实物的索要请求，很快将会有国家和具体专业的标准以及最佳方法来指导博物馆在这些领域的行为。接下来要处理的将是生物藏品（如基因探测、民族植物学、古生物标本）和知识财产（如传统医学方面的文化知识、歌曲、故事、宗教和文化仪式的所有权 / 知识产权）。

如何准备：首先分析博物馆为藏品文件记录所制定的内部标准。你们是否需要员工主动检查文件记录，以便发现潜在的问题？捐赠者或卖主提供的保证是否足够？确定博物馆经营中可能会在上述方面引起关注的各个领域（收藏、研究、借用、展示、出版）。时刻留意这些活动的道德意义，时刻留意文物来源国或土著文化的关切 —— 这将有助于制定正确行为的政策，而这反过来又将引导博物馆界对这些问题展开对话，帮助我们制定出相应的国家标准来指导博物馆、为它们的决定提供支持。

解决问题
问题

公众、媒体或政策制定者如果不喜欢某座博物馆或者整个博物馆界的所作所为，他们有许多非常有效的方法来施加压力。公众可以采取一些措施来停止对博物馆的支持，如不再参观博物馆，不再给博物馆捐钱，或者不投票支持一些对博物馆非常重要的地方提案（如公债征税或减免债务）。他们可以给媒体写信，或者给地方、州政府和联邦政府的议员写信。如果他们认为博物馆在法律上违背了自己作为公众信托对象所承担的义务，他们还可以要求州检查总长采取行动。

媒体在传播坏消息（不管是什么样的坏消息）方面能起到立竿见影的效果，引起公众和政策制定者的注意。新闻报道可能会也可能不会公正地代表你们在这件事情上的立场，可能会也可能不会准确地呈现事实真相。但是一则大新闻却能将你的博物馆完全暴露在公众面前，其影响远远超过你的任何公关努力 — 而且你还无法操控新闻内容。

政策制定者可以在州或联邦政府的层面上中止给博物馆的拨款（至少他们可以尝试这样做）。对于整个博物馆界而言，最重要的是他们可能会剥夺博物馆实行自治的自由。如果他们觉得我们自己制定的标准不够完善，或者觉得我们自愿遵守这些标准的力度还不够的话，他们完全可以这样做。

正是由于这些原因，博物馆在制定并应用指导经营的政策时必须考虑哪些方面可能会出现问题以及如何解决这些问题。最容易引起政策制定者、媒体和公众关注的问题为（不一定按重要程度排列）：

- 出售馆藏
- 出售馆藏品后所获资金的使用
- 高管的报酬
- 影响当地生活质量的博物馆外观变化（如停车场、风景、改变建筑物轮廓或高度的修缮活动）
- 影响当地生活质量的博物馆经营方式的变化（如增加特别活动的次数和参观人数，因而影响当地交通和停车，噪音等等）
- 引起争议的展览内容（最为敏感的主题是宗教和色情，既牵涉到宗教又牵涉到色情的主题尤为敏感）
- 让个人或私人企业获利的经营方式
- 牵涉到员工或治理机构成员的利益冲突

好消息是通过制定并遵守根据国家认可标准出台的政策，博物馆可以在很大程度上为自己的行动辩护，化解可能出现的不良局面。坏消息是问题一旦被放大，就来不及回头去参照国家标准进行弥补。下列建议可以帮助大家了解如何运用本书介绍的标准以及其他适用的标准指导决策过程和对关注博物馆的人做出回应。

如何避免问题

1) 预先制定政策。在出现危机时或者在出现争议性行为之后，任何为博物馆的决定进行辩护而制定的政策都缺乏说服力。

2) 起草任何政策时，要让不同背景的人参与进来，他们可以从不同角度来看待问题，帮助博物馆预见可能来自不同群体的关切。

3) 依照全国认同的博物馆标准和其他相关非营利机构的标准来制定政策。以文件的形式记录你决定采用以及（更为重要的是）不准备采用的标准的理由。如果你有意决定采用在某些方面与国家标准相冲突的政策，上述做法就显得尤为重要。一定要为决定背后的考虑提供明确、具有说服力的解释。

4) 确保各项政策得到博物馆治理机构的批准，并注明批准日期。

5) 在对所有员工和治理机构成员进行入门式培训时一定要重新分析关键政策，并且确保员工和董事都能立刻接触到所有政策。

6) 在做出影响博物馆标准并且有可能引起争议的决策时，要立刻开始思考沟通方案。指定有权代表博物馆发言的人（确保其他人都知道自己无权代表博物馆发言），确保这些人熟悉自己要传递的信息。

7) 做出决策时首先要分析博物馆的政策、相关标准和最佳做法宣言，以及博物馆的使命、远景宣言（如果有的话）、博物馆规划以及其他相关规划。要能够证明博物馆的决策符合所有这些文件的精神。

8) 博物馆员工和董事会成员也是人。谁也不能要求他们做出的所有决定都绝对正确，但你应该让大家看到这些人有远见卓识，了解情况，用心良苦，明白所涉及的法律和道德问题。

9) 考虑是否以及如何主动宣布决策。如果是必然会引起争议的决策，主动宣布会有助于你掌握信息，避免引起他人猜疑。

附 录

各项标准和最佳做法的批准日期

下面列出的是本书所介绍的每一种标准或最佳做法最初的名称和最初获得通过/进行修改的日期。这些文件在 2006 年 11 月由美国博物馆协会董事会通过时被统一称作"美国博物馆标准和最佳方法"。

《优秀标准的特点》(《通过认定的博物馆的特点》,1996 年通过,2005 年修改)

《美国博物馆协会的博物馆目标宣言标准》(《认证委员会对博物馆目标宣言的几点希望》,1999 年通过,2004 年修改)

《美国博物馆协会的博物馆规划标准》(《认证委员会对博物馆规划的几点希望》,1999 年通过,2004 年修改)

《美国博物馆协会的博物馆职业道德准则》(《博物馆职业道德:给美国博物馆协会的报告》,1978。《美国博物馆协会的博物馆职业道德准则》,1993 年通过)

《美国博物馆协会关于博物馆制定内部职业道德准则的标准》(《认证委员会对博物馆制定内部职业道德准则的几点希望》,1999 年通过,2004 年修改)

《美国博物馆协会的博物馆治理标准》(《认证委员会对博物馆治理的几点希望》,2004 年通过)

《美国博物馆协会的博物馆授权标准》(《认证委员会对博物馆授权的几点希望》,2000 年通过,2004 年修改)

《美国博物馆协会的藏品保管标准》(《认证委员会对藏品保管的几点希望》,2001 年通过,2004 年修改)

《美国博物馆协会关于纳粹统治时期非法侵占物件的标准》(《涉及纳粹统治时期非法侵占物件的指导原则》,1999 年通过,2001 年修改)

《美国博物馆协会关于向非博物馆机构出借藏品的最佳方法》(《认证委员会的最佳做法声明:向非博物馆机构出借藏品》,2006 年通过)

《美国博物馆协会关于展示借展物的标准》(《展示借展物的指导原则》,2000 年通过)

　　《美国博物馆协会关于开发和管理企业和私人捐赠资金的标准》（《博物馆开发和管理企业资助的指导原则》，2001年通过；《博物馆开发和管理个人资助的指导原则》，2002年通过）

　　《美国博物馆协会关于缩减规模或裁员的标准》（《关于通过美国博物馆协会认证的博物馆面临缩减规模或裁员的几点意见》，2003年通过）

　　《美国博物馆协会的设施和风险管理标准》（2007年通过）

术语表

Accession 入藏： (1)正式接受一件物品并且让其成为博物馆为公众代管的藏品的行为；(2)运用编号为博物馆保管或拥有的某个物件或同时来自同一渠道的一组物件立刻创建简单、永久的记录。入藏记录除了其他数据外，还应该包括入藏编号，获得藏品的日期和性质（赠物、出土、购买、遗赠等），来源，对物件特点的简单描述，物件的状况、价值，以及登记入藏的员工的姓名。

Benchmark 基准： 用来衡量和评判质量或价值的参照点。

Benchmarking 用标准衡量评估： 为制定目标、评估业绩和决定是否需要以及如何进行改变而将博物馆的经营情况与某个参照点进行比较的过程。参照点有三个：博物馆不同部门之间或者参照博物馆以往历史而进行的内部比较，与所选同行进行的外部比较，以及与整个博物馆界进行的外部比较。

Business support 企业资助： 由某企业（公司、合伙公司、代理公司、家族企业等）提供的慈善性的或者出于企业营销、广告或公共关系目的的资金或实物资助，不管企业能从博物馆方面得到何种性质和价值的利益，也不管这种资助关系涉及的税金有多少。

Bylaws 内部章程： 明确治理机构职责的法律文件，如董事会成员的类型，安排和举行公司和治理机构会议时的后勤保障，委员会职责和修订章程的规定。内部章程还包括对治理机构的自律规定，如机构的成员数、出席会议的次数要求、任期等。

Care 保管： 博物馆对藏品的来源、鉴定和存放位置进行正确、充分的记录，并且运用现有、行业公认方法来保证藏品的安全，将藏品的损坏和损耗降至最低。

Collections 藏品： 博物馆受公众之托保管的活体或非活体物件。物件一旦入藏，通常就会被视为博物馆藏品的一部分。有些博物馆会设置不同种类的藏品（永久性藏品、用于研究的藏品、用于教育的藏品），对它们进行不同类型的保管和使用。这些不同种类以及它们的下属类别会在博物馆的藏品管理政策中明确说明。

Collections management policy 藏品管理政策： 由博物馆治理机构批准的书面文件，具体说明博物馆针对所有涉及藏品的问题所制定的各项政策，包括入藏、记录、存放和除藏。政策是规范博物馆行为的总原则，为进行良好判断提供标准。

Collections plan 藏品规划： 指导博物馆收藏内容的规划，并且逐渐将员工引入统一协调的方向，以预先确定的方式来提高和拓展藏品的价值。规划具有时效性，能够明确需要达到的具体目标。规划还能为博物馆的抉择提供合理解释，具体说明博物馆如何达到目标、具体的执行人、达到目标的时间以及成本。

Community 服务对象： 每座博物馆都有自己确定的服务对象，可以是由地理位置决定的群体（如博物馆周边社区、大学校园、小镇、城市、县或地区），有共同兴趣爱好的群体（如科学界、国际商务界），被视为构成社会某一独特部分的群体（如同性恋群体、亚裔人群），或者所有这些群体。

Deaccessioning 除藏： 正式清除博物馆藏品中某一件或者某一组入藏物件的过程。博物馆在藏品离开之前仍然拥有该藏品，但藏品的性质是已不再为公众所有。清除博物馆藏品中的物件通常被称为"除藏（disposal）"。

Director 馆长： 被赋予博物馆日常经营管理权的人，他负责分配资源，也负责对博物馆进行有效的经营。该职位为首席执行官，职责包括但不限于聘用和解聘员工，执行预算，落实各项政策，管理各个项目和员工。也可以被称为首席执行官（CEO）、博物馆行政管理者、现场经理、馆长等。

Emergency/disaster-preparedness plan 应急/防灾规划： 书面政策和规定，旨在预防或者将危及建筑物以及建筑物内人员和财产的自然或人为事件对人员（员工和观众）、建筑物、藏品、档案材料或博物馆各种记录的损失降至最低。所有博物馆都应该有各种规划来处理博物馆在出现紧急情况时如何保护员工、观众和藏品等问题。这些应该包括灾难出现时疏散员工和观众的计划，以及保护、疏散或抢救藏品的计划。

Fiduciary 信托的：受他人之托保管某物而建立的关系；信托继承人；信托合同；受信托的；受委托的。

Governance manual 治理手册：供治理机构成员所用的参考手册，能够帮助他们熟悉情况、接受培训和开展工作。它可以包括博物馆的目标宣言、内部章程、现行机构规划、各项政策和以前的会议纪要。

Governing authority 治理机构：为博物馆承担法律和信托职责的机构。除非授权给另一机构或者为行政管理系统所取代，该机构还负责批准博物馆的政策。治理机构的名称包括但不局限于：监事会、董事会、监理会、理事会、市政委员会、委员会。

Health and safety training 健康与安全培训：针对一些问题进行的理论和实际操作培训，如办公室功效学、安全装卸、血液传播和空气传播病源的安全性、危险物流通，以及物资使用安全数据表。

Individual donor support 个人捐赠：来自个人、家庭或家族基金会的现金、房产或预定的捐赠物，不管资金用于何种目的，或捐赠物是否免税。在本书介绍的标准中，个人捐赠不包括捐赠的藏品。

Inspection related to facilities and risk 设施和风险检查：可以包括对建筑物使用许可证的检查、消防部门的检查、对餐饮服务进行的卫生检查、美国农业部对展出动物进行的检查，以及保险公司对安全问题的检查。

Institutional plan 机构规划：博物馆的综合性规划，明确机构的发展目标并提供足够细节来指导实施，确定工作重点，指导制定面向未来的重要决定。有些博物馆将机构规划分为两个部分：（1）多年规划：确定战略、目标和重点的"大"规划，有时也被称为战略规划或长期规划；（2）经营规划：为执行战略规划或长期规划中的决定而制定的详细规划，有时也被称为执行规划。通常以短时间为限，围绕博物馆的预算年度而制定。博物馆对这些规划文件的叫法以及区分它们之间独特功能的方法不尽相同，美国博物馆协会对此没有强行要求的格式或名称。

Integrated pest management(IPM)综合虫害管理：虫害信息、环境条件与现有虫害控制方法的协调工作，旨在预防虫害程度超过标准，同时将对人员、财产、藏品和环境的危害降至最低。IPM 项目在做出虫害管理决定时运用整体方法，考虑各种合适的选项，包括但不限于杀虫剂。

Joint governance 联合治理：一种两个或两个以上机构共同治理博物馆的治理形式。这涉及分配或分享一些重要的治理职责，如确定博物馆的使命和目标；聘任、支持和评估博物馆馆长；制定战略规划；获得并管理各种资源；监督博物馆的各种项目和服务。这可以是某市政府与某非营利性私人机构联合治理的某博物馆，市政府拥有藏品和馆舍并聘用员工，非营利性私人机构制定博物馆的政策并经营博物馆。这也可以是某大学拥有并管理博物馆，但是将制定各种项目和服务的职责托付给了某个顾问委员会。联合治理并不自动包括那些有单独的"博物馆之友"机构的博物馆，除非这些"博物馆之友"机构有书面协议规定其在博物馆的治理中承担重要职责。

Objects 物件：用于沟通并提高学习动力的材料，用于实现博物馆目标的工具。

Remote governance 非直接治理：博物馆馆长通过行政管理系统而非直接向治理机构汇报的治理形式。例如：某大学博物馆的治理机构可能是大学的董事会，博物馆馆长通过教务长向校长汇报，再由校长向董事会汇报。隶属于州公园部门的博物馆馆长可能会通过公园主管向州公园与娱乐部门负责人汇报，再由该负责人向州长汇报。

Risk management 风险管理：鉴别、控制不确定事件并将其影响降至最低的总体过程，以便降低这类事件发生的概率或减轻这类事件造成的后果的程度。

Supporting group 支持团体：一个主要目的是为支持博物馆但不参与博物馆治理或承担博物馆职责的团体。该团体可能会提供资金支持、志愿者、专业知识或游说能力来弥补治理机构在知识和技能上的不足。这类团体可以被称为顾问委员会、博物馆之友、联合会或附属委员会。

• 内部支持团体为博物馆自身的一部分，或者是非正式的协会，或者由治理机构指定。它们在博物馆的治理机构或治理机构指派的人员指导下开展工作。

• 外部支持团体为非正式协会或单独成立的非营利性机构。它们的治理完全独立于博物馆。美国博物馆协会要求外部支持团体与博物馆的治理机构签署谅解函、管理协议或其他详细规定双方关系的文件。

美国博物馆协会
博物馆职业道德准则
（2000 版）

前言

道德准则随着条件、价值观和理念的变化而不断发展，因此任何一种职业道德准则都必须定期更新，而且必须建立在人们普遍接受的价值观之上。虽然博物馆的经营环境正变得越来越复杂，博物馆的基本价值观 — 这种超越分歧将我们联系在一起的纽带 — 仍然竭力服务当今和未来的公众。这种价值观引导着我们制定出下列《博物馆职业道德准则》中最根本的原则，并且一直沿用至今。

博物馆职业道德准则

博物馆收藏、保护并诠释我们这个世界的各种物品，以此对公众做出独特的贡献。博物馆在历史上曾经拥有并使用过有生命和无生命的自然物品以及各种形式的人工制品来增加人们的知识并陶冶人们的情操。今天，博物馆所涉及的内容五花八门，而这正好体现了人类视野的范围之广。博物馆的使命包括收藏、保护、展示自己拥有或者租借和制造的物件，以此向公众传播知识。博物馆包括政府和私人所有的人类学、艺术史和自然历史博物馆、水族馆、树木园、艺术中心、植物园、儿童博物馆、历史遗址、自然中心、天文馆、科技中心和动物园。美国的博物馆界包括收藏型和非收藏型机构。尽管它们的使命各不相同，但它们均为非营利性组织，而且全都致力于为公众提供服务。它们的藏品以及它们借用或自己制造的物件是研究、展示和吸引公众参与的各种活动项目的根本。

总的来说，博物馆的藏品和展出物件代表着整个世界共有的自然和文化财富。博物馆作为这些财富的托管人，必须提高人们对各种自然物品和人类经历的了解。博物馆必须成为全人类的资源，并且通过它们的各种活动培养人们在掌握知识的基础上去欣赏我们所继承的这个富饶而多彩多姿的世界。博物馆还必须为子孙后代保护好这笔遗产。

美国的博物馆建立在为公众服务的传统之上。它们的组织形式为公益信托，藏品和信息要造福于它们创建时所服务的对象。董事会成员、雇员和志愿者们致力于为这些受益人的利益服务。博物馆经营的基本准则是各种相关法律。博物馆作为非营利机构，必须遵守相应的地方、州政府和联邦政府的法律以及国际法和有关公众所托职责的具体法律标准。本《博物馆职业道德准则》依据上述原则制定。但是遵纪守法只是基本要求，博物馆以及博物馆的负责人除了应竭力避免承担法律责任外，还必须采取积极措施来保持他们的诚信，以此来博得公众的信任。他们不仅要遵纪守法，还应具有职业道德精神。因此，本《博物馆职业道德准则》列出了一些道德准则，而这些常常比遵纪守法更为重要。

忠诚于博物馆的使命以及忠诚于博物馆所服务的公众是博物馆工作的核心，不管这种工作是义务的还是有报酬的。在发生（实际、潜在或察觉到的）利益冲突的地方，绝对不能把忠诚作为牺牲对象。任何个人都不能利用自己在博物馆的职位谋取私利，或者以牺牲博物馆、博物馆的使命、声誉以及博物馆所服务的公众的利益为代价来使另一方获益。

对于博物馆而言，为公众服务是至高无上的。为了确认这一道德准则，也为了阐述它在博物馆治理、收藏和活动项目中的应用，美国博物馆协会颁布了该《博物馆职业道德准则》。博物馆在签署该准则后将为其治理机构、雇员和志愿者在行使博物馆相关职责时的行为负责。博物馆此后将确认自己确定的目标，确保谨慎地使用自己的资源，提高自己的效率，保持公众的信心。这种集体性的努力将提升博物馆的工作，增加博物馆目前以及未来对社会所作的贡献。

治理

博物馆的治理无论采取何种形式均为受公众之托确保博物馆为社会提供服务。治理机构保护并扩大博物馆的藏品和项目，以及博物馆的实物、人力和资金资源；确保这些资源支持博物馆的使命，应对社会的多元化，尊重自然和文化共同财富的多元性。

因此，治理机构要确保：

• 所有为博物馆工作或者代表博物馆的人员都理解并支持博物馆的使命和公众托付的责任。

• 治理机构的成员理解并完成自己的托管责任，采取集体而不是个人行动。

• 以支持博物馆使命的方式来保护、维护和开发博物馆藏品和项目以及博物馆的实物、人力和资金资源。

- 响应并代表社会的利益。
- 与员工保持关系，相互明确分工并尊重对方的职责。
- 董事、雇员和志愿者之间的工作关系建立在平等和相互尊重之上。
- 用职业标准和习惯做法来告知和指导博物馆的经营。
- 阐明各项政策并进行慎重监督。
- 治理行为促进的是公共利益而不是个人的经济利益。

藏品

博物馆的职业道德具有与众不同的特点，这是因为博物馆拥有、保管和使用代表着全世界自然和文化共同财富的物件、标本和活体藏品。对藏品的这种保管关系代表着公众最高的信任，也意味着博物馆必须合法拥有、永久收藏、保护、记录、开放和负责地处理藏品。

因此，博物馆必须确保：

- 它所保管的藏品支持博物馆的使命和公众托付的职责。
- 它所保管的藏品为合法所有且不受任何附加条件的制约，藏品的保护、安全措施和保养符合法律规定。
- 它所保管的藏品来源明确并有文件记录。
- 允许并管理藏品及相关信息的对外开放。
- 藏品的获得、出售和租借活动在实施时尊重对自然和文化资源的保护和保管原则，严禁对这些资料进行非法交易。
- 藏品的获得、出售和租借活动与博物馆的使命和公众托付的职责相符。
- 通过出售、交易或研究等活动出售馆藏完全是为了提高博物馆的使命。出售非活体藏品后的所得在使用时与博物馆行业的现有标准相一致，绝对不能用于与藏品获得或直接保管无关的活动。
- 明确人类遗骸、丧葬物和圣物的独特性质，并据此做出涉及此类藏品的所有决定。
- 与藏品相关的活动促进的是公共利益而不是个人的经济利益。
- 公开、严肃、积极地处理针对博物馆某藏品的索要请求，并且尊重各方的尊严。

项目

博物馆通过各种展览、研究、学术成就、出版物和教育活动来提高公众对人类共同自然和文化财富的了解和欣赏力，以此来服务社会。这些活动项目进一步提高博物馆的使命，并对社会的关心、兴趣和需求做出反应。

因此，博物馆应该确保：

- 所有项目支持博物馆的使命和公众托付的责任。
- 所有项目都建立在学术成就之上，不弄虚作假。
- 所有项目都对外开放并且根据博物馆的使命和资源鼓励尽可能多的观众来参与。
- 所有项目尊重多元化的价值观、传统和关注。
- 创收性质的活动以及涉及博物馆之外其他机构的活动必须符合博物馆的使命并支持公众托付的责任。
- 所有项目促进的是公共利益而不是个人的经济利益。

颁布

《博物馆职业道德准则》于1993年11月12日由美国博物馆协会董事会正式通过。美国博物馆协会董事会推荐该协会的所有非营利性博物馆成员采用该准则，并根据自己的具体情况制定单独的道德准则。

由美国博物馆协会主席提名并得到美国博物馆协会董事会批准的职业道德委员会将承担下列两个职责：

- 创建信息、教育和协助项目来指导各博物馆制定自己的职业道德准则。
- 研究《博物馆职业道德准则》并定期向美国博物馆协会董事会提出修改意见。

后记

1987年，美国博物馆协会董事会决定修订该协会于1978年制定的职业道德宣言，因为整个美国博物馆界都认识到该宣言需要进一步提高和加强，需要考虑博物馆在社会中所扮演的更加重要的角色，需要考虑自然和文化遗产的收藏、保护和诠释所涉及的美国人民非常关心的一些问题。

经过美国博物馆协会董事会成员、认证委员会和全国各地博物馆领导人的一系列分组讨论和意见阐述，美国博物馆协会主席任命了一个职业道德特别工作组来起草职业道德准则。职业道德特别工作组努力将博物馆界对职业道德的共识汇集在一起，制定出一个基本框架，让每座博物馆在此框架内制定自己的职业道德准则。该特别工作组还参考了博物馆职业道德传统，从美国博物馆协会的第一部职业道德准则 —1925 年出版的《博物馆从业人员职业道德准则》中得到了灵感。该准则的前言有这样一段话：

博物馆从最广泛的意义上来说是受托为人类以及为人[类]未来福祉保管藏品的机构。它们的价值与它们给人们情感和求知生活提供的服务成正比。博物馆工作人员的生活本质就是提供服务。

这种致力于服务的理念来自十九世纪美国博物馆创建文件中所包含的促进和传播知识的观念。乔治·布朗·古德，这位著名的动物学家曾出任美国国家博物馆的第一任馆长，他在 1889 年阐述道：

这个民主国家未来的博物馆应该既能满足专业人士和悠闲阶层的需要，也能适应机械师、产业工人、普通劳动者、推销员和秘书的需要。……总而言之，公立博物馆首先必须造福于公众。

二十世纪初的博物馆界领袖和纽瓦克博物馆馆长约翰·科顿·达纳在其论文《增加博物馆的用途》和《服务性博物馆》中倡导博物馆为公众服务的理念。达纳认为博物馆存在的目的不完全是收集和保护藏品。在他看来，博物馆是传播知识的重要中心。

到二十世纪四十年代，西奥多·娄，这位博物馆教育的积极倡导者发现博物馆界重新将精力放在学术研究和博物馆方法研究上。美国博物馆协会 1978 年出版的《博物馆职业道德》反映了这些关注，详细介绍了员工、管理层和治理机构之间的关系。

二十世纪八十年代，美国人越来越关注美国的文化多元性、全球环境和对公共机构的监督。技术的高速发展、涉及非营利性机构的政府新政策、麻烦不断的教育系统、私有和公有财富的变化模式、越来越大的资金压力 — 这一切都在要求人们更加明确地阐明博物馆的职业道德责任。1984 年，美国博物馆协会的"新世纪博物馆委员会"重新将重点放到公众服务和教育上，1986 年由国际博物馆协会（ICOM）通过的职业道德准则将服务社会确定为博物馆职责的核心。国际博物馆协会给博物馆的定义为"为社会及社会发展服务"的机构，并且认为"无论是公众还是私人机构支持的博物馆，为其工作就是承担起公众托付的巨大责任"。

职业道德特别工作组以这些为基础，起草了几稿《博物馆职业道德准则》，并且将这些初稿递交给了美国博物馆协会的执行委员会和董事会，还两次转发给整个博物馆界，广泛征求大家的意见。一百多位个人、博物馆专业组织以及各种类型和规模的博物馆代表提出了富有远见卓识的意见。这些意见对于递交给美国博物馆协会董事会并于1991年5月18日通过的准则具有决定性意义。不过，尽管经过了讨论过程，在批准后的职业道德准则正式启用后，人们很快发现博物馆领域过于多样化，根本无法使大家立刻就准则的每一点达成共识。

因此，美国博物馆协会董事会在1991年的会议上表决后决定暂缓执行该《博物馆职业道德准则》至少一年。这次会议上还批准了美国博物馆协会主席提名的职业道德促进委员会。这个新任命的委员会除了负责创建教育项目来指导博物馆制定自己的职业道德准则以及制定处理违反该准则行为的规定外，还要仔细研究职业道德标准，就修改标准内容或修改标准的实施方法向董事会提出建议。

新的职业道德促进委员会在成立后的第一年中仔细分析了准则以及几百条由此产生的建议或意见，启动了新的对话机制。美国博物馆协会的会员被邀请来就一些分歧最大的问题发表看法，如实施方式和对除藏后所获资金使用的限制。职业道德促进委员会成员还在年度大会和地区性会议上亲自与博物馆同仁们进行沟通，美国博物馆协会董事会主席甚至召集博物馆馆长们举行特别会议，专门讨论准则中对除藏后所获资金使用部分的文字表述。

这一研究过程带来了两个结果，需要董事会在五月份的会议上认真考虑：（1）接受职业道德促进委员会制定的新准则，或者（2）重新起草涉及除藏后所获资金使用部分以及准则实施方式的部分的内容。经过非常激烈的讨论之后，大会终于通过了恢复使用修改后的1991年版道德准则的动议，并且成立一个规模不大的委员会单独负责对准则进行修改。

此外，大家还表决通过决议，将职业道德促进委员会更名为职业道德委员会，负责制定信息和教育项目、研究《博物馆职业道德准则》、定期向董事会提出修改标准的建议。上述的最后改动于1993年11月得到了董事会的批准，写进了美国博物馆协会的《博物馆职业道德准则》中。

美国博物馆协会的下属每一座非营利性博物馆成员都应该在美国博物馆协会的《博物馆职业道德准则》上签字，还应该以此为依据并根据具体情况来制定自己的内部职业道德准则。上述建议的目的是让这些博物馆成员的治理机构、员工和志愿者将美国博物馆协会的准则应用在它们的具体环境中，激励它们制定并保持所有机构以及所有为这些机构工作或代表这些机构的人理解并遵守道德行为所需的良好政策和规定。

在采取这些措施的基础上，美国博物馆界继续努力通过自我管理来促进博物馆工作。《博物馆职业道德准则》为博物馆、社区和整个社会的利益服务。美国博物馆协会的根本目标是鼓励博物馆管理治理机构成员、员工和志愿者的道德行为。正式通过的博物馆内部准则能够促进更高、更加一致的道德标准。为了实现这一目标，职业道德促进会将举办研讨会，制定示范准则，发表文章。以上这些以及其他形式的技术支持将激发整个博物馆界对职业道德进行一场对话，并且为博物馆制定自己的内部准则提供指导原则。

编后记

　　本书在引进出版过程中得到了美国博物馆协会出版社的出版人（Publisher, The AAM Press）John Strand先生的大力支持和帮助；湖南省博物馆编辑出版部门负责人聂菲女士参与了该书的出版工作并提出了许多宝贵的意见和建议；湖南省博物馆的研究馆员郑曙斌女士参与了中文版的校对工作，段炼和于海玲两位女士参与了英文版的校对工作，熊朝霞、杨慧婷和王超三位女士参与了部分出版工作。谨在此表示诚挚的感谢。

编者

2010年5月

美国博物馆协会会员信息

美国博物馆协会
— 您的资源、声音和大家庭

　　请加入最大的博物馆协会 — 代表您专业利益的全国性服务机构。成为会员后，您将得到下列这些难以想象的益处：

　　• 就博物馆的任何事务得到专家的帮助以及保密的、个性化的指导，包括财务、道德、设施管理和藏品保管等各个方面。— 美国博物馆协会的信息中心

　　• 在教育和职业发展机会方面享受较大的优惠。— 美国博物馆协会的年度会议和博物馆博览会，研讨会和网络论坛

　　• 接触到博物馆方面最全面、最精确和最及时的信息。— 博物馆期刊、网络期刊、美国博物馆协会的活动通知和最新法律规定

　　• 从观众研究到技术，在涉及到博物馆各个领域的专业文献方面享受极大的优惠。— 美国博物馆协会的书店

　　• 有机会与同一领域或具有相同兴趣的同行建立网络联系。— 美国博物馆协会常设专业委员会和专业兴趣委员会

　　• 在华盛顿有一个声音让国会、决策者和媒体了解博物馆。— 美国博物馆协会的政府关系部以及博物馆倡议日

　　• 凭借着两万多会员的集体购买力，在保险、运输和其他服务方面为您节省时间和金钱。— 美国博物馆协会的亲和伙伴项目

• 有机会申请美国博物馆协会的职业发展资助。—— 美国博物馆协会的研究基金

• 能够让您及时了解新的就业机会，并且将您的简历发到网上，让几百座博物馆能够找到您。—— 美国博物馆协会的就业总部

"我们的许多员工已经开始将网络系列论坛用作职业发展的机会。我们感谢你们创建这种学习方式，感谢你们以如此合理的价格让我们接触到这么多人和信息。这又是一个让我觉得成为美国博物馆协会会员真是物有所值的方面！"—— 科妮·博德纳，俄亥俄历史学会，俄亥俄州哥伦布市

马上加入美国博物馆协会！
欲想更多地了解如何成为会员以及会员可享受的益处和优惠，
请登陆：www.aam-us.org/joinus
电话垂询：866.226.2150

Foreword

Dear Museum Colleagues,

As the president of the American Association of Museums, it is my pleasure to make this book available to you and your fellow museum professionals. We at AAM hope that this book, and others like it, will help you do the vitally important work of serving the public through your museum.

Although we are the "American" Association of Museums, our work—and yours—does not stop at any national border. Museums hold and preserve the art and artifacts of the entire world. Our visitors come from every country on earth. Our responsibility is to welcome them, to educate and inspire them, and perhaps to broaden their understanding of the world we all live in. I know that you, as a museum professional, share this same responsibility.

It is my wish that this book will be a first step in a long and rich collaboration between American museum professionals and you, our friends and fellow professionals in China. I am certain that we have a great deal to learn from you, and we are eager to share our knowledge with you.

I welcome you and your colleagues to join us, and become International Members of the American Association of Museums. Please visit our website, www.aam-us.org to learn more, or turn to the last page of this book for more information about us.

Cordially,

Ford W. Bell
President
American Association of Museums

Preface

What makes for a great museum? We're all sure we know one when we see it. But if you went to a given institution and asked a trustee, an assistant curator, the director, a guy in marketing and a few randomly selected visitors some basic questions—what the museum's goals are, how well it's accomplishing them, what its goals should be—you might find that nobody agrees on what everybody knows.

Hence, this book. One of AAM's key roles is to provide the museum community with forums for discussion, education and exchange, from our annual meeting to our professional education seminars to publications like this one. National Standards and Best Practices for U.S. Museums synthesizes the experience and best thinking of leading professionals, looking both inward at how museums function and outward toward their role in society at large. Our goal: to offer specific ways to think more deeply about making your institution the best it can be and provide tools to bring your ideas to fruition.

Ford W. Bell, DVM
President
American Association of Museums

Acknowledgements

It is my privilege to write the commentary for the first print edition of National Standards and Best Practices for U.S. Museums. As part of my work at the American Association of Museums (AAM), I help the board of directors corral the widely dispersed standards and best practices documents that have accumulated over several decades, and herd them into a coherent whole. For many years the AAM Code of Ethics for Museums, standards in the Accreditation Program and other AAM statements have guided the behavior of museums in the U.S. Not until 2006 (fortuitously, AAM's centennial), however, did the board formally designate these as national standards for the field. This process is ongoing, as AAM ushers the standards and best practices developed through the 13 AAM Standing Professional Committees into this assemblage. And new standards will be written in the coming years to meet changing expectations and emerging challenges.

The standards and best practices are presented in Section 2. In the accompanying text, I provide context, drawing on my experiences in the museum field for more than twenty-three years, the last eight at AAM, where I work closely with the Accreditation and Museum Assessment Programs, and the ethics task force of the AAM board. In my position, I spend a lot of time talking with people about how museums should and do behave. If a museum director is upset about an accreditation decision, they call. If the press contacts AAM asking whether a museum has violated museum standards, media relations staff talk to me about it. When the Accreditation Commission wrestles over appropriate standards and how they should be applied, I listen and push them to dig deep into the hard questions.

I have summarized my observations of the real-life situations in which the standards are tested, how museums put them into practice and where the biggest problems are likely to arise. Much of it is drawn, practically verbatim, from conversations I have had over and over again with museum professionals across the country. In other words, this has been road-tested by your peers. I hope you find it to be useful to you, as well.

The commentary in this book reflects the collective wisdom of many, many people in the museum field. Any original contributions I have made are based on what I have learned from them. Chief among these are the members of the Accreditation Commission, who devote hundreds of hours each year to reading about and discussing museums under their review. I am particularly grateful to the past and current chairs of the commission, Marty Sullivan, director of Historic St. Mary's City, and Jim Welu, director of the Worcester Art Museum. Their patient tutelage, as we worked through hard decisions, has been an unparalleled education.

I thank my colleagues Eileen Goldspiel, Julie Hart, Kim Igoe, Erik Ledbetter and Helen Wechsler, whose deep understanding in the realms of accreditation standards, national and international museum ethics, government regulation and journalism has contributed enormously to the detail and accuracy of the information in this book. Any errors or omissions, should something have evaded their eagle eyes, are due to this author. I owe a particular debt to Victoria Garvin, who, when starting her job as AAM's first standards research/ writer almost a decade ago, first raised the question, "So where are the standards, anyway?" (At that time, AAM had not officially approved any!) While she has moved on to other challenges, in writing this book, I frequently heard Victoria's voice in my head critiquing the text, pushing me to be clear and precise in my explanations.

I have learned that nothing cultivates good writing like good editing, and I thank John Strand and Lisa Meyerowitz for gently shepherding an initially sprawling manuscript to coherence. I am a better writer and thinker for their mentoring. My thanks to Kirsten Ankers and Susan v. Levine for their design expertise, adding beauty to truth.

I am grateful to my husband, Cliff Duke, for his patient listening on the frequent mornings that I felt the need to dissect the coverage in the New York Times regarding museums and their (mis)behavior. Lastly, spasibo to my fencing coach, Vitali Pokalenko, for continually reminding me not to be so serious. I hope, in this text, I have followed his advice.

Elizabeth E. Merritt
Founding Director
Center for the Future of Museums

Contents

Section 1 Introduction

Who Should Use this Book and How?

This book provides an overview of national museum standards (things all good museums should do) and best practices (commendable actions for which they should get extra credit). It explains how the standards are developed, who uses them and for what purposes, and how your museum can use them to guide operations. By presenting standards and best practices in one place, together with a common-sense exploration of what they look like in application, this book lays the groundwork for any serious discussion of what a museum can or should do. So share it widely with people with whom these discussions take place. You may want to give copies to:

- *members of your governing authority*: to help them understand the standards guiding the decisions of the staff, and by which their performance as board members will be judged by the outside world;

- *staff*: to establish a common culture and a sound basis for developing museum policies and procedures;

- *people engaged in creating your institutional plan*: so that attainment of museum standards guides your long-term goals;

- *administrators in your parent organization (if you have one) such as a college, municipality, for-profit company or foundation*: to foster an environment in which the museum can flourish and administrators can help to achieve museums' goals;

- *journalists*: to inform the way they write about your museum and better equip them to educate the public about museums in general;

- *funders and granting agencies*: so that they know that you know the standards and to help them establish appropriate criteria for deciding whether your museum is deserving of support.

Section 2 presents the standards themselves, first the overarching Characteristics of Excellence, then each of seven areas of performance addressed by the Characteristics. Each of these seven sections restates the Characteristics related to this area of performance; presents more detailed standards related to this area; provides commentary on issues that frequently cause problems or provoke questions; and outlines any related best practices.

What Is a Museum?

A museum is a place which invites, in a special way, to contemplation and musing about our humanly strive after truth, goodness and beauty. This contemplation and musing brighten at one side the notion of our nullity and transitoriness, but reinforce at the other side the experience of our mysterious relationship and linking with the Imperishable.

—F. J. C. J. Nuyens, Dutch sociologist, 1981

Various attempts have been made over the years to draw firm boundaries around the category "museums," defining who gets in and who stays out. Some things people have tried to take into account are:

- Whether the organization is nonprofit (private or governmental) as opposed to for-profit. Left outside in the cold using this criteria are institutions such as the International Spy Museum, the Biltmore Estate, Graceland, the American International Rattlesnake Museum and the Museum of Sex, not to mention numerous very small museums that have not gotten around to being formally incorporated as nonprofits. (For example, the World's Smallest Museum, in Superior, Ariz., which has a total interior space of 134 square feet.) While museum professionals may feel strongly that nonprofit status is an important way to establish that the primary purpose of the majority of museums is serving the public benefit, the average person walking in off the street would recognize any of the institutions mentioned above as fitting his or her concept of a museum.

- Whether the organization has education as one of its core functions. Most everyone agrees this is an appropriate criterion, but when you realize that education can encompass almost any form of learning about anything, it becomes so broad as to be useless as a boundary. Would you argue about the educational nature or content of the Museum of Advertising Icons, the Dr. Pepper Museum and Free Enterprise Institute or the Museum of Jurassic Technology? They may not present traditional art, history or science, but they provide fascinating explorations of their topics of choice. And what to make of the Bloedel Reserve of Bainbridge Island, Wash., which identifies its purpose as "to provide people with an opportunity to enjoy nature through quiet walks in the gardens and woodlands"? It is undoubtedly a public garden, and hence a museum, but as education goes, it doesn't get much more low-key than that. And, for that matter, how does this help distinguish museums from libraries or schools or dance studios or other types of organizations that are clearly educational in nature?

- The care, preservation and display of objects. Historically, this may have been true, but the late twentieth century saw the proliferation of organizations broadly recognized as museums that do not care for, own or use collections—for example, many children's museums and science centers use objects as props but do not regard them as collections held in the public trust. Currently, 10 percent of museums identify themselves as not owning or using collections.[1]

- Whether the organization has a physical location (which may itself be a historic artifact) and delivers much of its interpretive content through experiences at that location. A growing number of museums, however, are virtual, existing only on the Internet. They may be grounded in a physical location with collections that are not open to the public, but for some there is no "there" there. They are completely virtual organizations of knowledge and images with no physical presence (other than the server on which the site is housed). (See, for example, the International Spaceflight Museum, which is "located" in the Internet-based virtual world Second Life.) Even traditional site-based museums serve a growing number of people through their websites—their site visitation far surpassing their physical visitors. If the physical site closed or went away but the website remained, would it be any less a museum?

We may have to live with the fact that "museum" as a concept is the intersection of many complex categories, resulting in an organization that people can identify intuitively but that cannot be neatly packaged in a definition.

Where does this leave us in creating standards for this ill-defined bunch? The American

Association of Museums takes a "big tent" approach. If an organization considers itself to be a museum, it's in the tent. This means the universe of American museums, from our point of view, includes the small cadre of for-profit museums, together with the vast majority of nonprofit; non–collections-based museums as well as the traditional collecting institutions; organizations that care for living collections (zoos, botanic gardens, aquariums); as well as the museums of art, history and science. Our intuitive judgment that this apparently diverse group belongs together is born out by the fact that they can, in fact, agree on standards that apply to all of them.

Why Standards?

Standard: something used as a measure, norm or model in comparative evaluations; a required or agreed level of quality or attainment.

—Compact Oxford English Dictionary

It is human nature to compare ourselves to others—we want to know that we are doing the right thing, and we want to know how we measure up. With personal conduct, we compare ourselves against cultural norms—unwritten rules of conduct, ethics, morality; and societal benchmarks—such as IQ tests, educational degrees, performance evaluations, salaries. Judging by popular magazines, Americans are irresistibly drawn to self-scored "How Am I Doing?" quizzes for everything from dating, appearance and sexual performance to achievement of life goals.

It is only natural that we carry this over into our jobs. Each specialized endeavor, from the moment it is founded, starts creating its own specialized points of comparison. For individuals, what does it mean to be a good mechanic, a good doctor or a good psychic? For organizations, what does it mean to be a good university, a good veterinary clinic or a good organic farm? In some ways these organizations have it easy. If they ask to be judged by outcomes, their effects are easy to describe: students who pass exams and get jobs; pets that are cured or comforted at the end of life; produce that is chemical-free. Museums have a harder time defining, as a field, the effect we are trying to produce, at least in any way that is clear and measurable. As providers of informal learning experiences, we may or may not be able to track and measure the effect we have on what people know or think. And the knowledge we provide is not always a concrete fact or way of thinking. Often it is an experience—the sum total of sights and sounds and smells, tactile impressions, emotions—that adds to the life experience that shapes who we are.

Yet the vast majority of museums in the U.S. are nonprofit and ask for public support in one form or another in return for providing some kind of public good. So it is important that we be broadly accountable for our conduct, not just to the users of our services but to society as a whole. While some individual museums measure and report the effect they have on their audience and communities, such practice is rare, and field-wide studies are scarcer still. That makes it all the more important that we have clearly agreed-upon standards that describe what it means to be a "good" museum, one worthy of public support and trust.

Also, as we are responsible for administering somewhere between $4.5 billion and $6 billion in government and private support, museums are understandably a subject of scrutiny by regulators.[2] Adherence to mutually agreed-upon standards enables museums to self-regulate, to a large extent, in a flexible and appropriate way that accommodates the huge diversity of our field. When standards are poorly articulated in an important area of operations, or a museum's conduct seems to contravene generally accepted (if unwritten) public standards, the government steps in, and we get federal or state or local laws and regulations that may or may not be sensible and applicable to museums of all types and sizes.

Last but not least, museums are closely watched by the some 67,000 members of the American media—self-appointed guardians of the public interest and government oversight. Journalists are society's watchdogs, and while we might not like it when we are at the receiving end of their scrutiny, their zealous attention to museum behavior (and museum misbehavior does make for great headlines) keeps us appropriately on our toes. They constantly test whether we are able to credibly explain our actions and justify to the general public why they are reasonable and appropriate in the context of our self-identified standards.

Some Characteristics of Standards

Standards reflect areas of broad agreement. If people have not come to consensus, or pretty close, there can't be a standard, because nothing has been generally agreed upon. That means there may be very important areas of conduct for which there are no standards, as museums try out different types of behavior, see how their colleagues, the general public, regulators and the media react to these experiments, and adjust their actions accordingly. Sometimes these discussions can go on for decades without a consensus.

Standards reflect areas where things actually go wrong. People don't write standards about behavior that doesn't happen. A situation recently arose in which the Los Angeles Museum of Contemporary Art included a Louis Vuitton boutique in the middle of its exhibition on the Japanese artist Takashi Murakami. Murakami is known for exploring the fuzzy boundaries between art and commerce, particularly his collaboration with Vuitton. The profits from the boutique went to the Vuitton company, not the museum. Some people started questioning whether this is ethical. Does it contravene standards? Well, no. At this moment the standards don't say anything about having a for-profit company running a store in the middle of an exhibit. As far as I know, no museum ever tried it before, so the issue hasn't come up and the broader ethical issue has not been debated.

Standards change over time. Museum standards arise out of technical knowledge (how to do things well, like conservation or education) and out of attitudes regarding what is right and appropriate (ethics). Both technical knowledge and attitudes evolve over time. As we come to appreciate the complexities of the effects of RH and temperature on objects and buildings, our technical standards for climate control become more and more nuanced. I remember when the rule handed down from on high regarding climate control was "55 percent humidity, +/- 3 percent." End of story. Now we recognize that you can't expect a museum housed in a brick building in Bishop, Calif. (average relative humidity 20 percent) to maintain an interior relative humidity of 55 percent—the brick would spall. Society changes, too, and museum standards evolve within this larger cultural environment. Fifty years ago it was simply accepted that museums owned human remains and sacred objects from other cultures. Now there is considerable debate about whether and when this is ethical. And because museums lagged behind societal expectations in this regard, failing to develop and apply credible self-imposed standards, Congress passed the Native American Graves Protection and Repatriation Act (NAGPRA), legislating how museums must deal with federally recognized tribes and Native Hawaiian organizations. NAGPRA has worked out pretty well, but maybe if museums had voluntarily worked with tribal representatives to develop a mutually acceptable solution, it would have been even better in terms of efficiency and effectiveness (two characteristics not usually attributed to government regulations). Implementation also might have been easier, starting from a premise of trust and goodwill.

Consequently, this book is a snapshot of a rapidly changing landscape. While you use it, pay attention to what may happen in the next week, month or year by reading professional publications, attending local, state and regional museum meetings, checking the websites of AAM and other museum professional associations, and talking to colleagues.

Standards come from broad dialogue. To be appropriate and credible, standards need to be created through a process that incorporates input of people in institutions expected to abide by the standards and of people who hold those expectations. For this reason it is important that you be an active participant in the ongoing discussion that culminates in written standards—to be appropriate for all museums, standards need input from professionals at museums of all types and sizes. Given the increasing pressure for public accountability, we also need input from members of the public, policymakers and media who use these standards to assess whether museums live up to their expectations. You can help by educating your museum's funders, local policymakers and media, and national representatives about museum standards, drawing them into this discussion, as well.

What Are "Standards and Best Practices"?

If it is hard to pin down one thing that identifies a museum, it is easy to characterize people who work in museums: We love to argue about the meaning of words. This book could be ten times as long and only begin to cover the debate that ensues from an open discussion of the definition of *standard*. To forestall that debate (and move quickly to the important business of determining what the standards actually are), the AAM Board of Directors approved the following definitions. Of course, we can't make the rest of the field adopt these definitions universally, but at least it establishes what they mean for the purposes of understanding the material in this book.

Standards are generally accepted levels of attainment that all museums are expected to achieve. *Best practices* are commendable actions and philosophies that demonstrate an awareness of standards, successfully solve problems, can be replicated and that museums may choose to emulate if appropriate to their circumstances.

Translated into plain English: Standards are things that all good museums should live up to, and they can expect to be criticized by colleagues, or supporters or the press, if they don't. Standards are not lofty goals that only a few will achieve. They are fundamental to being a good museum, a responsible nonprofit and a well-run business. Best practices are "extra credit." Museums deserve applause if they can implement them but shouldn't be faulted if they can't. Some best practices may not be suitable to a museum's particular circumstances, and some museums might not have the resources needed to go that extra mile.

Where Do Standards Come From?

There are more than 17,000 museums in the U.S., with more than 200,000 employees.[3] These museums range in size from all-volunteer to more than 300 paid staff. Their annual operating expenses can be counted in the hundreds of dollars or in the high millions. They include historic sites and houses, zoos, art museums, history museums, science centers, children's museums, nature centers and botanic gardens (to name but a few). It is truly daunting to imagine inventing a system to establish standards appropriate for all of these organizations.

Fortunately, the museum field did not have to create this system all at once—it evolved on its own, through almost four decades of experimentation. And the method, in concept, is very simple: Get enough people representing these diverse museums talking to each other, give them ways to look closely at a lot of different museums and how they operate, share observations about what works and what does not work, discuss what is and is not appropriate, write it down, report it to the field, see what gets accepted or shot down and revise accordingly. This takes place through the activities of the several dozen professional associations representing various parts of the museum field, with AAM representing the whole.

Within AAM, this ongoing exploration of standards principally takes place through the Accreditation Program, ethics task forces empanelled by the AAM Board of Directors and the Standing Professional Committees (which represent various segments of the museum profession: curators, registrars, educators, security staff, etc.)

Of these, the Accreditation Program has had the biggest influence in creating written standards for museums. We say more about the Accreditation Program's role in recognizing achievement and enforcing standards on page 13. Here we focus on its role in codifying museum standards. There are about 800 museums in the Accreditation Program (more than 770 accredited, a couple dozen applicants). To earn accreditation they complete a detailed self-study of all areas of their operations. Two peer reviewers (senior staff from comparable institutions) read the self-study, visit the museum and write a report summarizing their observations. Finally the self-study and report are reviewed by nine museum professionals who volunteer to serve on the Accreditation Commission. Based on this information, the commission decides to accredit the museum, to table its decision while asking the museum to make improvements in areas where it falls short of standards, or denies accreditation. There may be considerable follow-up discussion (as you may imagine) between the commission, museum and peer reviewers regarding these decisions.

When the program began in the early 1970s, it was pretty informal. Staff provided some minimal written guidance for the peer reviewers, focusing their attention on certain areas of operations, but there were no written standards per se. As the peer reviewers, the commissioners, and museums whose fates were being decided wrestled with how to make fair and equitable decisions, it became clear that it was necessary to have a set of objective criteria by which museums can be assessed—rules that everyone would know ahead of time so that the commission would have a common point of reference during the deliberations. These rules have evolved and expanded over time, forming the core of what has become *National Standards and Best Practices for U.S. Museums.*

The other document central to national museum standards is the Code of Ethics for Museums, written in 1978, and most recently revised in 2000, which guides museums' creation of their own individualized codes of ethics. This and other ethics statements approved by the AAM board are issued to the field for comment (and lively debate) before being approved. This process may include national colloquiums on a given topic (like those held in 2002 and 2005 on collections planning and interpretive planning, respectively); sessions at professional meetings; formal comment periods; and referral to specific related task forces or committees of other organizations.

This process is mirrored in the various discipline-specific museum associations that create standards applicable to the segment of the museum community that they represent—the American Association for State and Local History, Association of Children's Museums, Association of Science and Technology Centers, etc. Taken together, these written standards create an overlapping web of guidance that apply at the broadest level to all museums, and then drill down to practices or ethics specific to particular fields.

In sum, museum standards arise from a big, messy dialogue that corrals all this input into a form approved by the field as a whole, as represented by staff who are actively engaged in the work of their professional associations. In this way, we ensure that the standards are applicable to, appropriate for and achievable by all types of museums.

How Can Museums Use the Standards?

The board, staff and volunteers who govern and operate museums come from diverse backgrounds, cultures and training. Staff may be trained in museum studies programs, where they learn how nonprofits work in general, or they may come from specialized academic programs about their subject (art, science, history) and have little or no knowledge of the legal and ethical underpinnings of nonprofit operations. Some people primarily learn on the job, but practices vary from museum to museum. And particularly in small or isolated institutions, norms can drift away from those of the field as a whole. Some staff, many board members and volunteers—and with increasing frequency, the director—come from the for-profit world and bring an entirely different set of assumptions about what is right and appropriate behavior for the organization or its employees. Museums that exist inside non-museum entities (for instance, universities or city or state governments) may report to individuals whose instinct is to apply the conventions of the bigger entity to the museum, regardless of whether this would conflict with usual museum practice.

Many of the conflicts that arise in the course of running a museum happen in part because people assume they are all speaking the same language. In fact, nonprofits in general and museums specifically have a very detailed and arcane language that guides their thinking. Ensuring that all parties engaged in leading and operating the museum understand museum standards provides the beginning of a common vocabulary. As noted in Getting to Yes, a classic 1981 text on difficult negotiations, having objective criteria for decision making can help parties with disparate needs arrive at wise and efficient solutions. People usually can agree that nationally approved standards are an appropriate set of measures to guide their discussions.

Here are some opportunities to expose people to the standards in order to help build a shared culture:

- *When people are hired, elected to the board or recruited as volunteers*: Include a copy of the "Characteristics of Excellence for U.S. Museums" in your personnel policy, board briefing book, volunteer manual or the equivalent. Present an overview of the standards in orientation sessions for staff, board members and volunteers.

- *When the museum is engaged in planning*: Museum standards should inform the goals the museum sets in its planning process. Some museums make meeting standards, or gaining recognition for meeting standards through becoming accredited, a goal in and of itself. When the planning team begins to meet, include the standards with the other basic documents the team might review as it begins its work (e.g., the last plan, the museum's recent financial statement, feasibility studies, etc.).

- *When staff and board write policies*: The first thing a museum's conduct will be judged by is whether it is in alignment with the museum's own policies. These, in turn, should be consistent with all the applicable national and discipline-specific standards. While an individual may not like a museum's actions, it is hard to make a case for those actions being objectively "wrong" if they are in accord with policies established in advance by people acting in good faith, and ratified by the opinion of their colleagues. It is, of course, crucial that these policies have been established before the action took place. (There is nothing like after-the-fact ratification to make an otherwise innocent action smell like a dead fish.) It is also important that they be publicly available—showing that the museum feels they will stand up to public scrutiny.

- *When the museum asks for support*: It benefits individual museums and the field as a whole when private donors, foundations, grant-making agencies and policymakers understand what constitutes a "good" museum worthy of their support. When you cultivate donors, write grant proposals and work with your local, state or national political representatives, integrate information on the standards and how you meet them into your message.

- *When you make any important decision, and when you prepare the accompanying communications plan*: Will you be able to explain how the museum's actions are in line with national standards? As discussed in Section 3, often when a museum lands in the news for something the press or public regard as questionable, they call AAM and we refer them to the national standards to guide their assessment of the museum's actions. So test your decision against the standards before the fact.

- *When you assess and report on the museum's performance*: Museums are increasingly called upon to publicly account for what they do to deserve public support. While the most meaningful measures document how the museum delivers its mission (the good it does for its community and audience), showing that you comply with national museum standards is a powerful tool for demonstrating to the public, press, policymakers and funders that you make responsible use of the support they provide. Museums can measure and report on this themselves, engage outside consultants, participate in peer-based programs such as the Museum Assessment and Conservation Assessment Programs or receive outside certification of meeting standards by becoming accredited.

Who Else Uses the Standards, and How?

Increasingly, funders use nationally recognized criteria for assessing whether museums deserve support. Some take into account whether a museum is accredited—accepting this third-party certification that the organization meets national standards. Florida, for example, requires museums to be accredited to receive some kinds of state funding. The Kresge Foundation and other major funders consider accredited status when reviewing grant proposals. The Institute of Museum and Library Services weighs a museum's participation in the Museum Assessment Program and the priorities it establishes through peer review against standards in that program in awarding competitive Museums for America grants. We do not track how often local and regional funders use such criteria, but we know that there is trend to do so and it is likely to become more common in the future.

Policymakers look to museum standards in deciding whether and how to create legislation or regulations to govern museum behavior. Often the museum field tackles the creation of standards because of a contentious issue in order to forestall government regulation. AAM Guidelines on Individual Donor Support, for example, were written in the wake of the "Sensations" exhibition at the Brooklyn Museum of Art in 1999, which raised issues of whether the lender of the works in the show, Charles Saatchi, cxcrciscd undue influence over the content and presentation, and the museum's lack of transparency regarding his support and the extent of his involvement. The state of New York takes accreditation into account when considering whether to charter museums as state nonprofits. Attorneys General in all states consult national standards in weighing the conduct of the nonprofit museums under their oversight. When the AGs do step in to intervene on behalf of the public, either because the museum proactively asks them to or because there is a potential breach of the public trust (such as when the Museum of the City of New York proposed large-scale deaccessioning of its collections), they often take into account ethics and museum standards as well as the law in issuing their decisions and providing guidance to the museum.

Members of the media use museum standards to inform their coverage, particularly regarding controversial actions that some people perceive to be unethical or simply objectionable. AAM is frequently contacted by members of the press about this or that museum, asking whether its behavior aligns with national standards. We don't comment on the actions of individual museums, but we are happy to take the opportunity to educate journalists on museum standards and help them understand how to apply them to their coverage. The topics that most often attract the attention of the press are: deaccessioning, care of collections, executive compensation, financial distress (particularly if it may be a result of financial mismanagement), relationships with individual and corporate donors and conflict of interest.

Members of the public increasingly refer to the standards, as well, particularly if they are irritated by something the museum has done and want to bring it to the attention of the press. It used to be that specialized standards were relatively inaccessible to the general public unless someone was pretty serious about doing research through a library or writing to a professional association. The World Wide Web has made this material easily available to anyone with a browser and some knowledge of how to search the Internet. Museums need to understand that members of their communities and audiences have access to this information—and take this into account when they make decisions and explain them to the public.

Museum Accreditation

In the U.S., compliance with museum standards is voluntary. The pressure brought to bear by funders, regulators, the press and the public may be considerable, but in the end, museums choose to follow or not follow standards of the field.

There is a cadre of museums, however, that have pledged to abide by the standards in a formally certified manner through the AAM Accreditation Program. For the past decade, the number of accredited museums has remained pretty constant, between 750 and 770—about 5 percent of museums in the U.S. We should commend these museums for their commitment to public accountability. By opening up their operations to intense scrutiny by their peers, they burnish the reputation of all museums. They also play a key role in the development of the standards themselves—accreditation being a crucible in which important issues are examined, patterns of behavior are observed to be consistently successful or unsuccessful, and emerging standards are tested for consistency, applicability and appropriateness.

The Accreditation Program constantly changes with time and is undergoing significant revisions even as I write. The broad outline has remained, however, and likely will continue to remain the same since its inception in the early 1970s. In the program, museums:

- undertake an intensive self-study, documenting various aspects of their operations. This self-study includes assembling fundamental documents such as plans and policies approved by the governing authority;

- open themselves to examination by a committee of their peers, who review the self-study and attached documentation, as well as visit the museum and interview members of the board, staff and volunteers;

- are assessed by the Accreditation Commission, composed of museum professionals who volunteer their time to review the self-study, documentation and peer reviewers' report in order to determine whether the museum meets AAM standards.

AAM's website (www.aam-us.org) provides information on how these standards are applied in accreditation and what documents accredited museums must have to demonstrate they are meeting the standards.

In my estimation, from talking with museum staff over the years, for every one museum that has attained accreditation, another ten consciously use museum standards to guide their planning and operations. Some of these museums intend to become accredited eventually. Others feel that while the standards are appropriate and worthy of their attention, they don't need or want the certification per se. And there are a few museums that consciously opt out, deciding, for example, that their institutional culture is not compatible with some of the standards.

There is increasing pressure, however, from policymakers and funders for all nonprofits—museums included—to adhere to formal, widely accepted standards and to demonstrate that they are doing so. Given that this trend is likely to continue, museum accreditation—or certification in some way, shape or form—is likely to play a greater role in the future. In this context, the standards set forth in this book, and the methods that museums use to demonstrate that they adhere to these standards, assume an even greater importance. It is in the best interests of museums that the field determines the standards, and the processes by which they will be judged, rather than being subjected to standards or to reporting requirements that do not fit the quirky reality of our nature.

1. Elizabeth E. Merritt, ed., 2006 Museum Financial Information (Washington, D.C.: American Association of Museums, 2006).

2. Estimated from data gathered through the Museum Financial Information Survey 2005 and U.S. Census Bureau data on employer institutions.

3. Institute for Museum and Library Services estimates that there are 17,500 museums in the U.S., see www.IMLS.gov; employee estimate from AAM analysis of the 2000 Census, accessed through the Missouri Census Data Center http://mcdc2.missouri.edu/.

Section 2 Standards and Best Practices

Core Questions

Two core questions underlie any assessment of a museum against museum standards:

How well does the museum achieve its stated mission and goals? How well does the museum's performance meet standards and best practices, as generally understood in the field and as appropriate to its circumstances?

Commentary

These questions are crucial to the flexible and appropriate application of national standards to museums of all sizes and types.

Mission and Goals

Nonprofit museums exist to serve the public, and a museum explains whom it will serve and how in its mission statement. (See more about mission statements on page 41.) Therefore the principle question guiding any assessment of a museum, whether by the public, media, funders, accreditation reviewers or others, is whether it is successfully meeting this mission. Since a museum has selected its own mission, it has chosen for itself the principle benchmark by which it will be evaluated.

Two museums, essentially identical in their operations but having dissimilar missions, might measure up very differently in light of this principle. A small historic house museum that meets its mission of serving its local community through interpreting neighborhood history might be doing a fine job. Its clone in another city, with equivalent exhibits and programs but an ambitious mission of being a world-class museum advancing scholarship in the field of history, might be found to fall far short of its aspirations.

Mission statements are typically very broad, and most museums could meet their missions in many different ways. Each museum makes more specific choices through its plans, principally the institutional plan (see page 44). These plans establish specific goals, such as "open a new, state-of-the-art exhibition wing in three years," "attain museum accreditation" or "double the number of schoolchildren served through programs." The museum's goals, as established in its plans, become important, self-identified indicators of whether the museum is meeting its mission.

"As Appropriate to its Circumstances"

Clearly a rural arts center, primarily run by volunteers with annual operating expenses of $50,000, is not going to look in any way, shape or form like the Metropolitan Museum of Art. Yet both could be meeting national museum standards. How can this be? It is because they each make intelligent use of available resources to do their work in a way their peers will recognize, in context, as being appropriate to their circumstances. The small arts center might have a 400-square-foot storage room, with art racks made of galvanized pipe, equipped with a hand-filled humidifier for the winter and a dehumidifier (also emptied by hand) for the summer. Copies to the key for the sturdy lock on the door are held by the part-time director and the volunteer curator. Exhibit labels are neatly printed using a Laserjet printer, mounted on foamcore and stuck to the wall with double-sided tape. Most of the lighting is incandescent, and the few fluorescent lights have filters to screen art from harmful ultraviolet wavelengths. The museum's education programs are excellent, taught by a dedicated group of volunteers, each of whom has completed a home study course in art history. Each year they hold an open house for the community, featuring a barbeque in the parking lot and including the local fire and police personnel. Their board of trustees includes representatives of the rapidly growing immigrant communities in their region. What's not to like?

"Appropriate to its circumstances" also takes into account geographic location, audience and community values. For most museums, it would be highly irregular to offer deaccessioned material from the collections back to the original donor. Legally, that donor has no more claim to the object than any other member of the public (i.e., none). The museum's principal responsibility—to use its resources in the public interest—is usually best served by the material going to another nonprofit where it will still be publicly available, or by selling on the open market for the best price possible to give the museum more resources to develop and care for the collections. A number of small, community-based museums, however, have decided that, in some circumstances, offering collections back to the original donor is appropriate. How can they tell a donor, they say, that her grandmother's wedding dress has been sold to a collector halfway across the country? Or that the family Bible now will be in the state archives, 400 miles away?

Characteristics of Excellence for U.S. Museums

The following 38 points, grouped under seven categories, were originally drafted by the Accreditation Commission to provide the big picture of national museum standards. This overview is a good starting point for any examination of the national standards and best practices. The more specific statements branch out from here. Each category will be discussed in more detail in the rest of this section.

I. *Public Trust and Accountability*

- The museum is a good steward of its resources held in the public trust.

- The museum identifies the communities it serves and makes appropriate decisions in how it serves them.

- Regardless of its self-identified communities, the museum strives to be a good neighbor in its geographic area.

- The museum strives to be inclusive and offers opportunities for diverse participation.

- The museum asserts its public service role and places education at the center of that role.

- The museum demonstrates a commitment to providing the public with physical and intellectual access to the museum and its resources.

- The museum is committed to public accountability and is transparent in its mission and its operations.

- The museum complies with local, state and federal laws, codes and regulations applicable to its facilities, operations and administration.

II. *Mission and Planning*

- The museum has a clear understanding of its mission and communicates why it exists and who benefits as a result of its efforts.

- All aspects of the museum's operations are integrated and focused on meeting its mission.

- The museum's governing authority and staff think and act strategically to acquire, develop and allocate resources to advance the mission of the museum.

- The museum engages in ongoing and reflective institutional planning that includes involvement of its audiences and community.

- The museum establishes measures of success and uses them to evaluate and adjust its activities.

III. *Leadership and Organizational Structure*

- The governance, staff and volunteer structures and processes effectively advance the museum's mission.

- The governing authority, staff and volunteers have a clear and shared understanding of their roles and responsibilities.

- The governing authority, staff and volunteers legally, ethically and effectively carry out their responsibilities.

- The composition, qualifications and diversity of the museum's leadership, staff and volunteers enable it to carry out the museum's mission and goals.

- There is a clear and formal division of responsibilities between the governing authority and any group that supports the museum, whether separately incorporated or operating within the museum or its parent organization.

IV. *Collections Stewardship*

- The museum owns, exhibits or uses collections that are appropriate to its mission.

- The museum legally, ethically and effectively manages, documents, cares for and uses the collections.

- The museum's collections-related research is conducted according to appropriate scholarly standards.

- The museum strategically plans for the use and development of its collections.

- Guided by its mission, the museum provides public access to its collections while ensuring their preservation.

V. *Education and Interpretation*

- The museum clearly states its overall educational goals, philosophy and messages and demonstrates that its activities are in alignment with them.

- The museum understands the characteristics and needs of its existing and potential audiences and uses this understanding to inform its interpretation.

- The museum's interpretive content is based on appropriate research.

- Museums conducting primary research do so according to scholarly standards.

- The museum uses techniques, technologies and methods appropriate to its educational goals, content, audiences and resources.

- The museum presents accurate and appropriate content for each of its audiences.

- The museum demonstrates consistent high quality in its interpretive activities.

- The museum assesses the effectiveness of its interpretive activities and uses those results to plan and improve its activities.

VI. *Financial Stability*

- The museum legally, ethically and responsibly acquires, manages and allocates its financial resources in a way that advances its mission.

- The museum operates in a fiscally responsible manner that promotes its long-term sustainability.

VII. *Facilities and Risk Management*

- The museum allocates its space and uses its facilities to meet the needs of the collections, audience and staff.
- The museum has appropriate measures to ensure the safety and security of people, its collections and/or objects and the facilities it owns or uses.

- The museum has an effective program for the care and long-term maintenance of its facilities.

- The museum is clean, well maintained and provides for the visitors' needs.

- The museum takes appropriate measures to protect itself against potential risk and loss.

Each of the preceding 38 bullets represents a huge amount of reflection on the part of all the people involved in developing the standards. Each word was carefully chosen, and the meanings and implications discussed at great length. Still, the overall effect can be daunting. Sometimes people get too hung up on the wording for this very reason—they sense the work that went into them and try to parse every "the", "and" and "so".

To get past this hurdle and help people focus on the intent behind the careful wording, AAM staffs have taken the liberty of translating the Characteristics from official language into, well, plain English. This version, while a bit tongue-in-cheek, is actually a very useful way of showing people how commonsensical, achievable and necessary the Characteristics are. You may want to distribute this version when introducing museum standards to a new audience.

Characteristics of Excellence for U.S. Museums "in Translation"

I. *Public Trust and Accountability*

Accountability
- Be good.
- No really—not only be legal, but be ethical.
- Show everyone how good and ethical you are (don't wait for them to ask).

Community engagement
- Do good for people.
- Know which people.
- And to be on the safe side:
  —Be nice to everyone else, too. . .
  —Especially if they live next door.

Diversity and inclusiveness
- Avoid cloning your staff or board members.
- Look something like the people you are doing good for. . .
- And maybe a bit like your neighbors.
- Let other people help decide what games to play. . .
- And what the rules are.
- Share your toys.

II. *Mission and Planning*

Mission

- Know what you want to do. . .
- And why it makes a difference to anyone.
- Then put it in writing.
- Stick to it.

Planning

- Decide what you want to do next.
- When you are deciding what to do, ask lots of people for their opinions.
- Put it in writing. . .
- Then do it.
- If it didn't work, don't do it again.
- If it did work, do.

III. *Leadership and Organizational Structure*

Make sure everyone is clear about who is doing what

- The board knows it is governing.
- The director knows he/she is directing (and the board knows it, too).
- The staff knows it is doing everything else.
- And put it in writing.

IV. *Collections Stewardship*

- Know what stuff you have.
- Know what stuff you need.
- Know where it is.
- Take good care of it.
- Make sure someone gets some good out of it. . .
- Especially people you care about. . .
- And your neighbors.

V. *Education and Interpretation*

- Know whom you are talking to.
- Ask them what they want to know.

- Know what you want to say (and what you are talking about).
- Use appropriate language (or images, or music).
- Make sure people understand you.
- And ask them if they like it.
- If not, change it.

VI. *Financial Stability*

- Put your money where your mission is.
- Is it enough money?
- Will it be there next year, too?
- Know when you will need more money.
- Know where you are going to get it.
- Don't diddle the books.

VII. *Facilities and Risk Management*

- Don't crowd people. . .
- Or things.
- Make it safe to visit your museum. . .
- Or work there.
- Keep it clean.
- Keep the toilet paper stocked.
- And if all else fails, know where the exit is (and make sure it is clearly marked).

I. Public Trust and Accountability

Standards Regarding Public Trust and Accountability
Characteristics of Excellence Related to Public Trust and Accountability

- The museum is a good steward of its resources held in the public trust.

- The museum identifies the communities it serves and makes appropriate decisions in how it serves them.

- Regardless of its self-identified communities, the museum strives to be a good neighbor in its geographic area.

- The museum strives to be inclusive and offers opportunities for diverse participation.

- The museum asserts its public service role and places education at the center of that role.

- The museum demonstrates a commitment to providing the public with physical and intellectual access to the museum and its resources.

- The museum is committed to public accountability and is transparent in its mission and its operations.

- The museum complies with local, state and federal laws, codes and regulations applicable to its facilities, operations, and administration.

Commentary

Public trust and accountability is the newest section of the Characteristics, added in 2004. It reflects growing expectations on the part of the public that they be included in the process of deciding what will be done with the support they provide to museums, and of the public and policymakers that museums tell people what they are doing and why. Because these characteristics are so new, it is hard to say exactly what a museum should do to meet them. The following commentary reflects the reasoning and values underlying these standards. In the absence of the "case law," this may help you decide how best to apply them to your museum's operations.

In the big picture, this new section of the Characteristics of Excellence encompasses one of the first standards tackled by the museum field: ethics. Operating in an ethical manner is fundamental to earning the trust and support of the public. The code of ethics for museums as a field, and standards regarding institutional codes of ethics for individual museums, are presented beginning on page 31.

Stewardship of Resources

"The museum is a good steward of its resources held in the public trust." You could almost paraphrase Jewish scholar Hillel and declare, "This is the whole standard... the rest is commentary." A steward takes care of something on behalf of someone else. For nonprofit museums, that "someone else" is the public, and the museum is accountable to them for how it manages their property. (This is a slightly metaphorical explanation, but grounded in the law—read Marie Malaro's *Legal Primer on Managing Museum Collections* for a detailed explanation of the legal obligations of stewardship.)

This statement is a good, simple touchstone by which to judge any potential decision. Would a reasonable person consider the museum's action to be consistent with good stewardship of collections, funds, the building or anything else it cares for on his or her behalf? For example, is the compensation provided to the director appropriate in proportion to the museum's overall budget? Is the museum doing a credible job of preserving the collections entrusted to its care? Even if you think reasonable people could disagree on the answer to a particular question, framing it in this way can help clarify potential concerns.

Communities and Neighbors

Nonprofit status is granted to museums in recognition of the fact that our organizations provide a public service—in return for public support, we devote our "profits" to creating a better society. But thinking has changed dramatically in the last fifty years about who should benefit as a result of this support. It is not enough anymore to appeal to a small, homogeneous audience (e.g., older white male railroad enthusiasts), and say, "That's who benefits from our work." There is an expectation that any museum serve some broader slice of society.

In particular, there has been a growing consensus in the past couple of decades that museums need to be attentive to the needs of their neighbors—the people who live and work nearby. This may or may not be the same folks the museum has identified as its community of users. Take, for example, a small museum of botany housed in a historic townhouse, in what has become an economically depressed but ethnically diverse neighborhood. The museum preserves and interprets an archive, rare book collection and herbarium. Its mission identifies its audiences as scientists, historians and artists researching the collections. But that museum still affects the people who live around it, even if they never come through its doors. Its physical appearance, the visitors who come into the neighborhood to get to the museum, the accompanying effect on parking, traffic, litter or noise, all influence the quality of life of the museum's neighbors. This standard says that museums have to take these effects into account. The museum might be a good neighbor in ways related to its mission, such as training community gardeners and helping maintain a public green space. Or it might simply make its library, with its Internet-connected computers, available as a quiet, safe place for neighborhood children to do homework in late afternoons.

Happily, as museums put this into practice, they find it is often in their best interests in a business sense, as well. Being involved with your community may lead to your neighbors becoming visitors to your museum. It may build mutually beneficial partnerships with local businesses. It can connect you with people and foundations interested in supporting your museum as much because of your effect on the community as because of belief in your mission (though they may come to care about that, too). It may even inspire a neighborhood kid to grow up to be a botanist, helping with the next challenge on our plate, which is . . .

Public Service Role and Education
To be honest, one of the historical reasons that the standards emphasize education as central to the identity of museums is tied to money. Government funding of culture boomed in the 1960s, along with tax reform that forced foundations to give more of their earnings to charity, but this funding was channeled to cultural institutions. At the time, museums were still categorized by the IRS as "recreational," and to qualify for the burgeoning opportunities for tax benefits and grants they needed to position themselves firmly in the educational realm. That said, it is not an inaccurate statement. The history of museums in the U.S. documents their ambitions to educate all classes of society. That is still true today. It is equally true that government, foundations and private funders expect museums to maintain their commitment to filling this role.

Diversity
There is an emerging consensus that museums ought to better reflect the growing diversity of American society in their governance, staffing and audience development. This conver-

sation can quickly bog down in a struggle over what counts when measuring diversity (ethnicity, race, gender, culture, (dis)ability, age, etc.). These issues can't be settled at the national level—the "right" answer is specific to each museum and its circumstances. Clearly a museum in a small agricultural town in rural South Dakota is going to have a harder time recruiting ethnic and cultural diversity than a museum in downtown Chicago. And in any case, for the South Dakota museum, the biggest challenge for board diversity might be finding people under the age of sixty to take the reins.

As with community engagement, the issue is as much practical as it is ideological. According to U.S. Census Bureau projections, by 2050 our population will be "majority minority"—Caucasians of European descent will make up less than 50 percent of the population. If your museum's current audience is primarily composed of the descendants of the founding Europeans, what happens to your institution if only that population cares about your museum? Your base of support will shrink and shrink, and maybe it will become so small the museum is not sustainable. On the other hand, if your story is told in a way that makes it compelling and important to all American citizens, you can make a more diverse audience care about what you do. Or maybe your mission changes over time and addresses broader issues of immigration and celebrates the "founding fathers" (and mothers) of different immigrant groups. In either case, it is difficult for a homogeneous board and staff—however well intentioned—to have "street cred" with groups the museum is trying to reach. People want to see other people like them working in the museum and having a voice in how it is run. And the museum is unlikely to make the best choices about how to serve new audiences without members of those groups helping make the decisions.

Accessibility

As all U.S. residents provide support for the museum (through the subsidy of federal or state tax-exempt status, if nothing else, not to mention local bond levies, etc.), everyone should be able to benefit, as far as is practicable, from the museum's assets.

Beyond what is required by law—notably the Americans with Disabilities Act—museums have an ethical imperative to make their resources as accessible as possible. This includes physical assets such as the building and grounds, and intellectual assets—information about the collections, results of the museum's research, exhibits, programs and website.

There may be practical limits to accessibility, often arising from the tension between access and conservation, but museums must do their best to strike an appropriate balance.

Unlimited physical access could destroy a museum's ability to preserve its collections, land or historic building for future generations. (And in the case of living animal collections, it could be bad for the preservation of visitors, too.) Unlimited intellectual access might release information in a harmful way. Donors might be put at risk, for example, if museums share information that could lead criminals to target their personal collections. Small populations of threatened or endangered species can be wiped out by commercial dealers or hobbyists if the locations where museum specimens were collected are revealed.

But restricting access is now an exception rather than the rule. Museums are expected to proceed on the assumption that the right to access is a given, and if it is restricted, they should be prepared to answer these questions: What makes this a reasonable restriction? What higher purpose does it serve? No one should have to justify why their group deserves special treatment in order to get into the museum, or be treated with less respect than any other visitor. For example, mobility-impaired visitors should not be relegated to the loading dock or the freight elevator.

Accountability and Transparency

Gone are the days when museums could say, "Pay no attention to the man behind the curtain." The policies and procedures that guide the museum's operations, its plans for the future and information on how well or poorly it is performing are expected to be made available to anyone who cares enough to look for it. And, increasingly, made available by mail upon written request is not enough. It means making these things a matter of public record—publishing them in newsletters or posting them on the museum's website.

Frankly, most of this information is going to become public one way or another. The website Guidestar (www.guidestar.org) posts electronic copies of all nonprofits' IRS 990 statements, which will only become easier and timelier as the IRS moves toward requiring electronic filing. The IRS itself, aware that many people now use these forms to assess nonprofit performance, is in the midst of redesigning the 990 form to facilitate that kind of analysis. In the world of the Web, any policy or plan, however confidential, can be leaked and posted for the world to see. Far better for the museum to control the medium and the message and take the opportunity to provide context for information that could otherwise be misinterpreted or misunderstood.

Legal Compliance

You might be surprised that legal compliance has to be written into museum standards. But well-meaning individuals often assume their good intentions exempt them from the requirement to follow certain laws and regulations. A children's museum's volunteers may not realize that the kids' group they are running in the morning is, effectively, a daycare center and subject to the relevant codes and regulations. Staff may think that because the museum's closets contain nothing more hazardous than Elmer's glue, acrylic paint, acetone, Lysol, floor wax and drain cleaner, they don't need to provide material safety data sheets to staff and train them how to read them. Even staff of large institutions are vulnerable to this reasoning. Curators returning from field research abroad may think they don't have to declare their animal and plant specimens to Customs, U.S. Fish and Wildlife or U.S. Department of Agriculture personnel because they are scientists—they are doing this for the betterment of mankind, rather than for profit. Ensure that all your staff, board and volunteers are familiar with the relevant laws and regulations governing your museum's actions and know that "this means you."

Standards Regarding Ethics
Characteristics of Excellence Related to Ethics

- The museum is a good steward of its resources held in the public trust.

- The museum is committed to public accountability and is transparent in its mission and operations.

- The governing authority, staff and volunteers legally, ethically and effectively carry out their responsibilities.

Commentary
Ethical Standards

The following section addresses the two general standards statements regarding ethics: one detailing how each museum creates a tailored code of ethics that governs its actions, the other outlining the general ethical principles to which all U.S. museums subscribe. There are several other standards in this book that one could regard as ethical principles. Some might argue that all big-picture standards, as opposed to technical standards such as what kind of archival ink to use, are about ethics. In any case, these other statements are organized in the sections addressing the areas of operation in question. Section IV: Collections Stewardship addresses loaning collections to non-museum entities and treatment of objects that might have been misappropriated in the Nazi era. Section VI: Financial Stability covers developing and managing business and donor support and retrenchment and downsizing.

The AAM Code of Ethics for Museums

Museums make their unique contribution to the public by collecting, preserving and interpreting the things of this world. Historically, they have owned and used natural objects, living and nonliving, and all manner of human artifacts to advance knowledge and nourish the human spirit. Today, the range of their special interests reflects the scope of human vision. Their missions include collecting and preserving, as well as exhibiting and educating with materials not only owned but also borrowed and fabricated for these ends. Their numbers include both governmental and private museums of anthropology, art history and natural history, aquariums, arboretums, art centers, botanical gardens, children's museums, historic sites, nature centers, planetariums, science and technology centers and zoos. The museum universe in the United States includes both collecting and noncollecting institutions. Although diverse in their missions, they have in common their nonprofit form of organization and a commitment of service to the public. Their collections and/or the objects they borrow or fabricate are the basis for research, exhibits and programs that invite public participation.

Taken as a whole, museum collections and exhibition materials represent the world's natural and cultural common wealth. As stewards of that wealth, museums are compelled to advance an understanding of all natural forms and of the human experience. It is incumbent on museums to be resources for humankind and in all their activities to foster an informed appreciation of the rich and diverse world we have inherited. It is also incumbent upon them to preserve that inheritance for posterity.

Museums in the United States are grounded in the tradition of public service. They are organized as public trusts, holding their collections and information as a benefit for those they were established to serve. Members of their governing authority, employees and volunteers are committed to the interests of these beneficiaries. The law provides the basic framework for museum operations. As nonprofit institutions, museums comply with applicable local, state and federal laws and international conventions, as well as with the specific legal standards governing trust responsibilities. This Code of Ethics for Museums takes that compliance as given. But legal standards are a minimum. Museums and those responsible for them must do more than avoid legal liability, they must take affirmative steps to maintain their integrity so as to warrant public confidence. They must act not only legally but also ethically. This Code of Ethics for Museums, therefore, outlines ethical standards that frequently exceed legal minimums.

Loyalty to the mission of the museum and to the public it serves is the essence of museum work, whether volunteer or paid. Where conflicts of interest arise—actual, potential or perceived—the duty of loyalty must never be compromised. No individual may use his or her position in a museum for personal gain or to benefit another at the expense of the museum, its mission, its reputation and the society it serves.

For museums, public service is paramount. To affirm that ethic and to elaborate its application to their governance, collections and programs, the American Association of Museums promulgates this Code of Ethics for Museums. In subscribing to this code, museums assume responsibility for the actions of members of their governing authority, employees and volunteers in the performance of museum-related duties. Museums, thereby, affirm their chartered purpose, ensure the prudent application of their resources, enhance their effectiveness and maintain public confidence. This collective endeavor strengthens museum work and the contributions of museums to society—present and future.

Governance

Museum governance in its various forms is a public trust responsible for the institution's service to society. The governing authority protects and enhances the museum's collections and programs and its physical, human and financial resources. It ensures that all these resources support the museum's mission, respond to the pluralism of society and respect the diversity of the natural and cultural common wealth.

Thus, the governing authority ensures that: all those who work for or on behalf of a museum understand and support its mission and public trust responsibilities; its members understand and fulfill their trusteeship and act corporately, not as individuals; the museum's collections and programs and its physical, human and financial resources are protected, maintained and developed in support of the museum's mission; it is responsive to and represents the interests of society; it maintains the relationship with staff in which shared roles are recognized and separate responsibilities respected; working relationships among trustees, employees and volunteers are based on equity and mutual respect; professional standards and practices inform and guide museum operations; policies are articulated and prudent oversight is practiced; and that governance promotes the public good rather than individual financial gain.

Collections

The distinctive character of museum ethics derives from the ownership, care and use of objects, specimens and living collections representing the world's natural and cultural common wealth. This stewardship of collections entails the highest public trust and carries with it the presumption of rightful ownership, permanence, care, documentation, accessibility and responsible disposal.

Thus, the museum ensures that: collections in its custody support its mission and public trust responsibilities; collections in its custody are lawfully held, protected, secure, unencumbered, cared for and preserved; collections in its custody are accounted for and documented; access to the collections and related information is permitted and regulated; acquisition, disposal and loan activities are conducted in a manner that respects the protection and preservation of natural and cultural resources and discourages illicit trade in such materials; acquisition, disposal and loan activities conform to its mission and public trust responsibilities; disposal of collections through sale, trade or research activities occurs solely for the advancement of the museum's mission—proceeds from the sale of nonliving collections are to be used consistently within the established standards of the museum's discipline, but in no event shall they be used for anything other than acquisition or direct care of collections; the unique and special nature of human remains and funerary and sacred objects is recognized as the basis of all decisions concerning such collections; collections-related activities promote the public good rather than individual financial gain; and competing claims of ownership that may be asserted in connection with objects in its custody should be handled openly, seriously, responsively and with respect for the dignity of all parties involved.

Programs

Museums serve society by advancing an understanding and appreciation of the natural and cultural common wealth through exhibitions, research, scholarship, publications and educational activities. These programs further the museum's mission and are responsive to the concerns, interests and needs of society.

Thus, the museum ensures that: programs support its mission and public trust responsibilities;

programs are founded on scholarship and marked by intellectual integrity; programs are accessible and encourage participation of the widest possible audience consistent with its mission and resources; programs respect pluralistic values, traditions and concerns; revenue-producing activities and activities that involve relationships with external entities are compatible with the museum's mission and support its public trust responsibilities; and programs promote the public good rather than individual financial gain.

Standards Regarding an Institutional Code of Ethics

All museums are required to have a formally approved, separate and distinct institutional code of ethics. An institutional code of ethics should: put forth the institution's basic ethical responsibilities as a museum and nonprofit educational entity (not solely be about individual conduct, e.g., conflict of interest issues); be tailored to the museum (it cannot simply be a restatement of the AAM *Code of Ethics for Museums* (2000) or a declaration of adoption of AAM's code, or simply a copy of a parent organization's code); be consistent with the AAM *Code of Ethics for Museums* (2000); state that it applies to members of the governing authority, staff and volunteers; be a single document, not a compilation or list of references to other documents; and be approved by the governing authority.

In addition, the following may be incorporated into the institutional code of ethics, or exist as separate documents, in which case they should be referenced in the institutional code of ethics:

- Sections on individual ethics, personal conduct and conflict of interest issues that spell out such details for staff, volunteers and members of the governing authority. These sections may exist separately in, for example, a personnel policy.

- Sections on collections-related ethics. These sections may exist separately in the museum's collections management policies.

- The museum may also adhere to codes of ethics specific to its discipline/collections (see below) and/or professional museum functions (e.g., *AAM Curators Code of Ethics*). Adoption of these codes cannot replace a separate institutional code. However, if the museum chooses to adhere to these codes, its code of ethics either should incorporate appropriate language from those codes or cite them and indicate that the museum will abide by them.

Museums governed by a larger institution or organization that does not have museum management as its primary operating purpose are required to have an institutional code of ethics that addresses the museum-specific issues outlined in this standard.

Purpose and Importance

An institutional code of ethics is important to ensure accountability. The effectiveness of a nonprofit institution is directly related to the public's perception of its integrity. A formally stated institutional code of ethics is evidence of a critical internal process—to write an institutional code of ethics, an institution must collectively discuss the issues it faces and determine what ethical principles are needed to guide its operations and protect its integrity.

It also ensures informed decision making: Developing and implementing an institutional code of ethics leads to informed oversight and benefits the institution in several ways. It creates internal agreement about which actions are consistent with the institution's mission. It serves as a self-made reference point for institutional choices. It also is a practical and effective tool in risk management—protecting both assets and reputation.

An institutional code of ethics expresses the institution's policies, consistent with the public service it affirms in its mission statement. It puts the interests of the public ahead of the interests of the institution or of any individual and encourages conduct that merits public confidence. It acknowledges applicable laws (including the institution's own bylaws or charter) and appropriate discipline-specific professional practices in order to help museums meet or exceed them (see below).

Implementation

A museum's ethical guidelines—either as part of its institutional code or in other approved policies (e.g., personnel policies, collections management policy)—should address: ethical duties of the governing authority, staff and volunteers; ethics related to the relationship of the governing authority and director; conflict of interest (for example: disclosure, gifts and favors, loans, outside employment, personal collecting, purchases of museum property, use of assets, confidentiality); collections ethics issues (for example: acquisition, deaccession, care and preservation/conservation, appraisals, dealing, access to the collection, truth in presentation); museum management practices (for example: legal compliance, ownership of intellectual property/scholarly research, personnel management); and the museum's responsibility to the public. In addition, it is also considered best practice to have policies that address (where applicable): management of business or individual support; commercial activities; and political activities. The institutional code of ethics should also contain a section addressing how the code will be implemented.

Expectations to Abide by Discipline-Specific Ethics Statements

Museums are expected to abide by "standards and best practices as they are generally understood in the museum field." Some discipline-specific associations have issued ethics statements or guidelines applicable to their disciplines or members. Museums should adhere to these ethics guidelines if they are: broadly applicable to all museums in that segment of the museum field; nonprescriptive—describing desirable outcomes rather than endorsing particular methods of achieving these outcomes; based when possible on applicable existing, widely accepted principles in the field; developed through a broadly inclusive process that gathers input from museums of relevant disciplines, geographic location, size, governance type and other relevant variables.

For example, history organizations are expected to adhere to The Statement of Professional Standards and Ethics of the American Association for State and Local History. Art museums that are members of the Association of Art Museum Directors are expected to adhere to Professional Practices in Art Museums of that association. When developing their codes of ethics, general museums (those that encompass two or more disciplines) must decide how these discipline-specific codes apply to their overall operations and make the reasoning behind those decisions clear.

Commentary

The AAM Code of Ethics and the Standards Regarding an Institutional Code of Ethics, taken together, establish how museums develop ethical guidelines for their institution. The AAM Code of Ethics for Museums outlines the general ethical standards that the field has agreed apply to all museums. It is not, in itself, a code of ethics that can be adopted by a museum—each museum has to write an ethics policy for itself, in alignment with any applicable national standards but tailored to its particular circumstances.

Each museum, in writing its own institutional code of ethics in conformance with the AAM code, expands on it by addressing specific issues, ensuring it fits its circumstances. Engaging the governing authority, staff and volunteers in applying the AAM code to your museum will stimulate the development and maintenance of sound policies and procedures necessary to understanding and ensuring ethical behavior by institutions and all who work for them or on their behalf.

How to Tailor a Code of Ethics to Your Museum ?

The most common problem with codes of ethics developed by museums (other than not having one, or simply saying, "We subscribe to the AAM Code of Ethics for Museums") is that many only cover the issues mentioned in the AAM code. But the code talks about issues that may affect all museums, and for which there are standards broadly agreed upon by the field. On many points, the AAM code and other ethics guidelines simply say, "This is important, and each museum has to work out the right answer for itself, guided by the following principles." Some examples of actions (with ethical implications) that a museum might choose to take or not take, or to undertake only in certain ways, and that might be addressed in the museum's institutional code of ethics include: the sale, in the museum store, of work by artists or craftsmen represented in the museum's collection; or of natural history specimens (shells, butterflies, fossils); accepting or not accepting corporate or philanthropic support from particular sources (e.g., tobacco companies, arms manufacturers, the oil industry); disclosure/confidentiality of provenance information such as the identity of donors who wish to remain anonymous, or the collecting locality of rare or endangered species; employment/supervision of a relative of an existing staff or board member; exhibition of collections belonging to or created by staff, a board member or volunteer.

Discipline-Specific Standards

It can be challenging to determine whether and when your museum should abide by discipline-specific ethical guidelines. Take the case of a general museum that encompasses art, history and natural history. Should it conform to the AASLH restriction stipulating that funds from the sale of deaccessioned material be used only for acquisition or preservation? (The term, *preservation*, while vague, is still a little more focused than AAM's proviso regarding direct care.) Is this an appropriate restriction to apply to the natural history collections? Or will the museum have different policies for funds resulting from the deaccession and sale of different parts of the collection?

Or, say your institution is an art museum, but not one whose director has been invited to join the limited membership of the Association of Art Museum Directors. Will you abide by standards set by a group that represents only part of your discipline (albeit the largest and most prominent part)?

Use of Funds Resulting from the Sale of Material Deaccessioned from the Collections

This is a tremendously controversial issue in the museum field, so much so that it deserves considerable discussion here. When the AAM Code of Ethics for Museums was revised in 1991, it said such funds could only be used for the acquisition of new collections. This was one of two issues that were so contentious they led to the statement being recalled for further editing. (The other was the proviso that AAM would enforce its membership's compliance with the Code of Ethics, which went over like the proverbial lead balloon.) The version approved in 1993, after much wrangling, added the category of "direct care" to acquisitions as acceptable use of such funds, while leaving that term open to interpretation.

This question is not just an arcane, museum-profession issue—it is a hot button for the general public, as well. If you total all the controversies that land museums in the news, use of funds from the sale of deaccessioned material accounts for a large chunk of them. Even people not familiar with museum standards understand intuitively that museums hold collections in the public trust, and that collections are not financial assets to be used to balance the museum's books or make up for monetary shortfalls.

Further complicating matters is the fact that the federal government, specifically the Internal Revenue Service (IRS), together with the Financial Accounting Standards Board (FASB) and the Government Accounting Standards Board (GASB), takes an intense interest in this subject. FASB and GASB establish the standards that determine how auditors account for collections in financial reports, and the IRS establishes how museums report financial and nonfinancial assets on their tax forms. In the 1990s, FASB pushed hard to require museums to capitalize all collections on their balance sheets and report them as financial assets. AAM and others waded into this battle and managed to forestall the move to capitalize collections—this time.

It was a difficult battle because from the viewpoint of the IRS, museums are trying to have their cake and eat it, too. We take the moral high ground, claiming the collections are not financial assets and should not be treated as such in accounting. But then we want to be able to sell them and use the cash for various purposes. So FASB and GASB conceded this point only with the stipulations that museums have to make a choice: Either restrict the use of funds from deaccessioning to acquisition of new collections (therefore keeping the value in the same class of artistic/scientific/historic assets), or use the funds for other things, as well, in which case you have to account for them as financial assets. If there is a perception that museums are generally not abiding by these rules (for example, using funds from the sale of deaccessioned material for conservation or replacing the boiler but not capitalizing the collections), the issue may well be revisited. Next time, the battle might be lost.

If the money resulting from the sale of deaccessioned collections is so contentious, then why do museums sell collections? It took a long time for people inside and outside the field to decide that it is acceptable to deaccession material from the collections at all. There has long been a strong feeling that accessioning something into the collections meant it should remain there forever, particularly in the case of donated material. No matter what the fine print on the donation form says, such acceptance seems to donors to be an implicit guarantee that their treasures will be cared for by the museum forever. It has become clear over the past few decades, however, that this principle is often at odds with the museum's obligation to make good use of its resources to benefit the public and take good care of its collections. Sometimes people make bad choices, and objects end up in a collection where they don't do anyone any earthly good, yet deplete time and resources. Museum missions change over time, and sometimes things that were a good fit a hundred years ago now fall outside the museum's scope. Sometimes a museum's reach has simply exceeded its grasp, and it has amassed collections it is unable to care for—deaccessioning into public or private hands may be more responsible than letting it deteriorate from inadequate stewardship.

But because collections are a special category of asset (cultural, scientific, artistic, rather than financial) there is a strong feeling that when something leaves the collection, any funds resulting from its sale should be used to replenish the value or utility of that category. If museums can use such funds to pay for other things, like fixing the front walk, funding education programs or underwriting the museum journal, it becomes tempting to raid the collections to supplement operating funds or the endowment. There is clear consensus in the field that this is a violation of a museum's fiduciary responsibility to raise those funds in other ways. It is fundamentally unacceptable to use collections as financial assets to sustain operational need. Selling objects from the collections in order to achieve maximum profit and to dedicate the sale proceeds to addressing long-term financial instability is an abrogation of the public trust.

But the specifics of how to apply this principle remain murky. If you accept that the museum may have good reason not to purchase new collections (no suitable material is available on the market, it is unethical to purchase such material, the museum is not adding to its collections), what can the funds be used for? Conserving existing collections may seem solid, but does this apply only to active conservation (treatment) or also to preventive conservation (which may rely heavily on archival storage materials, appropriate climate control and regular monitoring for pests)? Can it include salaries or fees for labor (such as the time of a conservator, curator or collections manager) related to preservation activities, even if such monies would be a normal part of the annual operating budget? If it is appropriate to use funds to improve conditions in storage, why not in exhibit areas? And since the museum building is an integral whole, does it not benefit the collections when the roof or electrical/mechanical/alarm/fire suppression systems are upgraded?

There are also many situations in which it is very, very tempting to chip away at the principle itself. What if the museum is going broke? The collections can't be taken care of if the whole institution goes downhill. For that matter (and this has happened), what if the museum is disposing of its collections because it is becoming a non–collections-based organization? These are not easy questions, and there are no easy answers, but exceptional cases cannot be used to establish the ethical principle that guides the mainstream of museum conduct.

Museums Inside Non-Museum Parent Organizations

Museum ethics guide the conduct of museums. What about their parent organizations? Is a university obligated to abide by museum ethics when setting policy or practice for one of its museums? Functionally, it is impossible for a small part of an organization (the museum) to dictate to a parent how it should behave. At best the museum can persuade the parent that it is ethically appropriate to let the museum abide by museum standards. Or it may point out that forcing the museum to violate the ethical guidelines people expect museums to abide by will generate bad press or endanger relations with alumni. The parent may value accreditation, and the museum might use accreditation enforcement of standards as a way to leverage compliance. In any case, it is useful to initiate these discussions prior to it actually becoming an issue. Usually parent organizations only engage in behavior their museums consider unethical if there is a significant incentive (monetary, political). It can be difficult to initiate open, unbiased discussions regarding standards of conduct for the organization once these factors are already in play.

II. Mission and Planning

Standards Regarding Institutional Mission Statements
Characteristics of Excellence Related to Mission

- The museum asserts its public service role and places education at the center of that role.

- The museum is committed to public accountability and is transparent in its mission and its operations.

- The museum has a clear understanding of its mission and communicates why it exists and who benefits as a result of its efforts.

- All aspects of the museum's operations are integrated and focused on meeting its mission.

- The museum's governing authority and staff think and act strategically to acquire, develop and allocate resources to advance the mission of the museum.

Purpose and Importance

All museums are expected to have a formally stated and approved mission that states what the museum does, for whom and why. A museum's mission statement is the primary benchmark against which to evaluate the museum's performance. One of the two core questions underlying any assessment of compliance with national standards is: *How well does the museum achieve its stated mission and goals*? This emphasis acknowledges an effective and replicable practice: Museums that use clearly delineated mission statements to guide their activities and decisions are more likely to function effectively.

A clearly delineated mission statement guides museum activities and decisions by describing the purpose of a museum—its reason for existence. It defines the museum's unique identity and purpose, and provides a distinct focus for the institution. A mission statement articulates the museum's understanding of its role and responsibility to the public and its collections, and reflects the environment in which it exists. Activities of the museum should support, directly or indirectly, the mission.

Commentary

Length

Sometimes museums trip over terminology when interpreting this standard. Some museums nowadays write short, punchy mission statements that fit on a business card or the footer of the museum's stationary. These can be inspiring, but sometimes a little vague on the specifics:

The increase and diffusion of knowledge among men.

—Smithsonian Institution, 1826

To invite learners of all ages to experience their changing world through science.

—Science Museum of Minnesota

Statements like these can be problematic in terms of describing the purpose of a museum, defining its unique identity and focus, etc., if only because of their brevity. Which isn't to say that there's not a place for statements like this (for example, on a business card or stationary). When museums write missions this brief, they may have another document (sometimes called a statement of purpose) that goes into more detail about what the museum does, for whom and why. In practice this is fine, as long as sufficient detail is captured somewhere, "sufficient" being enough to guide specific choices or assess whether the museum is meeting its mission. Other solutions might be to make the short statement a preamble to a more detailed mission statement, and then use it as an excerpt when appropriate; or have a longer mission statement and create a punchy, informal tag line that captures the spirit of the mission.

Consistency

One of the most common problems with mission statements is that if they change over time, different versions appear in different places, fossilized at the time of a given document's approval. The current statement may be in the institutional plan, but the collections policy, last revised a decade ago, contains an old version. Yet another appears in the fundraising plan (the development staff took the liberty of jazzing up the language a bit). This can be mere housekeeping, though still important, if the differences are trivial. But if the difference is substantive, reflecting a shift in what the museum has chosen to do, collect, or who it will serve, it is an extremely serious issue. The disparate versions may reflect a broader failure to review plans and policies comprehensively to make sure they are all working toward the same goal. And it may mean that parts of the staff that look to these documents for their marching orders are being sent in different directions.

Realism

Another serious problem with mission statements arises when the goals they set for the museum exceed the museum's resources. It is wonderful to aspire to be one of the most important natural history museums in the country, but do you have the collections to support this? If not, do you have a big enough budget to build such a collection and support the necessary research? Assessment of museums against the standards is grounded in the mission-based goals they set for themselves—if the mission cannot plausibly be achieved, they have sunk themselves to begin with.

It may be more appropriate to write a mission statement that is within the museum's grasp, and capture the "blue sky" thinking in a vision statement that paints a picture of what the museum would like to be in the future. That way the museum is being judged in light of something it can do, while still presenting a compelling image of what the museum could become with sufficient support.

Alignment with the Parent Institution

Museums that exist within a larger parent organization—such as a college, university, foundation, religious institution or arm of government—face particular challenges. Since they probably don't have separate articles of incorporation, they did not have to declare a formal mission statement in order to receive nonprofit status. That leaves questions of who is going to write the mission statement, who is going to approve it and with what level of authority. This can create several different kinds of problems.

If the museum staff or advisory board is given considerable latitude, they may approve a good, realistic mission statement that they proceed to implement very well. This kind of benign neglect can sometimes seem like a blessing. But when money, space or staffing gets squeezed, the parent organization often looks at the museum and says, "Huh! Is that what you are doing? It is not crucially important to us, so you get cut first." On the other hand, the parent may exercise very tight control and create a mission statement for the museum that ignores great opportunities that the staff sees clearly and would like to pursue.

For example, a college might direct its museum to put its attention solely on serving the student body. Seems reasonable, on the face of it. But the museum may be the college's best potential ambassador to the neighboring community, an important role if the town-gown relationship is strained to begin with.

These kinds of issues are best addressed by ensuring that some person or group with an appropriate level of authority in the parent organization (e.g., provost, dean, vice president) works closely with the museum staff and advisory board (if one exists) in reviewing and approving the museum's mission, and the plans built upon it. There should be a shared understanding of the museum's mission before making decisions about planning and resource allocation.

Standards Regarding Institutional Planning
Characteristics of Excellence Related to Planning

- All aspects of the museum's operations are integrated and focused on meeting its mission.

- The museum's governing authority and staff think and act strategically to acquire, develop and allocate resources to advance the mission of the museum.

- The museum engages in ongoing and reflective institutional planning that includes involvement of its audiences and community.

- The museum establishes measures of success and uses them to evaluate and adjust its activities.

Purpose and Importance

Strategic planning produces a mutually agreed-upon vision of where the museum is going and what it wants to achieve. It ensures this vision meets the needs of its audiences and community and that the museum identifies how it will obtain the resources to fulfill this vision. Planning allows the museum to make sound decisions in response to changes in its operating environment.

Museums use planning to set goals and establish strategies by which it will achieve them; to ensure that the museum acquires, develops and allocates its resources (human, financial, physical) in a way that advances its mission and sustains its financial viability; to gather appropriate information to guide its actions, including input from stakeholders and data from benchmarking; and to establish measures by which the museum will assess its achievements.

Implementation

Museums should engage in current, comprehensive, timely and formal planning for their future. Planning is current when it is up-to-date, and reflective of an ongoing process; comprehensive when it covers all relevant aspects of museum operations (e.g., not just a facility master plan); timely when it is geared to significant events in the museum's lifecycle (e.g., changes in size, scope, purpose, governance, etc.); formal when the process and outcome are documented in writing and approved by vote of the governing authority. The process should be inclusive of all stakeholders: staff, governing authority, audiences and community; ongoing; reflective; documented.

Documentation

As evidence of its institutional planning, museums should have documentation of the planning process (e.g., committee lists, meeting minutes, planning schedules) and a current, comprehensive, timely and formal institutional plan that includes both strategic and operational elements. Each museum's written institutional plan should include a multiyear and an operational plan, a combination of the two or the functional equivalent.

Each museum's planning documents will look different. However, the plan(s) should: be captured in written documents and approved by the governing authority; be based on the mission; be tied to other relevant planning documents (e.g., financial plans, development plans, interpretive plans, collections plans); set priorities helping the museum make choices and allocate available resources; identify how the institution will secure the human and financial resources needed to implement the plan by bringing resources and goals into alignment; be living documents, continually used and updated by the staff and governing authority; establish measurable goals and methods by which the museum will evaluate success; and include action steps, establish timelines and assign responsibility for implementation.

Planning by Museums Within Non-Museum Parent Organizations

Museums operated by a parent organization for which museum management is not the primary purpose (e.g., a university, or government agency) are expected to have a museum/site-specific planning process and plan, both of which should be linked to the parent organization's planning. The parent organization's planning process and documents should also reflect support for the museum's mission and ensure that museum/site-specific goals can be achieved.

Commentary

Why Plan?

I am asked time and again, "Why does my museum need a plan? We are doing a great job without one." There are so many answers to this question it is hard to know where to begin. How do you know you are doing a great job if you have not decided as a group (board, staff, stakeholders) what that job is? If that decision is not written down and approved, how do you know you all really have the same understanding of what you intend to do and how to get there? What happens if the director (who is usually the driving force in the museum) leaves? How does the next director know what the plan is and how to keep it smoothly progressing in the right direction? Without a written plan, how do you convince (fill in the blank: the public, local government, philanthropists, charitable foundations, granting agencies) that what you intend to do is worth their support? This is just the short list—other reasons abound. The fact is, planning is necessary for your museum's continued survival—not only to increase the chances that you are going in the right direction but to leverage support. Very, very few foundations, corporations or granting agencies are going to give you funds nowadays unless you have a plan that meets the characteristics outlined in this standard.

Process

Half of the value of a plan (maybe more than half) derives from the process of creating it. It is possible for one person to lock themselves in a room and concoct something that looks like an institutional plan, but it is likely to be a hollow document. Plans are more likely to be realistic, successful and well-implemented if the process of planning includes a diverse group of stakeholders including board members, staff, key supporters, members of the museum's self-identified community and neighbors. Why? The people the museum serves are the experts on whether the museum is serving them well and the best reality checkers about ideas on how to do this better. Plus, a group of people with diverse backgrounds, experience and training will consider a broader range of possibilities and do a better job analyzing the pros and cons of each. And staff, board, volunteers and community members are more likely to support the plan and do a good job implementing it if they have been involved in its development.

Content

The standard regarding planning is one of the most specific standards developed through AAM. Why all the detail? It was principally written by the Accreditation Commission, which reviews about a hundred museums each year, sees the same museums once every ten years, and has tracked some museums for more than thirty years of their existence. This gives them extensive experience observing what causes museums to succeed (or fail), and how this ties to elements in their plans. Every specific element called for in the standard (priorities, timelines, resources, assignment of responsibility) is listed because its absence has been observed to be a stumbling block for many, many museums. Think of accreditation as a big, long-term scientific experiment. Accredited museums are the guinea pigs for all museums, testing what works and what doesn't work. And they are the highest-performing museums in the country, in the opinion of their peers. If planning is crucial to their success, why would it be any less important for the other 95 percent of museums?

If you are just beginning to write your plan, I suggest you use the standard to create an outline for its contents. If you have a plan, I suggest you review it against the standard and see if there are places it may need more detail.

III. Leadership and Organizational Structure

Standards Regarding Governance
Characteristics of Excellence Related to Governance

- The governance, staff and volunteer structures and processes effectively advance the mission.

- The governing authority, staff and volunteers have a clear and shared understanding of their roles and responsibilities.

- The governing authority, staff and volunteers legally, ethically and effectively carry out their responsibilities.

- The composition and qualifications of the museum's leadership, staff and volunteers enable it to carry out the museum's mission and goals.

There is a clear and formal division of responsibilities between the governing authority and any group that supports the museum, whether separately incorporated or operating within the museum or its parent organization.

Purpose and Importance

Good governance is the foundation that enables the museum to succeed. The effective operation of a museum is based on a well-functioning governing authority that has a strong working relationship with the museum director. Together, the governing authority and director set the direction of the museum, obtain and manage the resources needed for it to fulfill its mission and ensure that the museum is accountable to the public. These expectations apply to all museums regardless of governance type, structure or name.

Implementation

The governing authority fulfills the basic responsibilities of nonprofit governance by: determining the organization's mission and purposes; selecting the chief executive and supporting and assessing his or her performance; ensuring effective organizational planning and adequate resources; managing resources effectively (including exercising good stewardship of collections and historic structures, if applicable); ensuring that the organization's programs and services advance the mission; enhancing the organization's public standing; ensuring legal and ethical integrity and maintaining accountability; recruiting and orienting new members of the governing authority; and assessing performance of the governing authority. For museums that have remote governance, these responsibilities may be spread out along a designated chain of command. In such cases, responsibilities must be clearly assigned to particular positions. For museums with joint governance, these responsibilities may be partitioned between different entities. See below regarding national standards in these situations.

Standards for Museums With Joint Governance

In museums with joint governance, in which the basic responsibilities of governance are shared between two or more groups (e.g., a city and a private, nonprofit organization, or a university and an advisory board), or when a separate entity provides resources vital to the museum's operation (e.g., land, collections, building, staff), the standards require that the museum clearly identify all the groups that are engaged in governance or provision of these vital resources, and the responsibilities of each group. These relationships should be detailed in formal, written documents (e.g., memoranda of agreement, memoranda of understanding, operating agreement).

Documentation

As evidence that good governance practices are in place and to demonstrate that the museum is meeting the Characteristics of Excellence, museums should have the following documents: mission statement; institutional plan; articles of incorporation, charter, enabling legislation or other founding document; bylaws, constitution, will or other documentation under which the museum is governed. If the museum has a parent organization, it should have documentation regarding the importance of the museum to the parent, expressing its commitment to support the museum (e.g., resolution of permanence passed by parent, parent organization's bylaws or organizing documents, memorandum of understanding or management agreement between the parent and the museum). Museums should have documentation of operational relationships with other organizations integrally connected to the museum's governance or operations (e.g., written memorandum of understanding or other type of formal agreement) and evidence of delegation of authority for operation of the museum to the museum director or the equivalent position.

Standards Regarding the Composition of the Governing Authority

A governing authority is expected to: cycle in new people and new ideas; reflect the diversity of the communities it serves; provide opportunities for external input so that the governing authority is accountable to those communities; and ensure that members of the governing authority are evaluated on their performance and nonperforming members are cycled out. *There do not have to be term limits for the service of members of the governing authority*, though this is one method traditionally employed by museums to achieve these goals.

When it is not possible to control these factors within the governing authority itself (e.g., museums within parent organizations, those with remote governance or those that are government-governed), the museum needs to find other ways to accomplish the goals outlined above. This may include establishing supporting groups as needed to assist with governance (e.g., advisory boards, auxiliary groups, community boards).

Commentary

Responsibilities of the Nonprofit Board

This standard was written to focus board members' attention on the job that is uniquely theirs to do. The basic responsibilities of nonprofit governance listed under Implementation on page 46, are adapted from Richard Ingram's classic *Ten Basic Responsibilities of Nonprofit Governance*, and are widely accepted by all types of nonprofits, not just museums. But government and the public have ever higher expectations of the level of oversight provided by what are, essentially, untrained volunteers (they may be highly trained in their professions, but are rarely trained in nonprofit governance). Many of the scandals that have dogged nonprofits in general and museums in particular in the past decade stem from the failure of the governing authority to provide appropriate oversight. Examples include excessive compensation of the chief executive officer, provision of lavish perks or even outright fraud and abuse in reimbursement of expenses; failure to realize or act on the scope of the museum's financial difficulties or to detect misleading bookkeeping and reporting on the part of staff; and engaging in or allowing the museum to engage in actions that appear to involve conflicts of interest regarding staff, board, individual or corporate donors, lenders or for-profit entities. As board members rarely have formal training in nonprofit governance or museum standards, it usually falls to museum staff to educate them regarding these responsibilities, or at least to help establish the process by which each board trains incoming members.

Reflecting the Diversity of the Community

Diversity is one of many areas in which the national standards can provide general guidance, but each museum must decide for itself the appropriate way to apply the standards. Only the museum and its constituents can identify what aspects of diversity are relevant in their circumstances and what constitutes appropriate diversity for the museum's governance. We can say a bit about the opposite—common patterns of homogeneity, why they arise and persist, and the barriers they can pose to museum excellence.

A museum's founder or founders often influence the museum long after they have passed on. One way you can see this is to look at who serves on the board of trustees. Because most boards of separate 501(c)3 museums are self-perpetuating (though some are elected by the membership) they usually select members who look a lot like them. This is natural—people are usually more comfortable working with people who share their background and experiences. And they usually recruit new board members from their circle of existing acquaintances. But it is also a problem—see discussions of diversity on pages 28 and 72. And it can be self-perpetuating, as when the museum finally reaches out to groups that have not traditionally been invited to serve on the board, only to find that they have no interest in doing so. Some of the patterns of homogeneity that we often see in museums include: affluent, socially prominent older white men, and occasionally women, particularly in organizations that are prestigious and have considerable financial resources; enthusiasts/knowledgeable amateurs—for instance, railroad enthusiasts or antique car collectors; scholars/academics—such as historians or scientists; ethnically homogeneous members—particularly if the museum interprets a particular culture or ethnic group; genealogically linked members—notably found in museums run by groups such as the Daughters of the American Revolution, Colonial Dames, Sons of the Confederacy, etc. Any of these groups can bring strengths to governing their museums. But if they are the only people at the table, they are severely limited in their ability to see a bigger picture, access diverse resources, reach out to new constituencies and build the next generation of museum visitors and board members. This effect is made worse by the fact that any one of these variables (race, ethnicity, profession, interests) may bring with them other, unintended sources of homogeneity. For example, a board of academics and scholars may contribute formidable expertise about the museum's subject area but they may have limited financial resources or access to people with such resources.

Joint Governance

At least 4 percent of museums have some form of joint governance. This may be a college or municipal museum with a separate, private nonprofit friends group that raises essential funds, or even hires part of the staff and owns the collections. It may be a museum jointly run by a city, which owns the building and collections, and a private nonprofit group contracted to hire staff and operate the museum. Sometimes the entities are so intertwined it is impossible to point to just one of them and say, "That is the museum." The museum truly arises from their pooled efforts.

These arrangements are increasingly common as museums search for successful financial models. And they are frequently successful. However, they are vulnerable at the point of intersection. What if the arrangement between the two (or three or four) entities running the museum breaks down? What if the city says it wants to take its collections back and go make another museum elsewhere? What if the friends group decides it won't provide its annual contribution to the operating fund unless the museum exhibits the collections of the group's chairperson?

Many of these arrangements function in the first place because of the level of trust that exists between people in key positions of the cooperating entities. When those people eventually leave, everything can be thrown into the air. Personal relationships are transitory—legal agreements last (at least until they are dissolved by mutual agreement or broken in court). Some organizations hesitate to propose a formal agreement with the entity that partners with them to run the museum because "things work okay now, but we are afraid things will fall apart if we bring this up." This hardly inspires confidence about the stability of the arrangement. Often the best thing a museum can do to ensure that the relationship continues to function smoothly is to capture it in a written legal agreement, enabling both parties to work out, in advance of a dispute, how they mutually want things to function.

Standards Regarding Delegation of Authority

All museums should have a director or the functional equivalent, part time or full time, paid or unpaid, to whom authority is delegated for day-to-day operations. Furthermore, the governing authority, staff and volunteers should have a clear and shared understanding of their roles and responsibilities.

Purpose and Importance

Having clear delegation of authority means that the governing authority understands the main areas of its responsibility. Those areas are to collectively determine mission, set policies for operations, ensure that charter and bylaw provisions are followed, plan for the institution, approve budgets, establish financial controls and ensure that adequate resources are available to advance the museum's mission.

Delegation of authority leads to effective leadership and organizational structure by creating clarity about the distinct roles of governance and management; this clarity allows each to focus on the work they need to do. There is communication and collaboration but no duplication of effort. Since the governing authority has appointed a director (or equivalent position) with the expertise to run the museum, it should allow the director to perform his or her responsibilities without interference.

An unencumbered line of authority allows the institution to achieve more. It promotes good use of resources, including time. The director has the authority to act independently and oversee the day-to-day operations while the governing authority uses its time to make decisions that steer the institution. Staff at all levels should be clear about the chain of command.

Documentation

Documentation of the delegation of authority may be found in the bylaws of the institution, the formally approved job description of the director (or equivalent position) and, to apprise all staff, is often stated in the institution's staff handbook.

Commentary

Delegation of Authority

You can infer, from the fact that there is a whole standard just about delegation of authority to the director that it is frequent source of tension in museums. People who serve on the governing authority, after all, do so because they are passionately interested in what the museum does. But the role assigned to the board—approving policies and budgets, planning, finding money—can seem pretty dry. If board members are lucky, they get to serve on a collections committee and shop with other people's money. But the really fun part—designing exhibits and programs, choosing the carpeting for the new wing—belongs to the staff. Is it any wonder that board members often start nudging their way into these staff functions? But doing so fatally undermines the authority of the director and the professionalism of the staff.

Delegation of authority can be especially hard to enforce in small museums run mostly or entirely by volunteers, particularly if some board members also serve as volunteers (curators, exhibit preparators, development officers or salespeople, etc.). These dual roles put them simultaneously above the director (as his or her boss and supervisor) and below (as a staff member). Many small museums operate this way, and it works well if individuals wearing two very different hats remember to switch their headgear as appropriate.

Delegation of authority can also be problematic in museums within larger parent organizations such as universities and city or state governments. Sometimes the temptation to reach down and tinker with the fun parts (exhibits, again, are ever popular, as are collections and collecting) is just overwhelming to administrators. This standard can help museum directors explain to the (fill in the blank: provost, city manager, mayor, governor) why their direct intervention in museum operations is inappropriate.

IV. Collections Stewardship

Standards Regarding Collections Stewardship
Characteristics of Excellence Related to Collections Stewardship

- The museum owns, exhibits or uses collections that are appropriate to its mission.

- The museum legally, ethically and effectively manages, documents, cares for and uses the collections.

- The museum conducts collections-related research according to appropriate scholarly standards.

- The museum strategically plans for the use and development of its collections.

- The museum, guided by its mission, provides public access to its collections while ensuring their preservation.

- The museum allocates its space and uses its facilities to meet the needs of the collections, audience and staff.

- The museum has appropriate measures in place to ensure the safety and security of people, its collections and/or objects, and the facilities it owns or uses.

- The museum takes appropriate measures to protect itself against potential risk and loss.

Purpose and Importance

Stewardship is the careful, sound and responsible management of that which is entrusted to a museum's care. Possession of collections incurs legal, social and ethical obligations to provide proper physical storage, management and care for the collections and associated documentation, as well as proper intellectual control. Collections are held in trust for the public and made accessible for the public's benefit. Effective collections stewardship ensures that the objects the museum owns, borrows, holds in its custody and/or uses are available and accessible to present and future generations. A museum's collections are an important means of advancing its mission and serving the public.

Implementation

Museums are expected to: plan strategically and act ethically with respect to collections stewardship matters; legally, ethically and responsibly acquire, manage and dispose of collection items as well as know what collections are in its ownership/custody, where they came from, why it has them and their current condition and location; and provide regular and reasonable access to, and use of, the collections/objects in its custody.

Achieving this standard requires thorough understanding of collections stewardship issues to ensure thoughtful and responsible planning and decision making. With this in mind, national standards emphasize systematic development and regular review of policies, procedures, practices and plans for the goals, activities and needs of the collections.

How Does a Museum Assess Whether Its Collections and/or Objects Are Appropriate for Its Mission?

This is determined by comparing the institution's mission—how it formally defines its unique identity and purpose, and its understanding of its role and responsibility to the public—to two things: (1) the collections used by the institution; and (2) its policies, procedures and practices regarding the development and use of collections (see also the Standards Regarding Institutional Mission Statements).

A review of a museum's collections stewardship practices examines: whether the mission statement or collections documents (e.g., collections management policy, collections plan, etc.) are clear enough to guide collections stewardship decisions; whether the collections owned by the museum, and objects loaned and exhibited at the museum, fall within the scope of the stated mission and collections documents; and whether the mission and other collections stewardship-related documents are in alignment and guide the museum's practices.

Assessing Collections Stewardship

There are different ways to manage, house, secure, document and conserve collections, depending on their media and use, and the museum's own discipline, size, physical facilities, geographic location and financial and human resources. Therefore, one must consider many facets of an institution's operations that, taken together, demonstrate the effectiveness of its collections stewardship policies, procedures and practices, and assess them in light of varying factors. For instance, museums may have diverse types of collections categorized by different levels of purpose and use—permanent, educational, archival, research and study, to name a few—that may have different management and care needs. These distinctions should be articulated in collections stewardship-related policies and procedures. In addition, different museum disciplines may have different collections stewardship practices, issues and needs related to their specific field. Museums are expected to follow the standards and best practices appropriate to their respective discipline and/or museum type as applicable.

The standards require that:

- A current, approved, comprehensive collections management policy is in effect and actively used to guide the museum's stewardship of its collections.

- The human resources are sufficient, and the staff have the appropriate education, training and experience to fulfill the museum's stewardship responsibilities and the needs of the collections.

- Staff are delegated responsibility to carry out the collections management policy.

- A system of documentation, records management and inventory is in effect to describe each object and its acquisition (permanent or temporary), current condition and location and movement into, out of and within the museum.

- The museum regularly monitors environmental conditions and takes proactive measures to mitigate the effects of ultraviolet light, fluctuations in temperature and humidity, air pollution, damage, pests and natural disasters on collections.

- An appropriate method for identifying needs and determining priorities for conservation/care is in place.

- Safety and security procedures and plans for collections in the museum's custody are documented, practiced and addressed in the museum's emergency/disaster preparedness plan.

- Regular assessment of, and planning for, collection needs (development, conservation, risk management, etc.) takes place and sufficient financial and human resources are allocated for collections stewardship.

- Collections care policies and procedures for collections on exhibition, in storage, on loan and during travel are appropriate, adequate and documented.

- The scope of a museum's collections stewardship extends to both the physical and intellectual control of its property.

- Ethical considerations of collections stewardship are incorporated into the appropriate museum policies and procedures.

- Considerations regarding future collecting activities are incorporated into institutional plans and other appropriate policy documents.

Commentary

Collections Stewardship: The Big Picture, and Then the Details . . .

No other area of museum standards is backed up by more technical literature, interpreting every nuance to the nth degree. Perversely enough, this can make it more difficult, not less, to adapt the standards to the museum's mission, goals and circumstances, as specified by the "Two Core Questions." Reams of research have been published on the effects of temperature and humidity on a variety of materials. The pros and cons of wet pipe versus dry pipe (not to mention pre-action) fire suppression systems have been endlessly debated. None of this helps a small, local historical society clearly answer the question: "What climate control (if any) or fire suppression (ditto) should we install in our historic, one-room schoolhouse?" Because it is all too easy to become bogged down in a morass of detail, for this area of the standards it is particularly useful to start with the big picture, as baldly stated in the Characteristics of Excellence in Translation:

Know what stuff you have.

Know what stuff you need.

Know where it is.

Take good care of it.

Make sure someone gets some good out of it . . .

Especially people you care about . . .

And your neighbors.

This big-picture view keeps you focused on outcomes rather than methods. The museum staff can then thoughtfully choose benchmarks for the desired results, and work backwards from that to the appropriate details of implementation, factoring in the museum's resources, both human and financial.

For example, "Know what stuff you have" refers to records-keeping and inventory, of course. The museum needs records (paper and/or electronic) of what it owns, its origin, significance, history of use, location and condition. Before you leap into an online debate with your colleagues on Museum-L about the relative merits of cataloguing software, stop and assess the scope of your collection and what you are doing with it. Is your museum a small, all-volunteer historic house with 200 objects that does not loan or borrow material? Maybe it is enough for you to make a duplicate copy of your physical card catalogue (on archival card stock, of course) to keep off-site. On the other hand, if you have a paleontology collection with a few hundred thousand specimens, and its primary users are international researchers, you may need a first-class relational database capable of publishing catalogue data to the Web in a searchable format, compatible with any relevant data standards. If you curate an art museum, you may need digital visual documentation of every work of art, of a quality suitable both for scholarly use and insurance purposes. As with all areas of collections care, the appropriate solution can only be assessed relative to the collections, their needs, their users and the museum's mission and resources.

Climate Control

Climate control is a particularly contentious issue, both because the associated mechanical systems can soak up a seemingly endless supply of funds to design, build, adjust and maintain, and because there is no absolute standard for "correct" climate control. For one thing, museums usually store and display more than one kind of collection, and different materials (pottery, fabric, painted wooden panels, furniture, taxidermy specimens, minerals, fluid specimens) have different optimal conditions for temperature and relative humidity. It is rarely practical for museums to have a storage room with separately adjustable climate controls for each and every material type. Even if you can afford a climate-control system that can maintain precisely whatever climate you choose, the settings are a compromise between the needs of these different collections.

For another thing, climate control is a classic example of "the perfect is the enemy of the good." Climate-control systems are expensive, and complex systems are notoriously fin-icky and difficult to maintain. Many museums might be better off installing a serviceable, resilient system that does a pretty good job of maintaining a set point with acceptable fluctuations, and putting the money they did not spend on a "state of the art" system into materials and labor to create microclimates (cases, plastic bags, desiccants) or provide quality pest management or security. "Taking good care of it" is the cumulative effect of a balanced approach to all these actions.

For museums that exist in, or primarily are, historic houses or sites, climate-control systems can actually be destructive, not only to the historic integrity but also to the actual fabric of the house. While the historic house community is currently working to formulate standards on this issue, there is already consensus that minimal climate control is often the appropri-ate approach for certain historic structures. Opening and closing the windows at the right times of the year, thus using the "passive control" systems a house was designed to exploit, may be both historically appropriate and the most effective way to conserve some buildings. What about the furnishings, costumes, archives and other materials that may be housed in such a structure? It might be more responsible for the organization to make strategic choices about displaying replicas or storing and displaying certain works in a separate, climate-controlled modern building.

Even in buildings that are merely functional rather than intrinsically historic in value, theo-retical "best temperature and humidity" may be neither practical nor desirable. In climates with naturally very low humidity, trying to maintain 55 percent RH in the museum could be disastrous to the museum's energy bill and to the building. A brick building can literally pull itself to pieces in such conditions, as the interior moisture migrates through the walls to the outer, drier environment.

Collections Planning

The good news about collections stewardship is that most of the problems museums en-counter (overcrowded storage, need for climate control, staff for records-keeping, care, cleaning and pest control, etc.) can be solved simply with money. Not that money is neces-sarily easy to get, but at least the right solution is pretty straightforward once you consult the literature, confer with colleagues and make some rational choices. This is unlike some areas of performance such as governance, for which the problems tend to be interpersonal and political—and much harder to solve! (For example, a founding board that is unwilling to step aside for the new generation or adapt to the museum's changing needs—that one is not going to get fixed by something as simple as money.)

There is one big, thorny problem, however, in collections stewardship that money, per se, can't solve: "Know what stuff you need." Many museums (perhaps the majority) spend part of their precious resources taking care of materials that do not advance their mission, serve their audiences or support the exhibits, educational or research plans. This comes about for entirely understandable reasons. Many museums have legacy collections dating back to the founder, whose original vision for the museum may be far different from the role it plays now. Many museums built their collections over decades by accepting what was offered, often with no guiding template other than: "It fits our (very broad) mission, and it is neat stuff." With infinite resources, such materials would not be a problem. It might even (to paraphrase a frequent justification for keeping it) "be of some use someday." But no museum (not even the Smithsonian or the Getty) has infinite resources—there is always a limit to the time, space and money a museum has to care for collections and make them accessible, and all collections it cares for compete for these resources.

Collections planning is the process of making conscious, proactive choices about what belongs in the collections in light of the museum's mission, purposes and audiences. It actively shapes the collections to support the stories the museum intends to tell or the questions its users ask. While national standards do not yet call for all museums to have a collections plan, there is a growing consensus that it is a core document that helps the museum make wise choices and assures key supporters that the museum is making thoughtful use of the resources they contribute. Within the next decade, a collections plan will probably be as de rigueur as a collections management policy.

Best Practices Regarding Loaning Collections to Non-Museum Entities

Museums hold collections in trust for the public. As stewards, museums fulfill their fiduciary and ethical responsibilities by preserving, caring for and providing access to collection objects for the benefit of the public. AAM recognizes that some museums loan objects from their collection to non-museum entities and encourages museums that do so to consider best practices for collections care and accessibility, and public accountability.

In some instances, loaning objects from the collection to non-museum entities may jeopardize the level of care provided for the items. This may constitute a breach of a museum's public trust responsibility and be perceived as an inappropriate or unethical use of objects held and maintained for the benefit of the public. Further, loaning objects from the collection to non-museum entities may result in inappropriate or inadequate practices in collections documentation and limit public access to the items.

If a museum engages in the practice of loaning objects from the collection to organizations other than museums, such a practice should be considered for its appropriateness to the museum's mission; be thoughtfully managed with the utmost care and in compliance with the most prudent practices in collections stewardship, ensuring that loaned objects receive the level of care, documentation and control at least equal to that given to the objects that remain on the museum premises; and be governed by clearly defined and approved institutional policies and procedures, including a collections management policy and code of ethics.

Commentary

Museums are often pressured by key supporters to lend to non-museum entities. This could be another nonprofit (schools, universities, hospitals, foundations), a for-profit business or a government entity. For example, a local bank that is a major donor to the museum may request a loan of art to hang in its corporate headquarters. A municipal museum may be expected to loan fine or decorative art to the mayor's office or official residence. While some people wish museums could agree that this is wrong, which would enable staff to cite national standards when they deny such requests, it isn't that simple. In some cases these loans may advance the museum's mission by reaching key audiences and expanding their opportunities to exhibit collections. In some cases it is political reality that such loans will take place. Responsible practices call for the museum to distinguish between acceptable uses (for example, displays in a climate-controlled, secure public space of a school, business or government building) that serve the public, and uses that may benefit individuals or private companies at the expense of the public good.

Standards and Best Practices Regarding the Unlawful Appropriation of Objects During the Nazi Era

This area of collections stewardship is of such sensitivity and high importance that it has separate standards and best-practice statements regarding a museum's obligations. These statements have been promulgated by the field to provide guidance to museums in fulfilling their public trust responsibilities.

Standards Regarding the Unlawful Appropriation of Objects During the Nazi Era

The reader is directed to the AAM website (www.aam-us.org) for a text of the standards that includes an introduction and history of how they were formulated, as well as AAM's commitment to supporting implementation.

General Principles

The American Association of Museums (AAM), the U.S. National Committee of the International Council of Museums (ICOM-US), and the American museum community are committed to continually identifying and achieving the highest standard of legal and ethical collections stewardship practices. The AAM Code of Ethics for Museums states that the "stewardship of collections entails the highest public trust and carries with it the presumption of rightful ownership, permanence, care, documentation, accessibility, and responsible disposal."

When faced with the possibility that an object in a museum's custody might have been unlawfully appropriated as part of the abhorrent practices of the Nazi regime, the museum's responsibility to practice ethical stewardship is paramount. Museums should develop and implement policies and practices that address this issue in accordance with these guidelines.

These guidelines are intended to assist museums in addressing issues relating to objects that may have been unlawfully appropriated during the Nazi era (1933–1945) as a result of actions in furtherance of the Holocaust or that were taken by the Nazis or their collaborators. For the purposes of these guidelines, objects that were acquired through theft, confiscation, coercive transfer or other methods of wrongful expropriation may be considered to have been unlawfully appropriated, depending on the specific circumstances.

In order to aid in the identification and discovery of unlawfully appropriated objects that may be in the custody of museums, the Presidential Advisory Commission on Holocaust Assets in the United States (PCHA), Association of Art Museum Directors (AAMD), and AAM have agreed that museums should strive to: (1) identify all objects in their collections that were created before 1946 and acquired by the museum after 1932, that underwent a change of ownership between 1932 and 1946, and that were or might reasonably be thought to have been in continental Europe between those dates (hereafter, "covered objects"); (2) make currently available object and provenance (history of ownership) information on those objects accessible; and (3) give priority to continuing provenance research as resources allow. AAM, AAMD and PCHA also agreed that the initial focus of research should be European paintings and Judaica.

Because of the Internet's global accessibility, museums are encouraged to expand online access to collection information that could aid in the discovery of objects unlawfully appropriated during the Nazi era without subsequent restitution.

AAM and ICOM-US acknowledge that during World War II and the years following the end of the war, much of the information needed to establish provenance and prove ownership was dispersed or lost. In determining whether an object may have been unlawfully appropriated without restitution, reasonable consideration should be given to gaps or ambiguities in provenance in light of the passage of time and the circumstances of the Holocaust era. AAM and ICOM-US support efforts to make archives and other resources more accessible and to establish databases that help track and organize information.

AAM urges museums to handle questions of provenance on a case-by-case basis in light of the complexity of this problem. Museums should work to produce information that will help to clarify the status of objects with an uncertain Nazi-era provenance. Where competing interests may arise, museums should strive to foster a climate of cooperation, reconciliation and commonality of purpose.

AAM affirms that museums act in the public interest when acquiring, exhibiting and studying objects. These guidelines are intended to facilitate the desire and ability of museums to act ethically and lawfully as stewards of the objects in their care, and should not be interpreted to place an undue burden on the ability of museums to achieve their missions.

Standards
1. Acquisitions
It is the position of AAM that museums should take all reasonable steps to resolve the Nazi-era provenance status of objects before acquiring them for their collections—whether by purchase, gift, bequest or exchange.

a. Standard research on objects being considered for acquisition should include a request that the sellers, donors or estate executors offering an object provide as much provenance information as they have available, with particular regard to the Nazi era.

b. Where the Nazi-era provenance is incomplete or uncertain for a proposed acquisition, the museum should consider what additional research would be prudent or necessary to resolve the Nazi-era provenance status of the object before acquiring it. Such research may involve consulting appropriate sources of information, including available records and outside databases that track information concerning unlawfully appropriated objects.

c. In the absence of evidence of unlawful appropriation without subsequent restitution, the museum may proceed with the acquisition. Currently available object and provenance information about any covered object should be made public as soon as practicable after the acquisition.

d. If credible evidence of unlawful appropriation without subsequent restitution is discovered, the museum should notify the donor, seller or estate executor of the nature of the evidence and should not proceed with acquisition of the object until taking further action to resolve these issues. Depending on the circumstances of the particular case, prudent or necessary actions may include consulting with qualified legal counsel and notifying other interested parties of the museum's findings.

e. AAM acknowledges that under certain circumstances acquisition of objects with uncertain provenance may reveal further information about the object and may facilitate the possible resolution of its status. In such circumstances, the museum may choose to proceed with the acquisition after determining that it would be lawful, appropriate and prudent and provided that currently available object and provenance information is made public as soon as practicable after the acquisition.

f. Museums should document their research into the Nazi-era provenance of acquisitions.

g. Consistent with current practice in the museum field, museums should publish, display or otherwise make accessible recent gifts, bequests and purchases, thereby making all acquisitions available for further research, examination and public review and accountability.

2. Loans
It is the position of AAM that in their role as temporary custodians of objects on loan, museums should be aware of their ethical responsibility to consider the status of material they borrow as well as the possibility of claims being brought against a loaned object in their custody.

a. Standard research on objects being considered for incoming loan should include a request that lenders provide as much provenance information as they have available, with particular regard to the Nazi era.

b. Where the Nazi-era provenance is incomplete or uncertain for a proposed loan, the museum should consider what additional research would be prudent or necessary to resolve the Nazi-era provenance status of the object before borrowing it.

c. In the absence of evidence of unlawful appropriation without subsequent restitution, the museum may proceed with the loan.

d. If credible evidence of unlawful appropriation without subsequent restitution is discovered, the museum should notify the lender of the nature of the evidence and should not proceed with the loan until taking further action to clarify these issues. Depending on the circumstances of the particular case, prudent or necessary actions may include consulting with qualified legal counsel and notifying other interested parties of the museum's findings.

e. AAM acknowledges that in certain circumstances public exhibition of objects with uncertain provenance may reveal further information about the object and may facilitate the resolution of its status. In such circumstances, the museum may choose to proceed with the loan after determining that it would be lawful and prudent and provided that the available provenance about the object is made public.

f. Museums should document their research into the Nazi-era provenance of loans.

3. Existing Collections
It is the position of AAM that museums should make serious efforts to allocate time and funding to conduct research on covered objects in their collections whose provenance is incomplete or uncertain. Recognizing that resources available for the often lengthy and arduous process of provenance research are limited, museums should establish priorities, taking into consideration available resources and the nature of their collections.

Research

a. Museums should identify covered objects in their collections and make public currently available object and provenance information.

b. Museums should review the covered objects in their collections to identify those whose characteristics or provenance suggest that research be conducted to determine whether they may have been unlawfully appropriated during the Nazi era without subsequent restitution.

c. In undertaking provenance research, museums should search their own records thoroughly and, when necessary, contact established archives, databases, art dealers, auction houses, donors, scholars and researchers who may be able to provide Nazi-era provenance information.

d. Museums should incorporate Nazi-era provenance research into their standard research on collections.

e. When seeking funds for applicable exhibition or public programs research, museums are encouraged to incorporate Nazi-era provenance research into their proposals. Depending on their particular circumstances, museums are also encouraged to pursue special funding to undertake Nazi-era provenance research.

f. Museums should document their research into the Nazi-era provenance of objects in their collections.

Discovery of Evidence of Unlawfully Appropriated Objects

g. If credible evidence of unlawful appropriation without subsequent restitution is discovered through research, the museum should take prudent and necessary steps to resolve the status of the object, in consultation with qualified legal counsel. Such steps should include making such information public and, if possible, notifying potential claimants.

h. In the event that conclusive evidence of unlawful appropriation without subsequent restitution is found but no valid claim of ownership is made, the museum should take prudent and necessary steps to address the situation, in consultation with qualified legal counsel. These steps may include retaining the object in the collection or otherwise disposing of it.

i. AAM acknowledges that retaining an unclaimed object that may have been unlawfully appropriated without subsequent restitution allows a museum to continue to care for, research and exhibit the object for the benefit of the widest possible audience and provides the opportunity to inform the public about the object's history. If the museum retains such an object in its collection, it should acknowledge the object's history on labels and publications.

4. Claims of Ownership

It is the position of AAM that museums should address claims of ownership asserted in connection with objects in their custody openly, seriously, responsively and with respect for the dignity of all parties involved. Each claim should be considered on its own merits.

a. Museums should review promptly and thoroughly a claim that an object in its collection was unlawfully appropriated during the Nazi era without subsequent restitution.

b. In addition to conducting their own research, museums should request evidence of ownership from the claimant in order to assist in determining the provenance of the object.

c. If a museum determines that an object in its collection was unlawfully appropriated during the Nazi era without subsequent restitution, the museum should seek to resolve the matter with the claimant in an equitable, appropriate and mutually agreeable manner.

d. If a museum receives a claim that a borrowed object in its custody was unlawfully appropriated without subsequent restitution, it should promptly notify the lender and should comply with its legal obligations as temporary custodian of the object in consultation with qualified legal counsel.

e. When appropriate and reasonably practical, museums should seek methods other than litigation (such as mediation) to resolve claims that an object was unlawfully appropriated during the Nazi era without subsequent restitution.

f. AAM acknowledges that in order to achieve an equitable and appropriate resolution of claims, museums may elect to waive certain available defenses.

5. Fiduciary Obligations

Museums affirm that they hold their collections in the public trust when undertaking the activities listed above. Their stewardship duties and their responsibilities to the public they serve require that any decision to acquire, borrow, or dispose of objects be taken only after the completion of appropriate steps and careful consideration.

a. Toward this end, museums should develop policies and practices to address the issues discussed in these guidelines.

b. Museums should be prepared to respond appropriately and promptly to public and media inquiries.

Best Practices Regarding the Unlawful Appropriation of Objects During the Nazi Era

Public awareness of the extent to which cultural property was unlawfully appropriated during the Nazi era is greater than ever. Though much of the property was recovered and returned, or its owners compensated, there is still material unaccounted for. Therefore, the museum community strives to identify this material in order that restitution may be made.

Because they hold their collections in trust for the public, it is important for museums to identify this material. Stewardship of collections "carries with it the presumption of rightful ownership, permanence, care, documentation, accessibility and responsible disposal," as articulated in the AAM Code of Ethics for Museums. AAM views the issue of unlawful appropriation of objects during the Nazi era as one of high significance for all museums.

Museums are directed to the Standards Concerning the Unlawful Appropriation of Objects During the Nazi Era, developed in 1999 by a joint working group appointed by the AAM Board of Directors and ICOM-US Board. Museums are also directed to AAM Recommended Procedures for Providing Information to the Public about Objects Transferred in Europe During the Nazi Era, formulated pursuant to an agreement reached in October 2000 between AAM, the Association of Art Museum Directors (AAMD), and the Presidential Advisory Commission on Holocaust Assets in the United States (PCHA).

Museums are encouraged to register and participate in the Nazi-Era Provenance Internet Portal (NEPIP). This website (www.nepip.org) provides a searchable registry of objects in U.S. museum collections that were created before 1946 and changed hands in Continental Europe during the Nazi era (1933–1945). By participating in the Portal, museums that have such objects in their collections fulfill their responsibility under the Guidelines and Recommended Procedures adopted by the museum field to make Nazi-era provenance information accessible.

Commentary

Wrestling with the ethical dimensions of material that may have been unlawfully appropriated during the Nazi era has served as a prelude for the museum field to the more general issue of claims regarding cultural property. The standards regarding Nazi-era assets set an example for how such ethical decisions can be approached.

At the very least a museum should be aware of the origin of the material it might acquire, research these issues and make a thoughtful decision in alignment with its mission, policies and values that it is able and willing to explain to the public. Remember the Standards in Translation—being good means more than just following the law. Museums are obliged to consider ethical implications of their actions and weigh whether the outcomes they pursue are defensible in the court of public opinion, as well as the court of law.

The manner in which a museum treats claimants sets the tone for how this relationship will play out—and may determine whether the issue is resolved through mediation or goes to court. Handling claims promptly and respectfully can lead to relatively amicable and mutually productive discussions. Appropriate steps for a museum include promptly reviewing the claim, conducting its own research and asking for the claimant's research. If the object is in the museum's collection and there is credible evidence of unlawful appropriation without restitution, the museum should seek to resolve the matter with the claimant.

In many cases, a museum may have options to perfect its legal title to an object by invoking a narrow, technical defense in court (such as expiration of a statute of limitations). Museums should not resort to such defenses until they have first achieved an ethical determination based on an examination of all the available research. The availability of technical legal defenses is not an invitation to invoke the law to thwart an ethical outcome.

V. Education and Interpretation

Standards Regarding Education and Interpretation
Characteristics of Excellence Related to Education and Interpretation

- The museum clearly states its overall educational goals, philosophy and messages, and demonstrates that its activities are in alignment with them.

- The museum understands the characteristics and needs of its existing and potential audiences and uses this understanding to inform its interpretation.

- The museum's interpretive content is based on appropriate research.

- Museums conducting primary research do so according to scholarly standards.

- The museum uses techniques, technologies and methods appropriate to its educational goals, content, audiences and resources.

- The museum presents accurate and appropriate content for each of its audiences.

- The museum demonstrates consistent high quality in its interpretive activities.

- The museum assesses the effectiveness of its interpretive activities and uses those results to plan and improve its activities.

Commentary

Considering that education and interpretation are the core of all museums' activities, it may seem a bit surprising that there is little in the way of detailed standards, beyond the above Characteristics, elaborating on what museums must do to fulfill their basic obligations in this area of operation. (See Standards Regarding Exhibiting Borrowed Objects, which does provide additional commentary on a narrow but important issue, p.73.) I offer the following observations on why this may be so.

First, museums are generally pretty good at education and interpretation. Remember I said at the beginning of this book that standards evolve to address things that are actually problems. Perhaps, as a field, we have not developed standards in this area because we do not feel there is any difficulty to be addressed. Second, there is no consensus on objective criteria for what constitutes "good education" or "good interpretation." At the narrow, technical level there are guidelines on writing and designing labels or building accessible exhibits, but is there really only one good way to write an exhibit label? To teach a program? To deliver content via the Web? Finally, this standard is another area where "good" can only be assessed in the context of the museum's mission, audiences and resources. You can't measure it by volume—a little museum mounting one changing exhibit a year and producing four public programs may be doing a better job, and making better use of its resources, than a similar museum that strains its finances and staff to produce three changing exhibits and twelve programs.

I can offer a few observations, however, about aspects of education and interpretation that often present challenges to many museums.

Diversity of Audience

Some museums were founded to serve the interests of a rather specific, sometimes narrowly defined, community. The unifying characteristic might be culture (Swedish Americans), interests (aviation enthusiasts) or genealogy (Daughters of the American Revolution). From one perspective, this is a museum's choice—each museum identifies its own mission and audience. Many feel, however, that if this audience is too narrowly defined the museum is, in effect, excluding people potentially interested in their topic, and therefore not serving the interests of the public in a broad sense. And it is the public, as a whole, that supports the museum through its tax-exempt status. On a practical level, few museums can afford to serve a narrowly defined audience, particularly as the demographic of any community tends to change over time, through aging, migration and shifts in interest. The smaller the group served by the museum, the more likely it is to find itself marginalized and without viable support.

Thus the Characteristics specify that a museum "understand the characteristics and needs of... its potential audiences" and that "the museum strives to be inclusive and offers opportunities for diverse participation." This paints a picture of an institution that tries to engage a broad variety of users, which will influence the stories and messages the museum chooses to tell and how it delivers them. For example, a historic house museum that focuses solely on the business and political accomplishments of its well-off, Caucasian, male owner may be missing aspects of interpretation that would engage the attention of other audiences— the stories of the women who managed the household, or the servants or slaves who made this lifestyle possible. Railroad enthusiasts may focus primarily on technological achievements, when there are broader stories to be told about economics, migration and social and geographic mobility, to name a few.

Evaluation

In the absence of well-defined standards for education or interpretation, the most meaningful assessment is to measure whether it is working! The Accreditation Commission, in wrestling with standards for interpretation, has returned again and again to the thought that it would be sufficient if museums (a) defined what they wanted to achieve through their interpretive activities (interpretive planning); (b) measured whether they achieved their goals; and, of course, (c) took corrective action if necessary. Unfortunately, evaluation challenges many museums, even large ones with significant resources. There is an abundance of literature, many consultants and a plethora of evaluation schema to assist museums in this area. The best advice I have for museums wanting to demonstrate excellence in education and interpretation is to invest in a systematic, formal, ongoing program of evaluation for exhibits, programs and other interpretive activities, and to use the results of this evaluation to guide improvements in this area of operations.

Standards Regarding Exhibiting Borrowed Objects

The reader is directed to the AAM website (www.aam-us.org) for a copy of the standard that includes a preamble and history of the development of this standard.

Before considering exhibiting borrowed objects, a museum should have in place a written policy, approved by its governing authority and publicly accessible on request, that addresses the following issues:

1. Borrowing Objects
The policy will contain provisions:

a. Ensuring that the museum determines that there is a clear connection between the exhibition of the object(s) and the museum's mission, and that the inclusion of the object(s) is consistent with the intellectual integrity of the exhibition.

b. Requiring the museum to examine the lender's relationship to the institution to determine if there are potential conflicts of interest or an appearance of a conflict, such as in cases where the lender has a formal or informal connection to museum decision making (for example, as a board member, staff member or donor).

c. Including guidelines and procedures to address such conflicts or the appearance of conflicts or influence. Such guidelines and procedures may require withdrawal from the decision-making process of those with a real or perceived conflict, extra vigilance by decision makers, disclosure of the conflict or declining the loan.

d. Prohibiting the museum from accepting any commission or fee from the sale of objects borrowed for exhibition. This prohibition does not apply to displays of objects explicitly organized for the sale of those objects, for example craft shows.

2. Lender Involvement

The policy should assure that the museum will maintain intellectual integrity and institutional control over the exhibition. In following its policy, the museum:

a. should retain full decision-making authority over the content and presentation of the exhibition;

b. may, while retaining the full decision-making authority, consult with a potential lender on objects to be selected from the lender's collection and the significance to be given to those objects in the exhibition;

c. should make public the source of funding when the lender is also a funder of the exhibition. If a museum receives a request for anonymity, the museum should avoid such anonymity where it would conceal a conflict of interest (real or perceived) or raise other ethical issues.

Commentary

Why is the subject of borrowing objects—out of all the areas of performance related to education and interpretation—the one singled out for an explicit standard? Because it is one that often lands museums in the news, and not in a good way. It manages to hit many of the hot buttons that attract the attention of the press, the public, regulators and funders: conflict of interest, private profit subsidized by public support, integrity and trustworthiness of content.

And it illustrates the fact that we write standards to deal with things that actually happen. Notably, one famous incident that occurred just prior to the writing of this standard was the "Sensations" exhibition at the Brooklyn Museum. In that case, Charles Saatchi, noted collector of edgy, young British artists, lent his collection to the museum for a major exhibition. There were two areas of controversy surrounding this exhibit—the biggest public outcry was actually about content. (The Catholic community particularly objected to the work "Holy Virgin Mary" by Chris Ofili, which incorporated elephant dung and cutouts of female genitalia from pornographic magazines.) However, it also raised issues about process. The museum initially did not divulge that Saatchi, in addition to lending the works, both exerted considerable control over the curatorial content and provided significant financial support. Taken together with the fact that, to a degree unusual among collectors, Saatchi has a reputation for "flipping" collections (selling large portions after they have appreciated in value), it looked to the press, public and the mayor of the New York City as if Saatchi were perhaps using the museum, which receives considerable city funding, for his private benefit.

This case also illustrates one of the reasons compelling museums to develop their own voluntary standards. It is tempests like these that create the greatest risk of government (federal, state or local) stepping in to impose outside control over abuses of the public trust. And while the "Sensations" case may seem like a very specific (and extreme) example, the general issue arises quite often. Some other examples: A staff member, volunteer or board member is willing to lend a collection for an exhibit. Is there a perception that this inflates the potential selling price of these items, and could the lender have pressured the museum to include the collection? The museum is cultivating a major collector, hoping that the collection will be donated to the museum in the long run. As part of the courtship, the museum mounts an exhibit entirely consisting of works borrowed from this collector. The collector wants to exert considerable control over which works are displayed, and how, and what is said about them. When does this cross the boundary into exerting inappropriate levels of influence over intellectual content(Particularly if the museum staff disagrees with the donor's choices...) ?

VI. Financial Stability

Standards Regarding Financial Stability
Characteristics of Excellence Related to Financial Stability
- The museum legally, ethically and responsibly acquires, manages and allocates its financial resources in a way that advances its mission.

- The museum operates in a fiscally responsible manner that promotes its long-term sustainability.

Commentary
Short, sweet, to the point. While there are many standards from outside the museum field that impinge on this area of operations (e.g., Financial Accounting Standards Board standards, the Association of Fundraising Professionals' Code of Ethical Principles and Standards of

Professional Conduct, the Panel on the Nonprofit Sector's Principles for Good Governance and Ethical Practice), museums are mostly concerned that: (1) they have enough money; (2) it was raised in an appropriate way; and (3) it is spent in accordance with the mission. There are separate standards statements dealing with what to do if there is not enough money and how to insure that the money comes from appropriate sources (with no inappropriate strings attached). See the text of these standards below.

Executive Compensation

The third point, "spent in accordance with the mission," deserves special attention. In the past decade, the press, the public and regulators have become increasingly sensitive to the issue of nonprofit executive compensation. It is a matter of some concern if the museum director's compensation is much higher than that of his or her peers, disproportionate to the museum's overall expenditures or includes perks that seem unduly lavish or unrelated to his or her duties. The press and public become particularly outraged by the perks. Actual examples from recent stories in the news include swimming pool maintenance, high-end, handmade furnishings for the director's home and first-rate travel and accommodations.

The issue of unduly high salary is more pernicious, however. More and more often, museums are engaged in major expansions, new buildings by name-brand architects, new ventures and large capital campaigns. This means there is a lot of pressure on directors to bring in big money. Some boards decide the best way to do this is to hire chief executives from the private sector, people with a background in law or financial management. Such candidates bring with them business-sector expectations regarding compensation. Also, some directors from the nonprofit sector decide that the best way to cultivate high-end donors is to adopt their lifestyle. Even if the financial equation seems clear ("if we pay this guy $x, he can bring in $y with his contacts, which is a net gain"), there is still the issue of public perception, which cannot be ignored. The public regards nonprofit museums as charities and expects museum directors to display a degree of frugality in keeping with that status. It is, after all, the public's money that is being spent, to a large extent. It behooves museums to critically examine appropriate compensation levels for their chief executives, including benchmarking themselves with their peers and with other nonprofits supported by their community.

Standards Regarding Developing and Managing Business and Individual Donor Support

The reader is directed to the AAM website (www.aam-us.org) for the original, full version of this text that includes recommended procedures for documenting donor support, as well as notes regarding legal and tax compliance.

General Principles

- **Loyalty to mission.** To ensure accountability and informed decision making, museums should develop written policies, approved by their governing authorities, guiding the museum's development and management of business and individual support in a manner that protects their assets and reputation and is consistent with their mission.

- **Public trust and accountability.** The museum community recognizes and encourages appropriate collaborations with a variety of stakeholders, including a museum's donors. Such support often comes with expectations regarding involvement in the museum's activities. It is essential to a museum's public trust responsibilities that it maintain control over the content and integrity of its programs, exhibitions and activities.

- **Transparency.** Museums should provide business and individual donors with accurate information about mission, finances and programs.

- **Fidelity to donor intent.** Museums should use support from business and individual donors for purposes that are mutually agreed upon.

- **Ethics and conflict of interest.** In soliciting and managing business and individual support, the museum should comply with the AAM Code of Ethics for Museums and its own ethics policies, with particular attention to potential conflicts of interest.

- **Confidentiality.** A museum should ensure that information about donations is handled with respect for the wishes of the donor and with confidentiality to the extent provided by law.

Purpose and Importance

Not-for-profit, charitable, educational and scientific organizations and those they serve have always benefited from the business sector and the generosity of individual donors. Businesses and individual donors also have benefited from their relationships with the museum community. Through association with museums, businesses seek to positively affect their enterprise by showing their commitment to a not-for-profit's mission, generating goodwill within communities in which they operate and increasing the recognition of their business identity. Through their generosity, donors reaffirm their commitment to the arts, sciences, history and lifelong learning and to creating a stronger and more civil society by making objects and information accessible. In addition, individual donors often have family connections or other close personal relationships with the museums they support.

In light of often intricate museum-donor relationships, AAM has worked with the field to create these standards on developing and managing business and individual donor support. While these standards provide general guidance, it is essential that each museum draft its own policies appropriate to its mission and programs.

Managing Support

Museums should create policies regarding business and individual donor support either as separate documents or as part of other museum policies. A museum should be consistent in following its policy; any changes should be driven by evolving standards and best practices and the institution's mission and strategic direction. A museum should not change policy solely in response to a specific situation.

These policies should: identify the museum's goals for developing and managing support; define the responsibilities of the governing body and staff for decisions about business and individual donor support, including but not limited to solicitation, gift acceptance, fulfillment, recognition and public inquiry; ensure that the museum has the necessary human and financial resources for fulfilling its obligations in any donor relationship; and address conflicts of interest in situations involving business or individual donor support opportunities in which a member of the museum's governing authority or staff may have an interest.

Conflict of Interest

The policy should address the obligation of members of the staff or governing authority to disclose any interest in the relationship under consideration. Such disclosure does not imply ethical impropriety. The museum may require that the individual recuse himself from any discussion and/or action regarding support from a business or donor with whom he or she is associated or has an interest, and document the individual's role in any other aspect of the project or program supported by that donation.

Donor Communication and Relationships

The policy should clearly identify which staff or governing body members are authorized to make or change agreements with businesses or individual donors. In addition, a museum should have a clear policy concerning the level of financial, tax and legal information it will provide to supporters, including a policy of recommending that they consult their own legal and financial advisors.

Types of Support a Museum Will Accept

A museum should develop a gift acceptance policy outlining the types of support it accepts from businesses or individual donors and delineating a process for determining whether or not—from a mission, operational, business and legal perspective—to accept a gift as offered. A museum should determine whether it will exclude any business or category of business because of the business's products and services, taking into consideration the characteristics, values and attitudes of its community and audience, discipline and mission. In deciding whether to exclude certain supporters a museum may wish to consider: products and services provided by a business; the business practices of the potential supporter; and whether to associate certain exclusions with particular activities (e.g., children's programming).

Recognition

A museum should consider the range of recognition it may offer a business or individual donor. In doing so, it should consider general standards for recognizing donor support based on the level of support received, such as those relating to the use, placement, size of names and signage.

Confidentiality

A museum should ensure that a relationship of trust is established and maintained with its donors by respecting the private nature of information about the donor and the donation, if appropriate. In doing so, it may consider developing a system to control access to and handling of donor information; balancing the museum's obligation to maintain public accountability with its obligation to protect donors' privacy by outlining what type of information can and cannot be kept confidential; and collecting only relevant information about donors or potential donors.

Anonymity

A museum must determine whether and under what circumstances it will accept anonymous gifts. A museum should avoid agreeing to requests for anonymity that conceal a conflict of interest, real or perceived, or raise other ethical concerns.

Uncollectable Pledges

Situations may arise when donors cannot or do not honor a pledge. In determining the enforceability of a pledge that is not honored, a museum may consider legal and accounting implications; the overall impact of the gift on the museum; the museum's history and previous relationship with the donor; and the attitude of the community toward the situation.

Documentation

A museum should require that all documents relating to the development of donor support be maintained and retained in accordance with applicable law and record-retention policies.

Application of Policy

A museum should identify clearly all entities, such as friends groups, voluntary organizations, components of a museum system, etc., that must comply with its policies about business and individual donor support.

Public Accountability

A museum should respond to all public and media inquiries about its support from businesses and individual donors, including allegations of unethical behavior, with a prompt, full and frank discussion of the issue, the institution's actions and the rationale for such actions.

Issues Related Specifically to Business Support
Use of Museum Names and Logos

A museum should set clear parameters for the use of any of its names and logos by a business supporter. In creating such a policy a museum might address: the contexts in which it will permit such use; its responsibility to approve all uses of its names and logos; specific prohibitions; and conformity with its policies for protecting intellectual property (e. g., trademark, copyright).

Promotion of the Museum-Business Relationship

A business may wish to promote its relationship with a museum in its marketing, advertising and public relations activities. In its policy, a museum might address: limits on the scope of how and the extent to which a business may promote its relationship with the museum, and the responsibility of the museum to approve any such promotion.

Support from Vendors
Current or potential relationships between a museum and a vendor providing goods or services should not be contingent upon a contribution from the vendor.

Exclusive Arrangements
A museum should carefully consider whether or not it is willing to enter into a relationship with a business that restricts the museum from receiving support from the business's competitors or from using a competitor's products and services.

Commentary
Balancing Expectations
Because most nonprofit museums are tax exempt and receive so much of their income from public sources (government funding), they are held to a high standard of conduct. And yet U.S. museums rarely have guaranteed sources of government funding, unlike their European colleagues. They are expected to aggressively pursue other sources of support, as well, including private funding. These funders—individuals or businesses—bring their own expectations to this relationship. Corporations increasingly see sponsorships as a business rather than a charitable arrangement. They want value for their money in terms of publicity and exposure. Individual donors care deeply about the museum and its mission and may be deeply vested in a project and want to be involved in key decisions regarding its execution. And while these standards specifically cite individual donors, they are equally applicable to the family foundations some of these donors have created.

These motivations are not inherently bad, they are merely human. But it is the museum's obligation to acknowledge and manage these expectations in a manner that is consistent with the public trust. A typical situation that requires careful thought occurs when museums court major collectors by mounting shows devoted to works from their collections. In some cases the press or public have questioned whether these exhibits unduly benefit the collector by increasing the value of the featured works. Some have raised the issue of whether these exhibits represent the highest curatorial judgment regarding quality and the best use of the museum's space and time. Another situation occurs when a corporate sponsor may be perceived to have an interest in the message behind an exhibit: an oil company funding an exhibit examining conservation in Alaska, for example, or a pharmaceutical company supporting an exhibit exploring traditional versus alternative medicine. The public may presume (rightly or wrongly) that the funder influenced the content. Such doubts can erode one of museums' most valued assets—our reputation for accuracy and objectivity. Application of the standards in such instances will help museums identify potential conflicts before they blossom into controversies, make appropriate decisions consistent with their policies and conventions of the field and justify their actions to the public and press in a credible manner.

Donor Intent

Donor intent can become a point of controversy as a museum seeks to respond sensibly to changing circumstances while honoring the original terms of a gift. At the extreme end of the spectrum are high-profile situations such as that of the Barnes Foundation in Merion, Pa. Some contend it would be truer to the intent of Albert Barnes (and his curmudgeonly resolve to snub the artistic establishment) to abolish the institution than to move it to downtown Philadelphia, even if that were the only way to ensure its survival. Such people, like strict constructionists of the U.S. Constitution, believe that donor intent is so rigid as have no flexibility, even if the proposed use seems to adhere to the spirit of the gift. Unfortunately, if the donor is dead, there is no way to ask, though sometimes family members can be approached for a proxy blessing on a reasonable alteration to the purposes for the original gift. At some point this becomes a legal issue, as the administration of such gifts is supervised by the attorney general of the state in which the museum is incorporated. But, as with so many of the issues raised in this book, the museum should grapple with the ethical dimensions of its decision before the AG becomes involved.

Standards Regarding Retrenchment or Downsizing

In these challenging economic times many museums are experiencing a dramatic loss of income from multiple sources, including endowments, parent organizations, funding agencies, admissions and museum store sales. In response, many museums make changes in their governance, staffing and operations. These actions can be necessary and appropriate steps in securing the museum's future. Sometimes, however, downsizing or retrenchment is mistakenly assumed to be an indicator of bad management. This standard addresses the issues of downsizing and retrenchment, and how they may affect museums.

Downsizing and retrenchment can be responsible and necessary corrective actions in response to financial reductions. When preparing for retrenchment, museums: focus on retaining their ability to fulfill their mission and serve their community; take actions consistent with the highest ethical, fiscal and management standards in the museum field; and carefully consider the effect of their actions on their staff, their community and the collections they hold in trust for the public.

The following observations provide guidance regarding application of these standards to issues that commonly arise when a museum is considering downsizing or retrenchment.

Collections

Collections often receive special scrutiny during retrenchment either because of the expense of maintaining them appropriately or because of their potential as financial assets. In considering the role of collections in retrenchment, museums are guided by the following principles.

Collections are held in trust for the public, and a primary responsibility of the governing authority is to safeguard this trust. The museum may determine that it is unable in the long run to appropriately care for some parts of its collections. In such cases, the most responsible action may be to deaccession and transfer material to another suitable caretaker in an orderly manner that safeguards the collections and their documentation. Museums may carefully consider whether it is appropriate for the material to remain in the public domain at another nonprofit institution or whether it can responsibly be placed through public sale. Deaccessioning, however, is never a fast or simple solution. It may take a great deal of time and other resources to research the material in question, determine its provenance, identify any restrictions on the title and arrange for an appropriate and safe transfer. In the short run, it may actually require additional expenditures on the part of the museum to conduct the necessary research, prepare the documentation, arrange for disposition and affect the transfer. Deaccessioning is part of a long-term, thoughtful decision on the part of the museum about how best to fulfill its mission with available resources. It is conducted in accordance with standards and best practices in the field, and with the museum's own code of ethics, collections planning and collections policies.

Various statements of ethics in the museum field prescribe what can be done with the funds resulting from deaccessioning. All museums are expected to abide by the AAM Code of Ethics for Museums and by any additional codes of ethics particular to their discipline. The

AAM Code of Ethics for Museums specifies that proceeds from sales resulting from deaccessioning can be used only for acquisitions or direct care of collections. While the interpretation of "direct care" varies between museums and disciplines, there is a strong consensus that it does not include use of funds to pay operational expenses. The code of ethics of the Association of Art Museum Directors (AAMD) explicitly specifies that art museums can only use funds resulting from deaccessioning for the acquisition of new collections, and that of the American Association of State and Local History (AASLH) specifies that history museums can use such funds only for acquisition or preservation.

There is increasing pressure on museums to capitalize their collections and to use them as collateral for financial loans to the museum. The AAM Code of Ethics for Museums requires that collections be "unencumbered," which means that collections cannot be used as collateral for a loan. The AAMD code of ethics also precludes using collections as collateral, and further bars museums from capitalizing collections. The AASLH has also issued a position statement that declares that capitalizing collections is unethical.

A museum's collections are valuable only insofar as they are accessible to the public and to scholars and the information inherent in them is preserved through documentation and the knowledge of those who care for them. "Mothballing" collections, i.e., putting them in storage and eliminating or minimizing curation and use, may seem a desirable short-term strategy for cost reductions, but it carries measurable risks. Many kinds of collections are not stable in storage without constant monitoring and attention. Often, collections can be made accessible in a meaningful way only through the mediation of an experienced, knowledgeable staff that, once dismantled, may not easily be rebuilt.

Human Resources

Museums often reduce staff size in response to financial reductions. This may be accomplished by leaving positions temporarily unfilled, eliminating individual positions or eliminating whole departments or program areas. In considering the reduction of staff as a part of retrenchment, museums consider the short-term and long-term needs of the institution. Leaving a position vacant when a staff member departs is less traumatic than laying off existing staff. It can also, however, leave key positions and vital roles unfilled at a crucial time. Museums weigh the needs of the staff and the needs of the institution in choosing a strategy for staff reductions.

Museums also consider the impact of downsizing on the museum's programs and operations.

The museum's mission is accomplished primarily through its staff, but many museums also rely on volunteers and partnerships with other institutions. Staff reductions are planned in light of the overall impact on the museum's mission and activities and as part of an overall strategy for scaling back operations, supplementing paid staff with volunteers or partnerships or other strategies for accomplishing the museum's goals.

Museums in Non-Museum Parent Organizations

Museums that are part of a college or university or organized under municipal, county or state government have additional factors that affect their response to a financial crisis. When parent organizations need to make financial cuts, the museum may bear a disproportionate portion of the burden. Many museums within larger parent organizations have increased their financial stability by cultivating diverse sources of income. This is particularly important to museums in parent organizations. Museums that derive significant portions of their income from outside sources are less dependent on funding from their parent organizations. This minimizes the impact of funding cuts from the parent and the likelihood that the parent will see eliminating the museum as an attractive financial strategy.

Museums can also develop a separately incorporated friends organization. A separate 501 (c)3 support group can provide significant income, serve as an advocate for the museum and buffer it against sudden organizational changes. A formal memorandum of agreement between the parent and the friends group can ensure that the support organization has a voice in any decisions concerning the museum's future.

Another strategy is to embed the museum in the parent organization's operations. A museum that is an integral part of its parent organization is less likely to be an immediate target for financial reductions by the parent. By being strongly connected to the community served by the parent, reaching out to a broad constituency, attracting new sources of funding, garnering positive publicity and, most of all, being valued by a large number of people, a museum makes itself less vulnerable to cutbacks. An active and engaged constituency will encourage the parent organization to continue its support.

Parent organizations usually have no legal obligation to continue to operate a museum. They may not consider the possibility that the museum can lose accreditation as a result of changes made as part of retrenchment. AAM, representing the public's interest of stewardship of collections held in the public domain, urges parent organizations to take into account the following moral, ethical and practical issues. First, museums are a part of an institution's long-term strategy of civic engagement. Any decisions regarding the future of museums operated by a parent organization should take into account their long-term role in serving the broader public good. While in the short run, cutbacks to a museum may result in financial savings, in the long run they may damage the parent organization's ability to serve its community and reach out to a broad audience. And second, museums operate in the public interest and hold their collections as a public trust. If a parent organization is considering downsizing or closing a museum, it has an ethical obligation to do so in a manner that safeguards the public's interest. The fate of the collections must be carefully considered. Having taken on the obligation of caring for collections, the parent must plan to transfer this stewardship to another suitable caretaker in an orderly manner that safeguards the collections and their documentation. The new caretaker should be carefully chosen with attention to its ability to care for the collections and to continue to provide public and scholarly access. As discussed earlier in this standard, this process may require additional resources in the short term and may not be a useful strategy for immediate cost savings.

VII. Facilities and Risk Management

Standards Regarding Facilities and Risk Management
Characteristics of Excellence Related to Facilities and Risk Management

- The museum is a good steward of its resources held in the public trust.

- The museum demonstrates a commitment to providing the public with physical and intellectual access to the museum and its resources.

- The museum complies with local, state and federal laws, codes and regulations applicable to its facilities, operations and administration.

- The museum allocates its space and uses its facilities to meet the needs of the collections, audience and staff.

- The museum has appropriate measures to ensure the safety and security of people, its collections and objects and the facilities it owns or uses.

- The museum has an effective program for the care and long-term maintenance of its facilities.

- The museum is clean, well maintained and provides for visitors' needs.

- The museum takes appropriate measures to protect itself against potential risk and loss.

Purpose and Importance

Museums care for their resources in trust for the public. It is incumbent upon them to ensure the safety of their staff, visitors and neighbors, maintain their buildings and grounds, and minimize risk to the collections that they preserve for future generations. Conscious, proactive identification of the risks that could potentially harm people and collections, and appropriate allocation of resources to reduce these risks are vital to museum management.

Implementation

Simply put, a museum should manage its facilities, e.g., buildings and grounds, in such a manner as to ensure that they are clean, well maintained, safe and accessible.

Risk management is an institution-wide activity encompassing functions as diverse as building and site security, visitor services, integrated pest management, storage and use of hazardous materials, and insurance. A museum should manage risk to ensure: that risks to people (visitors, staff, neighbors) and to collections are accurately identified and assessed; that appropriate methods are employed to avoid, block, mitigate, share and assume or insure against risk; and that resources are appropriately allocated so as to have the greatest effect on reducing risk to people, facilities and collections.

Museums should also have regular, adequate training of staff in implementing an emergency-preparedness plan, including practice or drills; inspections related to facilities and risk (fire, health and safety, etc., as appropriate to the institution's circumstances); a process for addressing deficiencies identified in these inspections; and a program of health and safety training for staff and volunteers, as appropriate to the institution's circumstances. Museums are expected to comply with all applicable local, state and federal laws, codes and regulations.

Standards for Facilities and Risk Management as Related to Contractors

When museums contract key services related to facilities (e.g., food service, museum store, housekeeping, security), they are expected to require contractors to abide by national standards regarding facilities and risk management. If the museum does not have control over the contract governing this relationship (e.g., a city hires and supervises contractors operating in the museum's building), the museum should educate contractors on national standards and encourage them to abide by them.

Standards for Museums Housed in Historic Structures

Museums housed in historic structures should balance the preservation needs of the building with actions necessary to mitigate risk to people and to the collections housed in the building. The standards do not dictate specifically how this is achieved; they focus instead on the outcome of appropriate risk management. For example, a historic house museum needs to weigh all relevant factors (mission, resources, impact on the structure, alternative mitigation techniques) when deciding whether to install an automated fire suppression system. In order to be accountable, the institution should be able to explain how its decisions are appropriate to its circumstances.

Documentation

Museums should have a current, comprehensive emergency/disaster-preparedness plan that is tailored to the institution's needs and specific circumstances; covers all relevant threats; addresses staff, visitors, structures and collections; includes evacuation plans for people; specifies how to protect, evacuate or recover collections in the event of a disaster; and delegates responsibility for implementation. Museums should also have certificates of inspection related to facilities and risk, as appropriate to their circumstances, when such certificates are provided by the inspecting agency.

Commentary

Emergency Preparedness

Recent research by Heritage Preservation revealed the appalling state of emergency-preparedness planning in the United States. Only 20 percent of museums have an emergency-preparedness plan that covers collections and staff trained to implement it. Yet such plans are essential to museums fulfilling their roles as good stewards of the cultural, artistic, historic and scientific resources they hold in trust for the public. As a museum works toward meeting national standards, AAM strongly urges that it prioritize the development of an emergency-preparedness plan and training of staff in implementation.

Insurance

Museums frequently ask whether museum standards require them to carry insurance on their collections. The answer is no, they don't. What they do mandate is a well-considered, balanced approach to risk management that provides appropriate protection overall for people, facilities and collections. For most museums, some level of collections insurance is one element in this approach. Even if the collections are unique and in that sense irreplaceable in the event of a loss, insurance enables the museum to acquire new collections that provide some comparable benefit to its audience. It is far preferable, however, to prevent such a loss to begin with, and in allocating resources the museum should carefully examine how to balance prevention and mitigation (human and automated security systems, climate control, fire suppression, conservation) with insurance.

Section 3 Completing the Picture

The Universe of Museum Standards and Best Practices

When Are Other Standards Applicable to Your Museum?

There are many, many standards promulgated by groups large and small, inside and outside the museum field, which may influence museums. The most prominent of these are discussed below. Museums may come across or be presented with standards, however, from a variety of sources. It may help to examine the following criteria in deciding whether these standards are appropriate guides for your museum's policies and procedures.

Are the standards in question formally adopted or endorsed by at least one nonprofit organization that is broadly representative of the field, or of the segment of the field to which the standards apply? Are they broadly applicable to museums of all types and sizes? Or if only applicable to particular segments of the museum field (e.g., discipline-specific standards), then are they broadly applicable to all museums of that segment? Are they nonprescriptive—describing desirable outcomes, rather than endorsing particular methods of achieving those outcomes? Are they based, when possible, on applicable existing, widely accepted principles and practices in the field? Have they been developed through a broadly inclusive process that gathers input from museums of relevant disciplines, geographic location, size, governance type and other relevant variables? Have they been reviewed through a broadly inclusive process that invites, formally reviews and incorporates input? Are they restricted to areas of practice for which there exists broad consensus in the field? And finally, are they consonant with sound management of the museum as a whole?

Consider these questions, assess whether your museum is represented by the group promulgating the standards and decide whether it is appropriate for you to adopt them as voluntary standards. A general museum, for example, that includes both history and natural history collections should consider whether it will abide by both the American Association for State and Local History's standards and those of the Society for the Preservation of Natural History Collections. An art museum that has not been invited to participate in the Association of Art Museum Directors should consider whether it will abide by these standards even though they have been developed with the input of only a segment of the field.

It is very important to discuss these options in advance of any actual decision that would be influenced by the standards, as the looming real-world consequences of such decisions can have unfortunate effects on people's judgment. Also, creating or revising policies while a controversial decision is in play can lead the public to question the integrity of the process.

Other Major Sources of Standards Relevant to Museums

The following is a list of other major sources of standards relevant to museums and the most prominent of the policy documents they present to the field. Consult the AAM website for a more extensive list and for links to these documents.

Museum-Related Professional Associations (Discipline or Function Specific, Regional)

American Association for State and Local History (AASLH)

- Statement of Professional Standards and Ethics

- Ethics Position Paper #1: Capitalization of Collections

- Ethics Position Paper #2: When a History Museum Closes

American Institute for Conservation of Historic and Artistic Works

- Code of Ethics and Guidelines for Practice

American Public Gardens Association

- Voluntary Code of Conduct for Botanic Gardens and Arboreta

- Code Regarding Invasive Plant Species

Association of Art Museum Directors (AAMD)

- Professional Practices in Art Museums

- Report on Sacred Objects

- Report on Incoming Loans of Archaeological Material and Ancient Art

- Report of the AAMD Task Force on Collecting
- Report of the AAMD Task Force on Nazi Looted Art, Addendum

Association of Children's Museums

- ACM Standards Document **Association of Railway Museums**
- Recommended Practices for Railway Museums

Association of Science-Technology Centers

- Accessible Practices

Association of Zoos and Aquariums

- Code of Professional Ethics

International Council of Museums

- ICOM: Code of Ethics for Museums

International Committee for Documentation (CIDOC) of the International Council of Museums (ICOM)

- International Guidelines for Museum Object Information

Midwest Open Air Museums Coordinating Council

- Statement of Professional Conduct

Museum Store Association

- Code of Ethics
- Ethics Policies for Archaeological and Ethnological Resources
- Ethics Policies for Endangered Natural Heritage

National Initiative for a Networked Cultural Heritage and the Humanities

- Guide to Good Practice in the Digital Representation and Management of Cultural Heritage Materials

National Park Service's Northeast Region

- NPS: Guidelines for the Treatment of Historic Furnished Interiors in Accordance with the Secretary of the Interior's Standards for the Treatment of Historic Properties

The Secretary of the Interior

- Standards for the Treatment of Historic Properties Includes Standards for Preservation, Rehabilitation, Restoration and Reconstruction

Society for the Preservation of Natural History Collections

- Guidelines for the Care of Natural History Collections

Southeastern College Art Conference

- Guidelines for College and University Museums and Galleries

Tri-State Coalition for Historic Places

- Standards and Practices for Historic Site Administration

Associations Representing the Broader Nonprofit or Academic Sector

American Historical Association

- Standards for Museum Exhibits Dealing with Historical Objects
- Statement on Standards of Professional Conduct

Association of Fundraising Professionals

- Code of Ethical Principles and Standards of Professional Practice
- The Accountable Nonprofit Organization

BBB Wise Giving Alliance

- Standards of Charitable Accountability

College Art Association

- Guidelines Concerning Part-Time Professional Employment
- Guidelines Adopted by CAA Regarding the Hiring by Museums of Guest Curators, Exhibitors/Artists and Catalogue Essayists as Outside Contractors
- Professional Practices for Art Museum Curators
- Resolution Concerning the Acquisition of Cultural Properties Originating in Foreign Countries

- Resolution Concerning the Sale and Exchange of Works of Art by Museums

Independent Sector
- Principles for Good Governance and Ethical Practice: A Guideline for Charities and Foundations

National Council on Public History
- NCPH: Ethics Guidelines

AAM Standing Professional Committees and Standards

AAM currently has 13 Standing Professional Committees representing professional segments of the field (registrars, curators, security, educators, managers, public relations and marketing staff, evaluators, media and technology staff, exhibit designers, development and membership) as well as small museums, professionals involved in museum training programs and people concerned about the issue of staff diversity. Many of these committees have developed standards or best practice statements related to the areas of museum operation that fall within their purview. As of this writing, these standards have not yet been reviewed and approved as national standards and best practices by the AAM board, Accreditation Commission and Council of Standing Professional Committees. For this reason, they are not yet endorsed by AAM as an association. However, they represent the best thinking of professionals in these fields of endeavor on the issues faced in their work. As they are reviewed, revised and approved by AAM's governance, they will be posted to the AAM website and added to future editions of this book.

The major documents promulgated by the Standing Professional Committees are:

Code of Ethics for Registrars, developed by the Registrars Committee (RCAAM)

Code of Ethics, 1991, developed by the Development and Membership Standing Professional Committee (DAM)

Code of Practice for Couriering Museum Objects, developed by the Registrars Committee (RCAAM)

Curators Code of Ethics, 1996, developed by the Curators' Committee (CurCom)

Professional Standards for the Practice of Audience Research and Evaluation in Museums, developed by the Committee on Audience Research and Evaluation (CARE)

Standards and Best Practice in Museum Education, developed by the Committee on Education (EdCom)

Standards for Museum Exhibitions and Indicators of Excellence, developed by the Standing Professional Committees Council

Suggested Guidelines in Museum Security, developed by the Museum Association Security Committee in collaboration with the Museum, Library and Cultural Properties Council of American Society for Industrial Security International

Trends and Potential Future Standards

We can't foresee the future, but we can make some pretty good guesses based on monitoring discussions among the museum field, coverage by the press, legislative efforts by regulators and expectations of funders. Based on these observations, it is likely that the following trends will influence standards in the coming years.

Transparency and Accountability

Policymakers at the state and federal level will continue to raise the bar for nonprofit accountability. If nothing else, as long as Sen. Charles Grassley (R-Iowa) continues to be re-elected, nonprofits in general, and some museums in particular, will continue to receive close scrutiny. In order to avoid inappropriate or overly prescriptive legislative mandates governing our behavior, museums will need to develop more stringent voluntary standards regarding reporting their own financial and programmatic performance as well as compensation of directors and board members. Groups like BBB-Wise Giving, Charity Navigator and GuideStar are encouraging private donors to require a good deal of performance information from museums before handing over their funds. If museums don't develop voluntary standards for what they report to the public and how, it is likely to be imposed upon us.

What you can do to be prepared: Think about what the public, press, policymakers and funders want to know about your museum, and what you want them to know. Start designing ways to make this information available. The World Wide Web is a fabulous medium for sharing information at relatively low cost. Documents you might want to share broadly include your mission statement, institutional plan, audited financial statements, IRS 990 reporting form and key policy documents (ethics, collections management, etc.). Think about designing your own measure of success—a score sheet, as it were—to shape how your constituents assess your progress. Basic information might include simple "outputs" (counts) of attendance, acquisitions, number of exhibits, programs and publications. It is even more powerful to report on results (outcomes) based on evaluation data. How did your major new exhibit change the knowledge, beliefs and attitudes of visitors? How has your high school internship program affected the career choice of participants? Did your marketing partnership with local merchants help direct visitor spending into the local economy? Taking charge of how such information is compiled and shared both demonstrates appropriate stewardship of public resources and ensures that you maintain control of your museum's image.

Planning, Planning and Yet More Planning

You may have noticed the recurring phrase in the Standards in Translation that reiterates that museums should "decide what they are going to do... and put it in writing." Grant makers and philanthropic foundations are increasingly concerned that recipients of their funding demonstrate that they know what they are going to do with the funds, and that their plan is part of an integrated, sustainable vision for the museum. The Institute of Museum and Library Services used to give general operating support—but that time is gone forever. The Government Performance and Results Act (GPRA) sounded the death knell for that era in the realm of federal grants when it became law in 1993. Federal granting agencies need to be able to demonstrate what, precisely, the public's money is being used to accomplish. Private foundations are increasingly adopting the same approach.

What you can do to be prepared: Planning isn't rocket science; it doesn't have to require expensive consultants or massive amounts of staff time. A small museum can make planning part of the institutional culture by starting to write things down as decisions are made, and ensure these written versions are approved by the board and shared with everyone. No elaborate template is necessary—just start simple and build from there. A bigger museum with more complex operations can devote more resources to formal planning, and probably needs to. The larger the staff and budget and the more projects the museum is engaged in at one time (exhibits, programs, publications, research, fundraising), the more important it is that these activities be integrated, prioritized and understood by all involved. The time you put into planning will be repaid by the increased effectiveness of your activities and increased ability to raise support to make the plans a reality.

Evaluation

At the other end of the pipeline, both government and private funders increasingly expect formal evaluation data to demonstrate that the plan actually worked and had measurable effects (whether the evaluation addresses the knowledge and attitude of visitors or the economic health of the community). Frankly, there is already strong consensus in the museum field that evaluation is necessary and desirable. The only thing that has kept it from being codified in national standards is the fact that so many museums, even accredited ones, would immediately flunk the standard. This is evidently a very difficult thing to do well (even at large museums with a lot of resources), but the day is coming when museums are going to have to figure it out.

What you can do to be prepared: Evaluation isn't rocket science, either, but it may be chemistry lab—a little more complex and harder to master than planning, judging from the progress (or lack thereof) of the field in adopting it. Take small steps first. Think about the desired outcomes of any given project or activity and decide, at least conceptually, how you would measure whether it was successful. Identify your most important projects and activities, and start implementing an evaluation program for these areas of operations. Include at least a small line item for evaluation in the budgets for these projects and activities, identify who on staff is responsible for designing and conducting the evaluation and make sure the results are actually shared and used to make decisions. Help is often available from local colleges or universities. Find out whether students in related fields of study are required to do individual or class projects and enlist their aid. Use free online project evaluation resources such as that available from the Institute of Museum and Library Services.

Green Design

There is increasing pressure from within and outside the field for museums to take greater responsibility for the health of our environment by adopting eco-friendly principles for operation and design. There is not any national standard regarding "green" design at this time, but it will be an item for discussion by the field in the coming decade.

What you can do to be prepared: Discuss with the board and staff whether they value and feel the museum ought to adopt ecologically conscious business practices. Are such practices related to your mission? Even if the answer is "no," do people feel that these practices are in alignment with your values as a business and with the expectations of your community? If so, then start considering ecological impact as one aspect of decision making and start identifying small steps that can make a difference. First steps can be as simple as providing recycling bins in public and staff areas, using recycled materials for office and program supplies, supporting low-impact commuting (car pools, public transport, bicycling) among staff in tangible ways and using low-energy appliances and office equipment. As opportunities for larger impact arise (renovations, a new building project, upgrades to building systems), factor green design into your decision making and budgeting. Some museums are designing buildings to Leadership in Energy and Environmental Design (LEED) standards, either with or without formal certification.

Collections Planning

There is not yet an expectation that each museum have a collections plan, but it is highly likely that in the near future this will become a document required by national standards—and will be as fundamental as an institutional plan or a code of ethics. (See the discussion of this issue under Collections Stewardship.)

What you can do to be prepared: Consider starting collections planning in advance of it becoming a standard. A collections plan can help your museum build a shared vision for the collections, set priorities for acquisitions and improvements to care, and convince collectors to donate specific material or funders to support collections care needs. Even if you feel you already have this vision, having it in writing and formally approved by the governing authority helps you make a compelling case for support. It can give the museum the energy boost it needs to tackle necessary, appropriate (but usually not enjoyable) deaccessioning. And you may well find that when you bring staff, board members and external constituents into the planning discussion, there is not as much of a shared vision as you thought.

Cultural/Biological/Intellectual Property Issues

If you follow the news at all, you are aware of the heightened international concern regarding ownership and repatriation of cultural property. Recently Italy, Greece and Peru have all aggressively pursued claims against museums for material that they feel was acquired, exported or retained in contravention of the laws of its country of origin. The legal aspects of this fall outside the scope of our discussion. Of course museums are expected to abide by the law, though with cultural property questions, picking your way through the morass of national and international laws and treaties is itself a challenge. The ethical aspects, however, are very much our business and will affect how the legal aspects play out, both in terms of the potential for new treaties or regulations and in how foreign governments (or the U.S. government) choose to pursue legal claims. The museum field is currently grappling with the ethical dimensions of acquisitions and claims regarding antiquities and archaeological materials. Soon there will be national and discipline-specific standards and best practices guiding museum conduct in these areas. The next frontiers will be biological material (e.g., genetic prospecting, ethnobotany, paleontological specimens) and intellectual property (e.g., cultural knowledge regarding traditional medicine and ownership/intellectual control of songs, stories, religious and cultural ceremonies).

What you can do to be prepared: Start by reviewing your internal standards for documentation of acquisitions. Do you require staff to aggressively check documentation to uncover potential problems, or is it sufficient that the donor or seller provide assurances? Identify all areas of your operations (collecting, research, loans, exhibits, publications) that potentially trigger concerns in any of the areas mentioned above. Being aware of the ethical dimensions of these activities and the concerns of source countries or native cultures enables you to begin creating your own policies regarding appropriate behavior. This, in turn, will shape the field's dialogues on these issues and help us to develop appropriate national standards to guide museums and provide support for their decisions.

Troubleshooting
Problems . . .

When the public, press or policymakers don't like the way an individual museum or museums in general are behaving, they have a number of very effective ways to apply pressure. Members of the public can withhold their support in the form of attendance, donations or their vote on local initiatives important to the museum, such as bond levies or easements. They can write letters to the press and to representatives at the local, state and federal levels of government. They can also ask the attorney general of their state to take action if they feel a legal abuse of the museum's obligations as a servant in the public trust has occurred.

The press can do an extremely effective job of spreading bad news, whatever it is, catching the attention of the public and policymakers. News outlets may or may not fairly represent your position in the matter, and they may or may not accurately present the facts. But one big story can expose more people to your museum than any single piece of PR you have paid for—without your having control over the message.

Policymakers can withhold funds at the state or local level (or at least they can try). Most importantly for the field as a whole, they may take away the freedom of museums to self-regulate if they feel that our self-imposed standards are insufficient or that our voluntary compliance is ineffective.

For all these reasons, it is extremely important that museums consider what can go wrong and how to deal with it when creating and applying policies that guide their operations. The issues that most often attract the attention of policymakers, press and the public are (though not necessarily in rank order):

- Deaccessioning of collections items

- Use of funds resulting from the sale of deaccessioning collections

- Executive compensation

- Changes to the exterior of the museum that affect local quality of life issues (e.g., parking lots, landscaping, renovations to the building that change its footprint or height)

- Changes to museum operations that affect local quality of life issues (e.g., increasing attendance or frequency of special events, thus affecting local traffic, parking, noise, etc.)

- Controversial exhibit content (with particular hot buttons being religion and pornography, and especially anything that combines the two)

- Operating in a manner that benefits an individual or private company

- Conflicts of interest on the parts of staff or members of the governing authority

The good news is that by writing and following policies based on nationally recognized standards, a museum can go a long way toward defending its actions and defusing potentially damaging situations. The bad news is that once the problem has blown up, it is usually too late to go back and consult the standards to fix things. Here is a brief guide on how to use the standards presented in this book, and other applicable standards, to guide your decision making and shape your response to concerned constituents.

. . . *And How to Avoid Them*

1. Create policies ahead of time. Policies prepared during a crisis or after controversial actions, retroactively validating the museum's decision, lack credibility.

2. When drafting the policies, involve a diverse group that can look at the issue from a variety of perspectives and help foresee potential concerns from various constituencies.

3. Base policies on nationally recognized standards in the museum and related nonprofit fields. Document your reasoning regarding the standards you choose to adopt and (more importantly) those you choose not to adopt. This is particularly important if you consciously choose to adopt a policy that is in conflict with national standards in some regard. Be prepared to make a clear and compelling case for the reasoning behind your choice.

4. Ensure that policies are formally approved by the museum's governing authority and marked with the date of approval.

5. Review key policies in the introductory training given to all staff and members of the governing authority, and make sure all policies are readily accessible to staff and board.

6. When making a decision that bears on museum standards and is potentially controversial, start thinking about your communications plan right away. Designate who will be empowered to speak on the museum's behalf (making sure everyone else knows they are not authorized to do so) and ensure that they are well briefed on their message.

7. When making the decision, start by reviewing the museum's policies and the relevant standards and best-practice statements, as well as the museum's mission, vision statement (if you have one) and institutional and other relevant plans. You should be able to demonstrate that the decision aligns with all these documents.

8. The staff and board of museums are only human. No one can reasonably expect their decisions to be perfect, but you should be able to demonstrate that they are judicious, well informed, well intentioned and grounded in an understanding of the legal and ethical issues involved.

9. Consider whether and how you want to proactively communicate the decision. Especially with an inherently controversial decision, breaking the story yourself can help you control the message and avoid any appearance of secrecy.

Appendix

Dates of Approval of Standards and Best Practices

The following list provides the original title and dates of initial approval/revision for each standard or best practice statement included in this book. As a group, these documents were approved as "Standards and Best Practices for U.S. Museums" by the AAM Board of Directors in November 2006.

Characteristics of Excellence (Characteristics of an Accreditable Museum. Approved 1996, revised 2005.)

AAM Standards Regarding Institutional Mission Statements (The Accreditation Commission's Expectations Regarding Institutional Mission Statements. Approved 1999, revised 2004.)

AAM Standards Regarding Institutional Planning (The Accreditation Commission's Expectations Regarding Institutional Planning. Approved 1999, revised 2004.)

The AAM Code of Ethics for Museums (Museum Ethics: A report to the American Association of Museums, 1978. AAM Code of Ethics for Museums, approved 1993.)

AAM Standards Regarding Institutional Codes of Ethics (The Accreditation Commission's Expectations Regarding an Institutional Codes of Ethics. Approved 1999, revised 2004.)

AAM Standards Regarding Governance (The Accreditation Commission's Expectations Regarding Governance. Approved 2004.)

AAM Standards Regarding Delegation of Authority (The Accreditation Commission's Expectations Regarding Delegation of Authority. Approved 2000, revised 2004.)

AAM Standards Regarding Collections Stewardship (The Accreditation Commission's Expectations Regarding Collections Stewardship. Approved 2001, revised 2004.)

AAM Standards Regarding the Unlawful Appropriation of Objects During the Nazi Era (Guidelines Regarding the Unlawful Appropriation of Objects During the Nazi Era. Approved 1999, revised 2001.)

AAM Best Practices Regarding Loaning Collections to Non-Museum Entities (Accreditation

Commission Statement Regarding Best Practices: Loaning Collections to Non-Museum Entities. Approved 2006.)

AAM Standards Regarding Exhibiting Borrowed Objects (Guidelines on Exhibiting Borrowed Objects. Approved 2000.)

AAM Standards Regarding Developing and Managing Business and Individual Donor Support (Guidelines for Museums on Developing and Managing Business Support. Approved 2001. Guidelines for Museums on Developing and Managing Individual Donor Support. Approved 2002.)

AAM Standards Regarding Retrenchment or Downsizing (Considerations for AAM Accredited Museums Facing Retrenchment or Downsizing. Approved 2003.)

AAM Standards Regarding Facilities and Risk Management (Approved 2007.)

Glossary

Accessioning: (a) Formal act of accepting an object(s) into the category of materials that a museum holds in the public trust; (b) the creation of an immediate, brief and permanent record utilizing a control number for an object or group of objects added to the collection from the same source at the same time, and for which the museum has custody, right or title. Customarily, an accession record includes, among other data, the accession number; the date and nature of acquisition (gift, excavation, expedition, purchase, bequest, etc.); the source; a brief identification and description; condition; provenance; value; and name of staff member recording the accession.

Benchmark: A point of reference used in measuring and judging quality or value.

Benchmarking: The process of comparing your museum's operations to some point of reference for the purpose of setting goals, evaluating performance and making decisions about whether and how to change. There are three points of reference: internal comparison between departments or against the museum's history, external comparison to selected peers and external comparison to the museum field.

Business support: Any support, financial or in-kind, that is philanthropic or driven by marketing, advertising or public relations provided by a business (corporation, partnership, agency, family business, etc.), regardless of the nature and value of the benefit provided by a museum, or the tax implications of the relationship.

Bylaws: Legal documents that describe matters delegated to the governing authority, such as membership categories, the logistics of scheduling and holding meetings of the corporation and the governing authority, committee charges and provisions for amendments. Self-regulatory provisions for the governing authority, such as membership in the organization, attendance requirements and termination, also are in the bylaws.

Care: The museum keeps appropriate and adequate records pertaining to the provenance, identification and location of the museum's holdings and applies current, professionally accepted methods to their security and the minimization of damage and deterioration.

Collections: Objects, living or nonliving, that museums hold in trust for the public. Items usually are considered part of the museum's collections once they are accessioned. Some museums designate different categories of collections (permanent, research, educational) that functionally receive different types of care or use. These categories and their ramifications are established in the museum's collections management policy.

Collections management policy: A written document approved by the governing authority that specifies the museum's policies concerning all collections-related issues, including accessioning, documentation, storage and disposition. Policies are general guidelines that regulate the activities of the organization. They provide standards for exercising good judgment.

Collections plan: A plan that guides the content of the collections and leads staff in a coordinated and uniform direction over time to refine and expand the value of the collections in a predetermined way. Plans are time-limited and identify specific goals to be achieved. They also provide a rationale for those choices and specify how they will be achieved, who will implement the plan, when it will happen and what it will cost.

Community: Each museum self-identifies the community or communities it serves. This may be a geographically defined community (e.g., neighborhood, academic campus, town, city, county or region), a community of interest (e.g., the scientific community, the international business community), a group viewed as forming a distinct segment of society (e.g., the gay community, the Asian community) or a combination of these types.

Deaccessioning: Formal process of removing an accessioned object or group of objects from the museum's collections. A museum still owns a deaccessioned object until it disposes of it but no longer holds it in the public trust. Removing the object from the museum's possession is commonly referred to as *disposal*.

Director: The individual who is delegated authority for the day-to-day operations of the museum and allocated resources sufficient to operate the museum effectively. Functionally, this position is the chief executive officer with responsibilities including, but not limited to, hiring and firing staff, executing the budget, implementing policies and managing programs and staff. May be called CEO, museum administrator, site manager, curator, etc.

Emergency/disaster-preparedness plan: Written policies and procedures intended to prevent or minimize damage to people (staff and visitors), buildings, collections, archival materials or organizational records resulting from natural and man-made events that threaten the building and the people and objects inside it. All museums are expected to have plans that address how the museum will care for staff, visitors and collections in case of emergency. This includes evacuation plans for staff and visitors, and plans for how to protect, evacuate or recover collections in the event of disaster.

Fiduciary: Of or relating to a holding of something in trust for another: a fiduciary heir; a fiduciary contract; of or being a trustee or trusteeship; held in trust.

Governance manual: Reference manual assembled for use by members of the governing authority to assist with orientation, training and ongoing work. It may include, for example, copies of the museum's mission statement, bylaws, current institutional plan, policies and minutes of past meetings.

Governing authority: The body with legal and fiduciary responsibility for a museum. Unless delegated to another body or through a chain of command, also responsible for approving museum policy. Names of the governing authority include but are not limited to: board of commissioners, board of directors, board of managers, board of regents, board of trustees, city council, commission.

Health and safety training: Theoretical and practical instruction regarding such issues as office ergonomics, safe lifting, blood-borne and airborne pathogen safety, hazards communication and use of material safety data sheets.

Individual donor support: Cash, real property or planned gifts from an individual, family or family foundation, regardless of the use of the support or the tax implications of the gift. For the purposes of these standards, individual donor support does not include donations of collections.

Inspections related to facilities and risk: May include, for example, building occupancy permits, fire department inspections, health inspections of food service operations, USDA inspections of animal displays and insurer inspections for safety issues.

Institutional plan: Comprehensive plan that broadly delineates where the institution is going and provides sufficient detail to guide implementation. Sets priorities and guides important decisions that are oriented toward the future. Some museums split this into two parts: (1) multiyear plan: a "big picture" plan that sets strategies, goals and priorities and is sometimes referred to as a strategic or long-range plan; and (2) operational plan: a plan that provides the details needed to implement the decisions in the strategic or long-range plan. This usually focuses on a short period of time, typically geared toward the museum's budget year. Sometimes referred to as an implementation plan. There is great variability in how museums refer to these planning documents or divide particular functions between them. AAM does not mandate a particular format or nomenclature.

Integrated pest management (IPM): The coordination of information about pests and environmental conditions with available pest control methods to prevent unacceptable levels of pest damage while minimizing hazards to people, property, collections and the environment. IPM programs apply a holistic approach to pest management decision making and consider all appropriate options, including but not limited to pesticides.

Joint governance: A governance structure in which two or more entities share governance of a museum. This involves dividing or sharing basic governance responsibilities such as determining mission and purpose; hiring, supporting and evaluating the director; strategic planning; obtaining and managing resources; and monitoring the organization's programs and services. For example, this could be a museum jointly governed by a city government, which owns the collections and the building and employs the staff, and a private nonprofit, which determines museum policy and operates the museum. Or it could be a university that owns and manages a museum but delegates responsibility for determining programs and services to an advisory board. Joint governance does not automatically include museums that have separately incorporated friends organizations, unless the friends organization has significant responsibility for governance of the museum delegated to it in writing.

Objects: Materials used to communicate and motivate learning and instruments for carrying out the museum's stated purpose.

Remote governance: Governance in which the museum director reports only indirectly, through a chain of command, to the actual governing authority. For example: The governing authority of a university museum might be the board of regents, and the director reports through the provost, to the university president, to the regents. The director of a museum in the state parks department might report through a parks manager, to the head of the state department of parks and recreation, to the governor.

Risk management: The overall process of identifying, controlling and minimizing the impact of uncertain events in order to reduce the likelihood of their occurrence or the severity of their impact.

Supporting group: A group whose primary purpose is to support the museum but that has no governing authority or responsibility for the museum. The group may provide financial support, volunteers, expertise or advocacy to complement the knowledge and skills of the governing authority. Supporting groups may be called, for example, advisory boards, friends, guilds or auxiliary boards.

- Internal supporting groups are part of the museum itself, either as an informal association or by appointment of the governing authority. They serve at the pleasure and under the direction of the museum's governing authority or its designee.

- External supporting groups are informal associations or separately incorporated nonprofit entities. They are independent of the museum in their own governance. AAM expects there to be a letter of understanding, a management agreement or other document detailing the relationship between an external supporting group and the museum's governing authority.

AAM Code of Ethics for Museums
(2000)

Introduction

Ethical codes evolve in response to changing conditions, values, and ideas. A professional code of ethics must, therefore, be periodically updated. It must also rest upon widely shared values. Although the operating environment of museums grows more complex each year, the root value for museums, the tie that connects all of us together despite our diversity, is the commitment to serving people, both present and future generations. This value guided the creation of and remains the most fundamental principle in the following *Code of Ethics for Museums*.

Code of Ethics for Museums

Museums make their unique contribution to the public by collecting, preserving, and interpreting the things of this world. Historically, they have owned and used natural objects, living and nonliving, and all manner of human artifacts to advance knowledge and nourish the human spirit. Today, the range of their special interests reflects the scope of human vision. Their missions include collecting and preserving, as well as exhibiting and educating with materials not only owned but also borrowed and fabricated for these ends. Their numbers include both governmental and private museums of anthropology, art history and natural history, aquariums, arboreta, art centers, botanical gardens, children's museums, historic sites, nature centers, planetariums, science and technology centers, and zoos. The museum universe in the United States includes both collecting and noncollecting institutions. Although diverse in their missions, they have in common their nonprofit form of organization and a commitment of service to the public. Their collections and/or the objects they borrow or fabricate are the basis for research, exhibits, and programs that invite public participation.

Taken as a whole, museum collections and exhibition materials represent the world's natural and cultural common wealth. As stewards of that wealth, museums are compelled to advance an understanding of all natural forms and of the human experience. It is incumbent on museums to be resources for humankind and in all their activities to foster an informed appreciation of the rich and diverse world we have inherited. It is also incumbent upon them to preserve that inheritance for posterity.

Museums in the United States are grounded in the tradition of public service. They are organized as public trusts, holding their collections and information as a benefit for those they were established to serve. Members of their governing authority, employees, and volunteers are committed to the interests of these beneficiaries. The law provides the basic framework for museum operations. As nonprofit institutions, museums comply with applicable local, state, and federal laws and international conventions, as well as with the specific legal standards governing trust responsibilities. This *Code of Ethics for Museums* takes that compliance as given. But legal standards are a minimum. Museums and those responsible for them must do more than avoid legal liability, they must take affirmative steps to maintain their integrity so as to warrant public confidence. They must act not only legally but also ethically. This *Code of Ethics for Museums*, therefore, outlines ethical standards that frequently exceed legal minimums.

Loyalty to the mission of the museum and to the public it serves is the essence of museum work, whether volunteer or paid. Where conflicts of interest arise — actual, potential, or perceived — the duty of loyalty must never be compromised. No individual may use his or her position in a museum for personal gain or to benefit another at the expense of the museum, its mission, its reputation, and the society it serves.

For museums, public service is paramount. To affirm that ethic and to elaborate its application to their governance, collections, and programs, the American Association of Museums promulgates this *Code of Ethics for Museums*. In subscribing to this code, museums assume responsibility for the actions of members of their governing authority, employees, and volunteers in the performance of museum-related duties. Museums, thereby, affirm their chartered purpose, ensure the prudent application of their resources, enhance their effectiveness, and maintain public confidence. This collective endeavor strengthens museum work and the contributions of museums to society — present and future.

Governance

Museum governance in its various forms is a public trust responsible for the institution's service to society. The governing authority protects and enhances the museum's collections and programs and its physical, human, and financial resources. It ensures that all these resources support the museum's mission, respond to the pluralism of society, and respect the diversity of the natural and cultural common wealth.

Thus, the governing authority ensures that:

- all those who work for or on behalf of a museum understand and support its mission and public trust responsibilities

- its members understand and fulfill their trusteeship and act corporately, not as individuals

- the museum's collections and programs and its physical, human, and financial resources are protected, maintained, and developed in support of the museum's mission

- it is responsive to and represents the interests of society

- it maintains the relationship with staff in which shared roles are recognized and separate responsibilities respected

- working relationships among trustees, employees, and volunteers are based on equity and mutual respect

- professional standards and practices inform and guide museum operations

- policies are articulated and prudent oversight is practiced

- governance promotes the public good rather than individual financial gain.

Collections

The distinctive character of museum ethics derives from the ownership, care, and use of objects, specimens, and living collections representing the world's natural and cultural common wealth. This stewardship of collections entails the highest public trust and carries with it the presumption of rightful ownership, permanence, care, documentation, accessibility, and responsible disposal.

Thus, the museum ensures that:

- collections in its custody support its mission and public trust responsibilities

- collections in its custody are lawfully held, protected, secure, unencumbered, cared for, and preserved

- collections in its custody are accounted for and documented

- access to the collections and related information is permitted and regulated

- acquisition, disposal, and loan activities are conducted in a manner that respects the protection and preservation of natural and cultural resources and discourages illicit trade in such materials

- acquisition, disposal, and loan activities conform to its mission and public trust responsibilities

- disposal of collections through sale, trade, or research activities is solely for the advancement of the museum's mission. Proceeds from the sale of nonliving collections are to be used consistent with the established standards of the museum's discipline, but in no event shall they be used for anything other than acquisition or direct care of collections.

- the unique and special nature of human remains and funerary and sacred objects is recognized as the basis of all decisions concerning such collections

- collections-related activities promote the public good rather than individual financial gain

- competing claims of ownership that may be asserted in connection with objects in its custody should be handled openly, seriously, responsively and with respect for the dignity of all parties involved.

Programs

Museums serve society by advancing an understanding and appreciation of the natural and cultural common wealth through exhibitions, research, scholarship, publications, and educational activities. These programs further the museum's mission and are responsive to the concerns, interests, and needs of society.

Thus, the museum ensures that:

- programs support its mission and public trust responsibilities

- programs are founded on scholarship and marked by intellectual integrity

- programs are accessible and encourage participation of the widest possible audience consistent with its mission and resources

- programs respect pluralistic values, traditions, and concerns

- revenue-producing activities and activities that involve relationships with external entities are compatible with the museum's mission and support its public trust responsibilities

- programs promote the public good rather than individual financial gain.

Promulgation

This *Code of Ethics for Museums* was adopted by the Board of Directors of the American Association of Museums on November 12, 1993. The AAM Board of Directors recommends that each nonprofit museum member of the American Association of Museums adopt and promulgate its separate code of ethics, applying the *Code of Ethics for Museums* to its own institutional setting.

A Committee on Ethics, nominated by the president of the AAM and confirmed by the Board of Directors, will be charged with two responsibilities:

- establishing programs of information, education, and assistance to guide museums in developing their own codes of ethics

- reviewing the *Code of Ethics for Museums* and periodically recommending refinements and revisions to the Board of Directors.

Afterword

In 1987 the Council of the American Association of Museums determined to revise the association's 1978 statement on ethics. The impetus for revision was recognition throughout the American museum community that the statement needed to be refined and strengthened in light of the expanded role of museums in society and a heightened awareness that the collection, preservation, and interpretation of natural and cultural heritages involve issues of significant concern to the American people.

Following a series of group discussions and commentary by members of the AAM Council, the Accreditation Commission, and museum leaders throughout the country, the president of AAM appointed an Ethics Task Force to prepare a code of ethics. In its work, the Ethics Task Force was committed to codifying the common understanding of ethics in the museum profession and to establishing a framework within which each institution could develop its own code. For guidance, the task force looked to the tradition of museum ethics and drew inspiration from AAM's first code of ethics, published in 1925 as *Code of Ethics for Museum Workers*, which states in its preface:

Museums, in the broadest sense, are institutions which hold their possessions in trust for mankind and for the future welfare of the [human] race. Their value is in direct proportion to the service they render the emotional and intellectual life of the people. The life of a museum worker is essentially one of service.

This commitment to service derived from nineteenth-century notions of the advancement and dissemination of knowledge that informed the founding documents of America's museums. George Brown Goode, a noted zoologist and first head of the United States National Museum, declared in 1889:

The museums of the future in this democratic land should be adapted to the needs of the mechanic, the factory operator, the day laborer, the salesman, and the clerk, as much as to those of the professional man and the man of leisure. . . . In short, the public museum is, first of all, for the benefit of the public.

John Cotton Dana, an early twentieth-century museum leader and director of the Newark Museum, promoted the concept of museum work as public service in essays with titles such as "Increasing the Usefulness of Museums" and "A Museum of Service." Dana believed that museums did not exist solely to gather and preserve collections. For him, they were important centers of enlightenment.

By the 1940s, Theodore Low, a strong proponent of museum education, detected a new concentration in the museum profession on scholarship and methodology. These concerns are reflected in *Museum Ethics*, published by AAM in 1978, which elaborated on relationships among staff, management, and governing authority.

During the 1980s, Americans grew increasingly sensitive to the nation's cultural pluralism, concerned about the global environment, and vigilant regarding public institutions. Rapid technological change, new public policies relating to nonprofit corporations, a troubled educational system, shifting patterns of private and public wealth, and increased financial pressures all called for a sharper delineation of museums' ethical responsibilities. In 1984 AAM's Commission on Museums for a New Century placed renewed emphasis on public service and education, and in 1986 the code of ethics adopted by the International Council of Museums (ICOM) put service to society at the center of museum responsibilities. ICOM defines museums as institutions "in the service of society and of its development" and holds that "employment by a museum, whether publicly or privately supported, is a public trust involving great responsibility."

Building upon this history, the Ethics Task Force produced several drafts of a *Code of Ethics for Museums*. These drafts were shared with the AAM Executive Committee and Board of Directors, and twice referred to the field for comment. Hundreds of individuals and representatives of professional organizations and museums of all types and sizes submitted thoughtful critiques. These critiques were instrumental in shaping the document submitted to the AAM Board of Directors, which adopted the code on May 18, 1991. However, despite the review process, when the adopted code was circulated, it soon became clear that the diversity of the museum field prevented immediate consensus on every point.

Therefore, at its November 1991 meeting, the AAM Board of Directors voted to postpone implementation of the Code of Ethics for at least one year. At the same meeting an Ethics Commission nominated by the AAM president was confirmed. The newly appointed commission — in addition to its other charges of establishing educational programs to guide museums in developing their own code of ethics and establishing procedures for addressing alleged violations of the code — was asked to review the code and recommend to the Board changes in either the code or its implementation.

The new Ethics Commission spent its first year reviewing the code and the hundreds of communications it had generated, and initiating additional dialogue. AAM institutional members were invited to comment further on the issues that were most divisive — the mode of implementation and the restrictions placed on funds from deaccessioned objects. Ethics Commission members also met in person with their colleagues at the annual and regional meetings, and an *ad hoc* meeting of museum directors was convened by the board president to examine the code's language regarding deaccessioning.

This process of review produced two alternatives for the board to consider at its May meeting: (1) to accept a new code developed by the Ethics Commission, or (2) to rewrite the sections of the 1991 code relating to use of funds from deaccessioning and mode of implementation. Following a very lively and involved discussion, the motion to reinstate the 1991 code with modified language was passed and a small committee met separately to make the necessary changes.

In addition, it was voted that the Ethics Commission be renamed the Committee on Ethics with responsibilities for establishing information and educational programs and reviewing the *Code of Ethics for Museums* and making periodic recommendations for revisions to the board. These final changes were approved by the board in November 1993 and are incorporated into this document, which is the AAM *Code of Ethics for Museums*.

Each nonprofit museum member of the American Association of Museums should subscribe to the AAM *Code of Ethics for Museums*. Subsequently, these museums should set about framing their own institutional codes of ethics, which should be in conformance with the AAM code and should expand on it through the elaboration of specific practices. This recommendation is made to these member institutions in the belief that engaging the governing authority, staff, and volunteers in applying the AAM code to institutional settings will stimulate the development and maintenance of sound policies and procedures necessary to understanding and ensuring ethical behavior by institutions and by all who work for them or on their behalf.

With these steps, the American museum community expands its continuing effort to advance museum work through self-regulation. The *Code of Ethics for Museums* serves the interests of museums, their constituencies, and society. The primary goal of AAM is to encourage institutions to regulate the ethical behavior of members of their governing authority, employees, and volunteers. Formal adoption of an institutional code promotes higher and more consistent ethical standards. To this end, the Committee on Ethics will develop workshops, model codes, and publications. These and other forms of technical assistance will stimulate a dialogue about ethics throughout the museum community and provide guidance to museums in developing their institutional codes.

American 🔊 Association of Museums
Your Resource, Voice, Community

Be a part of the largest museum association—the national service organization that represents your professional interests. Membership brings you exceptional benefits:

· Expert help and confidential, customized guidance on any museum matter, from finance and ethics to facilities management and collection stewardship — AAM's Information Center

· Deep discounts on education and professional development opportunities — AAM's Annual Meeting and MuseumExpo^{TM}, Seminars and Webinars

· Access to the most complete, accurate and timely information for and about museums — Museum magazine, Aviso Online and AAM Action Alerts & Legislative Updates

· Significant discounts on professional literature covering every museum subject from audience research to technology — The AAM Bookstore

· Opportunities to network with colleagues who work in the same field or have similar interests — AAM's Standing Professional Committees and Professional Interest Committees

· A voice in Washington to make the case for museums with Congress, policymakers and the media — AAM's Government Relations Department and Museum Advocacy Day

· Collective buying power of more than 20,000 members to save you time and money on insurance, shipping and other services — AAM's Affinity Partner Program

· Opportunities to apply for funding assistance for AAM professional development — AAM Fellowships

· Ability to receive instant alerts about new job opportunities and post your resume so that hundreds of museums can find you — AAM's JobHQ

"The wheels are in motion to use the webinar series as a professional development opportunity for many of our staff. We thank you for modeling this way of learning and for making great information and people available to us at such reasonable prices. It is yet another way my AAM membership gives me value" — Connie Bodner, Ohio Historical Society, Columbus OH

Join AAM Today

For more information on becoming a member and all the member benefits and discounts

www.aam-us.org/joinus or call 866.226.2150

图书在版编目（CIP）数据

美国博物馆国家标准及最佳做法：汉英对照 / 湖南省博物馆译.
北京：外文出版社，2010
ISBN 978-7-119-06416-1

Ⅰ.①美… Ⅱ.①湖… Ⅲ.①博物馆—国家标准—美国—汉、英
Ⅳ.①G269.712-65

中国版本图书馆CIP数据核字（2010）第074998号

出版策划：胡开敏　陈建明

翻　　译：路旦俊
审　　校：黄　磊
责任编辑：杨春燕　佟　盟
装帧设计：唐　玺
印刷监制：张国祥

美国博物馆国家标准及最佳做法

美国博物馆协会　　　　　编著
伊丽莎白 E 梅里特　　　　评述

该书最初由位于美国首都华盛顿的美国博物馆协会出版
© American Association of Museums
ISBN 978-1-933253-11-4

© 2010外文出版社
出 版 人：呼宝民
总 编 辑：李振国
出版发行：外文出版社出版
　中国北京百万庄大街24号
　邮政编码100037
　http://www.flp.com.cn
印　　刷：恒美印务（广州）有限公司
开　　本：178mm×255mm 1/16　印张：15.5
2010年第1版第1次印刷
　（汉英）
ISBN 978-7-119-06416-1
12000